# Contents

# Acknowledgments

It seems to me that when you're young, you think you can take on the world alone. As you get older, you realise you can't achieve anything without the support of your family and friends. I'm getting older, slowly, and I owe a great deal to many people.

First, I would like to acknowledge the infinite support and belief invested in me, through so many years, by my parents, Johan and Valerie, and my brothers, Kobus, Deon and Gerritt. Whatever we have been, we have always been a family.

I am not sure how I will ever repay Nerine, my wife, for the gift of our children and for being my best friend, but I'll keep trying.

John and Miemie Winter, my 'outlaws', have been supportive at all times, becoming another father and mother to me. Riaan and Karien, my brother- and sister-in-law, have proved themselves time and time again to be friends beyond description. To them all, I can only offer my deepest and most sincere gratitude.

Etienne and Anita de Villiers have been wonderfully kind since Nerine and I arrived in London. They have been the ultimate friends indeed at a time of need.

I am also massively grateful to Edward Griffiths for the time and care he has taken in assisting me with this book, and for his patience and advice through many hours' work.

Nigel Wray, the man who brought me to Saracens, has been a tower of strength ever since, and his family – Linda, Lucy, Little Joe and Granny Wray – have felt like a family to me.

I am grateful to all those rugby followers who have supported and encouraged me over the years, both in South

# RAINBOW WARRIOR

## DEDICATION

*To my Mother and Father
for their love and support*

Africa and in London, perhaps most particularly to Robbie Schlemmer, the boot room man at Ellis Park and my most loyal supporter.

It was, of course, the Transvaal Rugby Union who gave me many great times in rugby, and I am grateful to Dr Louis Luyt, the officials and players for their friendship and support. Rand Afrikaans University is another institution to whom I owe a considerable debt, specifically to Koos Ehlers and Johan Gouws. And I cannot omit the South African Rugby Football Union, particularly those players and management who shared in my Springbok career.

Ian McIntosh, Jannie Engelbrecht, Morne du Plessis, all 28 members of the 1995 World Cup squad: they all made me look good, and I am profoundly grateful.

There were awkward times as well, and I must pay tribute to Hennie le Roux, the most loyal and courageous of friends, and to Gary Janks for always providing cautious and wise advice.

Since 1996, in England, my path has been smoothed by the support of the players and officials of Saracens, to whom I am duly grateful. With them, I know, many great days lie ahead.

Finally, I thank 'coachie', Kitch Christie, my partner and my mentor. I miss you. The game of rugby misses you too.

François Pienaar
London
July 1999

# *Foreword*
## *by Nelson Mandela*

As South Africans enter the second of phase in the life of their democracy, they can look back with considerable pride on the achievements of the first period. The manner in which the people and the political leadership of the country had confounded all the prophets of doom by achieving a peaceful transition from apartheid minority rule to non-racial democracy will forever stand recorded as one of the social and political miracles of our time. South Africans, long divided and in conflict with one another, rallied around and came together spectacularly during our first elections. Then began in earnest the process of nation building and national reconciliation. Today we can claim that we are truly one people, united within the treasured richness of our diversity.

None of this could have been achieved by the political leadership on its own. The South African achievement is that all its people, from different backgrounds, walks of life and sectors of society, contributed to the cause. The sportsmen and women of our country played a very crucial role in this regard, for sport reaches where politicians can never hope to. Our national sporting teams in all codes have done so much to instil in our people a sense of common national pride and nationhood.

Amongst those sports leaders, François Pienaar stands out. It was under his inspiring leadership that rugby, a sport previously associated with one sector of our population and with a particular brand of politics, became the pride of the entire country. A beacon in our process of nation-building will always remain the Springboks under his captaincy winning the World Cup in 1995. Seldom before or since has the country celebrated in such harmony and togetherness. François Pienaar's leadership extended way beyond the rugby field, and he truly represented all South Africans.

Even after his departure from the national rugby side, François has continued to be an excellent ambassador for his country and the values it cherishes as a nation. He continues to be a fighter for a united and non-racial South Africa – a true rainbow warrior.

We are confident that the spirit of François Pienaar will continue to live and grow from strength to strength in rugby and all the sporting codes of our country.

# *Introduction*

*Whatever you can do, or dream you can, begin it.*
*Boldness has genius, power and magic in it.*
*Begin it now.*
Johann Goethe

It was the first time I had seen my father cry. He is a hard man who has led a hard life in which everything has been earned and nothing has come for free. He is not normally a man who shows emotion, but the tears welled in his eyes because his oldest son was leaving South Africa. It was too much.

The international departures area at Johannesburg airport was crowded with families saying goodbyes. My mother was crying too.

'This is all Markgraaff's fault,' she said. 'It's his fault that you have to go and live in England. I hate him and I will hold it against him forever.' I told her not to worry and to think of the opportunities she would have to visit London. It was a lame response, but it was the best I could offer.

Riaan Winter, my wife's brother and my closest friend, had driven us to the airport. The Winters are a close family. He would miss his sister terribly. That much was clear. We had sat in silence as the highway flashed by, while bravery and sadness wrestled within each of us. Sadness was winning. It was a difficult time. As our family stood together in the terminal, Riaan suddenly left the group and walked away, simply to be alone. The goodbyes were becoming too much for everyone.

When Riaan composed himself and returned, I gave him a copy of Edward Griffiths' account of the 1995 Rugby World Cup – *One Team, One Country*, the book which tells of a much happier time in my life. I had written an inscription inside the cover which quoted Muhammad Ali's words when he was asked what he thought of Mike Tyson: 'The kid is good, but he's never been hit.' I added: *This kid has been hit, but he ain't going down.*

Then I shook hands with my three brothers, and said goodbye to my mother and father. I was trying hard not to cry. It was time to go, to pass through customs and wait in the passengers' lounge.

Our luggage happened to weigh 135 kilograms and we were carrying a huge framed photograph for Nigel Wray, chairman and owner of Saracens, but the South African Airways manager waved us through and wished us luck. We had been overwhelmed by public support.

I sensed people were watching us but Nerine, my wife, squeezed my hand as we walked. As our passports were being stamped, I glanced back through the glass partitions and saw my parents still watching us. The lump was growing in my throat. This was a difficult time, a wretched time.

I was a professional rugby player in South Africa and, three months earlier, the Springbok coach, Andre Markgraaff, had emphatically declared I was not part of his plans for the future. That was that. He had been appointed until the 1999 Rugby World Cup. My international career was over.

Dead end.

Nerine and I had decided to seek a new challenge, and we accepted Nigel Wray's offer to play for Saracens in England. As we settled in our seats on the flight to London, we momentarily doubted whether this change of direction was worth the heartache for us and our families.

Nerine ordered some champagne. She had been tremendously strong and clear throughout the decision-making process. There was no challenge left for us in South Africa. Markgraaff had ruled out any reprieve. We needed to move forward, maybe to make a sacrifice, to keep going. If Nerine had not been so resolved to move on, I would have stayed at home.

'Here's to our new adventure,' she said, raising her glass.

The champagne served its purpose, and soothed the lumps in our throats.

We slept soundly and arrived at Heathrow airport to find Nigel Wray, himself, waiting to meet us in the Terminal One arrivals' hall. We had trouble locating our luggage, but Nigel had waited for two hours simply to welcome us to London and to offer any assistance we might require. Immediately, our spirits soared. It was a remarkable gesture from a fine man.

It was a cold Sunday morning in London, but it was bright. I had told Nigel we would bring the sunshine, and we had; a pity about the temperature. Our bags successfully retrieved, we headed for a rented home in Windsor. There were only 13 days before my debut for Saracens, a league match against Orrell.

Our last fortnight in South Africa had been a frantic blur of removal men, last-gasp planning and farewells … and lunch with the President. The call from Nelson Mandela's private secretary had come out of the blue. She wanted to know if we would have lunch with the President before leaving for England. We accepted. Friday at 12.30? That would be fine.

I wore a black suit, not because I was in mourning but because all my other clothes had been packed, and, upon arrival, we were surprised to find few cars parked outside the Presidential guest house near the Union Buildings in Pretoria. Nerine and I had no idea what to expect, but we were shown to one of the grand drawing rooms and asked to wait. It was the same room where the Springbok World Cup squad had happily posed for a formal photograph before attending the State banquet held in our honour. That seemed a long time ago.

We sat quietly. The silence was eventually broken by the sound of a familiar chuckle from the hall. Escorted by Graca Machel, his future wife, the President arrived in the room and immediately made us feel at ease.

'How are you?' he enquired, beaming. 'How are you?'

He said he was sorry we were leaving South Africa, but added he fully understood the reasons for our decision. As we spoke, Nerine and I gradually realized we were the only guests invited for lunch. It would be just the four of us at the table. It was a huge compliment. We both felt extremely privileged.

After ten minutes or so, the President said the media were waiting outside and he suggested we go to answer their questions. I had no idea at all that a press conference was planned, and was profoundly touched when the President publicly thanked me for what I had done for the nation and wished me good luck in England. It was a warm, summer day and we stood for some minutes before the bank of photographers.

Having satisfied the media, the President led us to lunch. He drank *Peche Royale*, a sparkling peach drink, and we were amused by the manner in which he gently rebuked the waiter who wanted to take his glass before he had drunk every drop. I had previously read how the President manages to treat every person, be they a waiter or a head of state, with the same respect; now I was seeing this quality with my own eyes. He is a man of consummate dignity, and he reflects that dignity on everyone he meets.

We spoke about living in London, and were interested to hear Mrs Machel's stories of the years she spent studying in England. The President appeared so relaxed and happy, absolutely content to sit back and listen to the woman he loved.

He related a story on this occasion which I will not forget, an African tale with as many meanings as you want. President Mandela's home village is a small place called Qunu, in the Transkei and, during his visits, he is expected to discharge not only the duties attached to being President of the Republic of South Africa, but also those expected of the leading authority in Qunu. To the local population, he is still *their* leader.

His visits to Qunu are scheduled as periods of rest but, on one occasion, this calm was repeatedly disturbed by a woman complaining that her chicken had been stolen and eaten by her neighbour. She was initially told the President was too busy, but she eventually attracted his attention. 'What is the matter?'

he asked one of his guards. He was told about the persistent woman. All right, he declared, he would see her.

After listening to the woman's story, President Mandela requested that her neighbour be brought to answer the charge. The man arrived, dressed in his very best clothes, and offered his version of events. Mandela eventually decreed the man should replace the chicken. But the woman was not satisfied, saying she needed to be compensated for the time and money she had spent rearing the chicken. Mandela reconsidered and decided the man should pay the woman twice the value of the deceased chicken.

The conclusion of the story was then all but lost in laughter as the President mimicked the woman's excited reaction to his decision. He told the tale at length and much more colourfully than I have done here. He laughed and giggled infectiously, evidently enjoying himself.

After lunch, the President was called away to his office, and Nerine and I walked down the corridor behind him and Mrs Machel. He was holding her hand. It seemed the ultimate romantic act. As he said goodbye, he said he was already looking forward to the day I returned home, and he asked that I continue to represent South Africa with pride.

A thousand thoughts flooded my mind. Here I stood with the head of state of my country. Here I stood with a man who, for two thirds of my life, had been regarded as public enemy number one by many South Africans. Here I stood with a man who, all over the world, was regarded as one of the outstanding personalities of the twentieth century. And now, on this warm, soft December day in Pretoria, this man was speaking to me as a grandfather. I listened.

'And, François,' he concluded, 'thank you for everything you have done for South Africa. It is very much appreciated.'

'*Everything you have done.*'

It was not much when set aside the historic achievements of his life but, in 29 hectic years, it seemed that I had done something...

# CHAPTER ONE

# *Steel Foundations*

*Everyone has talent. What is rare is the courage to
follow that talent to the dark place where it leads.*
Erica Jong

Amid the excitement and euphoria, I had hoped the 1995 Rugby World Cup would, truly, unite all South Africans. Perhaps I was naïve. But the years of racial division and enmity had seemed literally to melt away as the fledgling democracy found an extraordinary event in which every South African could share and celebrate. I still believe that on 24 June 1995 South Africa did stand together, as one country united behind one team.

I won't easily forget the electric atmosphere at Ellis Park when President Nelson Mandela emerged from the tunnel wearing the Springbok jersey. An overwhelmingly white South African crowd in the stands chanted his name with real conviction – '*Nel-son! Nel-son! Nel-son!*' Shivers went up and down my spine. I could feel the country changing – eyes being opened, hearts being won, long-held prejudices being exposed.

The rainbow nation came alive that sunny afternoon.

More than four years on, it seems to me the 1995 Rugby World Cup offered nothing more than a glimpse of paradise, a glimpse of what South Africa can become. It did not represent the end of a journey, as we had hoped; it offered a tantalizing taste of one possible destination.

Wherever we, as South Africans, eventually go as a country, one thing seems certain: a long voyage stretches ahead of us.

On 24 June 1995, it all seemed so easy.

In many ways, many millions of South Africans, both black and white, appear to have returned to the trenches of the past.

In simple terms, whites seem to be increasingly impatient with the African National Congress government and concerned by what they see as falling standards, blacks are impatient with the inevitably slow delivery of improved lives while the coloured and Indian communities appear to feel as vulnerable and caught in the middle as ever. People on all sides are losing faith in the rainbow dream.

Patience and calm are required all round. The land is beautiful and the potential of all the people remains boundless, but the process takes time. For now, South Africa remains a country on a tightrope.

The truth is that if you travel through conservative rural towns today, you will very likely hear the fierce language of the 1970s and 1980s returning to predominantly Afrikaner communities. The predominantly black government is blamed for everything and credited for nothing. There is a sense of hope fled, of hard times ahead, of a new struggle, of more and more decent and talented people psychologically battening down the hatches.

I understand these communities, I can even understand – though no longer share – these views. This is a time to move forward, not back.

It was in just such a rural South African town that I was bred. I am proud to say I hail from typical Afrikaner working-class stock. There have been times in my life when, foolishly, I have been ashamed by the modesty of my upbringing. As a boy, I would ask my mother to drop me some distance from school so my friends wouldn't see our battered family car. But I am older and wiser now, and indebted for the support of my family.

People have variously described me as an 'enlightened' Afrikaner, somehow implying that I have left the Afrikaner rump far behind; and, from my current home in Hampstead, north London, I suppose it would appear as if I have moved some distance from the harsh suburbs of Vereeniging, south of Johannesburg, but I hope I have managed to retain the central principles of my formative years: a strong Christian faith, a sense of honesty, a deep love of family, a capacity for hard work, a determination to succeed and pride in being an Afrikaner.

Jan-Harm Pienaar, my father, was the second of seven children reared in Orange Free State farming lands. He lost his father in a drowning accident, when a truck carrying milk to Johannesburg burst a tyre and careered off the Barage bridge, and saw his mother married four times. Quiet and resolute by nature, his social views have changed little over the years.

As a young man, he found work in the steel industry and has remained there ever since. First for USCO, then SASOL, ISCOR, and now Highveld Steel he has taken his place in the engine room of these vast state-owned organisations which constructed South Africa's powerful industrial backbone.

My first impression of my father was as a pillar of authority. When he worked the night shifts, he would sleep during the afternoons and we would be repeatedly reminded to play in silence so as not to wake him. He watched Transvaal rugby, but more frequently with his friends than his children. That was the pattern of fatherhood in those days. That was how it was.

On 21 January 1966, Jan-Harm Pienaar married Valerie Diana du Toit, the fifth of 11 children from the rural Western Transvaal town of Orkney and, just under a year later, on 2 January 1967, I was born at the hospital in the district of Drie Riviere (Three Rivers), outside Vereeniging.

It was a time of floods – the Taaibos, Klip and Vaal rivers were all swelled beyond their banks by the summer rains – and my mother recalls setting my cradle by the river bank and constantly having to check the water level did not rise and wash me away on the flood.

We led a simple life, a happy life.

Throughout my youth, I was consistently aware of the reality that our family was not as wealthy as others. On one occasion, my mother took us to visit my grandmother before Christmas and I was excited to see presents laid out beneath the tree for my cousins and myself. We waited, and waited and were eventually told we could open the bright gifts.

My present turned out to be a small red bus, but I was amazed to see my cousin parading with the latest battery-operated car. The incident stayed with me for many years: it had seemed as if we were the poor relations and were treated as such. I was desperately sad, and desperately determined to prove to my grandmother that I would not be second rate.

My father's mother seemed a far more sympathetic figure until her death from cancer when I was 17. On one occasion, at the age of only eight, I playfully 'escaped' from our family home in Vanderbijlpark and travelled eight kilometres alone to reach the 'refuge' of her house in Vereeniging. The incident caused some alarm at the time, but it demonstrated the type of free and adventurous nature of my childhood.

There was room to roam.

We were encouraged to play outside, to explore and experiment. We were not wrapped in cotton wool, and protected. The result was we learned to stand alone from a very young age. People often ask why so many Afrikaners become outstanding rugby players, and I believe it is primarily because we are bred into an outdoor life. The warm climate helps, of course, but it felt as if we were brought up to be fit, strong and adventurous.

By 'we' I mean the four of us, the four Pienaar boys. I was the oldest, born at the start of 1967, followed by Kobus, born 22 months later, Deon born nine years later in 1976 and Gerrit, born 12 years later in 1979. The age gaps threw Kobus and me together, with Deon and Gerrit developing later as a second pair. We fought and played, laughed and argued. We were typical brothers and I relished the rough-and-tumble of the family.

I must confess, however, that rough-and-tumble was not my game in my early years. Kobus claims I was extremely close to my mother, whom I set above everyone else, and that I needed his protection at times. I know that was true. We used to play with toy cars in a sandpit at the park opposite our house and, when I was five, a larger boy pushed me in the sand. In tears, I ran home to find Kobus, who was only three at the time. He took me by the hand, marched me back to the sandpit and proceeded to beat up the larger boy on my behalf. I was mightily impressed.

In line with Afrikaner tradition, I had been named after my grandfather on my father's side and, in line with the popular consensus, I emerged as the quiet, serious older brother expected to guide his young siblings. We lived in a house of strict discipline: respecting adults, saying please and thank you, and striving to grow up according to Christian principles.

My parents were unable to attend church because my father usually worked on weekends to earn double pay; so, one Sunday morning when I was five, I decided to take Kobus to church. We sat in the gallery overlooking the main body of the church, but my younger brother was not the type to sit still. My Bible was perched on the ledge in front of us and the restless Kobus bumped the book. It fell on the congregation below. I stood back, so the people wouldn't be able to see me when they looked up. But I was angry with my brother, so I pinched Kobus as hard as I could.

'Eina!' he shouted.

And the entire congregation turned to stare at us. From that moment of supreme humiliation, I decided I would attend church on my own; and I did, although I was not actually christened into the faith until I was 17. Then, I was confirmed on the same day, barely a few minutes later.

As we grew older, the children in the suburb divided themselves into makeshift gangs, and we would spend long, warm days exploring the veld, catching snakes and finding mischief. When once we discovered a load of discarded wax, we spent weeks colouring the wax and moulding it into a reasonable set of crayons. We manufactured our own fun.

If such a lifestyle seems precarious, it was. I almost died at the age of seven when a rival gang captured me and, for fun, placed a noose around my neck. They left me hanging from a tree. I was starting to feel dizzy when one of our teachers happened to be passing by and rescued me. The prank would otherwise have gone disastrously wrong, but I escaped with cuts and welts on my neck, and I was back, playing in the veld, the next day.

My first school was AJ Jacobs primary school in Vanderbijlpark, where I fell in love with a teacher named Miss Haarhof, and I started playing rugby among just another horde of barefooted boys running around sun-scorched fields. I began as a centre and was swiftly moved to No. 8, but failed to be selected for the Transvaal Primary Schools side. My father was extremely disappointed and said the selectors were biased against us because we came from a poor and unfashionable school. He might have been right, but it is widely understood the strongest provincial school side never gets selected. There are too many other factors – self-interest and ego – in the equation.

Within a couple of years, my father went to work for Sasol, the family moved to Sasolburg and I enrolled at Voorslag primary school. Sport, each and every available sport, had seized my complete attention, but it appeared that my main talent lay in athletics, specifically the high jump. I was selected to represent Transvaal at the South African junior championships which, that year, were being held in Bloemfontein. The structure of junior sport in South Africa has, for some time, been as strong and efficient as any in the world. Marshalled by an army of dedicated and blazered schoolteachers, I was just one of many thousands to thrive within the organization.

I finished third in the event, despite slipping and cutting my foot when I fell at the back of the landing area, and found myself sitting next to an older athlete, a sprint champion, on the bus back to Sasolburg. We lived near each other and decided we would travel home together.

Participation at the national junior athletics championships had been restricted to whites. Enrolment at my school was restricted to whites. In fact, I had scarcely had any contact with black South Africans at all. This was the nature of my upbringing. Our young lives were simply designed in such a way that races were kept apart. There was no interaction at all.

It was not our choice. It was our reality.

At any rate, the sprint champion and I were scheduled to arrive back in Sasolburg at eleven o'clock that night, but the bus travelled quickly and we were back in the town by quarter-past ten. After some discussion, we decided we would walk home, a distance of no more than four kilometres, rather than wait for our parents to arrive and collect us, as arranged.

I had collected all the empty Coke bottles from the bus, to trade them in for a few cents at the local shop, and I was carrying these in a plastic bag when I became aware of a man, wearing an overcoat, standing in the path ahead of us. As I walked past in the dark, I felt his hand grab the back of my neck and there was a sharp pain in my hand. He had seized the bag of empty bottles. Instinctively, I swung my fist at his face, broke free and ran as fast as I had ever run. I actually left the sprint champion in my wake.

After a kilometre or so, we reached a café. The sprinter stopped to call the police but I wanted to keep running until I reached home. I was scared. At one point, I ran right into a girl who was just standing eating chips, and knocked her over. It was an accident. I just wanted to get home.

My parents were obviously concerned when they saw me, and my father went to call the police from our neighbours' house because we didn't have a telephone. Later that night, I looked out of my bedroom window and was certain the same black man was standing across the street.

I was scared beyond words.

It later transpired that a man matching the description that I eventually gave the police had murdered a newly-wed off-duty policeman and his wife in their car the previous night. The

21

incident knocked me back. I was nine years old and, for a few months, felt reluctant to go out alone.

This had been my first experience of crime, and it had also been my first meaningful interaction with a black South African. We did have maids working in the house – and we were close to Joyce and Maria who would call me *klein baas* (little boss) – but the narrow boundaries of my upbringing were such that we never dealt with black people as equals. We didn't 'connect' in any way. On reflection, it seems so foolish and unnecessary.

When my parents bought me a bicycle, a green model with white tyres, I was terrified it would be stolen and insisted to the teachers that I be allowed to keep the bicycle in the classroom, rather than the shed. I almost became obsessive about crime.

Life soon returned to normal: playing in the veld, indulging in every sport and studying only when there was nothing else to do.

Uncle Kobus, my father's younger brother, had started to play an increasing role in my daily existence. He was an entrepreneur, with his own tyre business in Johannesburg, and he attracted my attention and admiration by virtue of the fact that he drove a Mercedes Benz car.

During school holidays, I would go to work at his garage, helping with wheel alignment to earn a few extra rand. When I received my first wages, I immediately went to buy an electric carving knife and an electric fan for my mother.

On one occasion, Uncle Kobus came to watch me play rugby and said he would sponsor me one rand for every try I scored that afternoon. The financial incentive worked, even in those days, because I scored no fewer than eight tries and became the richest boy at school, or so it felt!

Rugby played an important role in our family. I remember vividly how we all woke early in the morning, like almost every other white South African family, and watched the third Test between the Springboks and All Blacks at Eden Park in 1981. The flower bombs and the demonstrations were beyond our comprehension. To us, it was just a game of rugby. That was the way my father thought, that was the way I was thinking.

The first senior match I ever saw was a club fixture between Iscor and the Rand Afrikaans University. Wim Hollander and Lee Barnard were playing for RAU and I remember being hugely impressed by the spectacle.

For most of my teen years, however, my first sport was neither rugby nor athletics. At that stage, I was a cricketer. While at primary school, I had been selected to play at the Triomf Cricket week, sponsored by a man with whom I would have many dealings in the future, Louis Luyt.

By the time I moved on to Transvalia high school, there was no doubt in anyone's mind that cricket was my first sport, ahead of rugby and athletics. As a medium fast bowler and a big-hitting batsman, I had been selected to represent Vaal Triangle at the annual South African Country Districts week in Malmesbury, a town in the Boland north of Cape Town. A national Country Districts team chosen at the end of the week would go on to participate at the prestigious Nuffield Week for provincial high school teams.

Piet Botha, who later played for Transvaal and Border, played at the same event and we were together when the national Country Districts team was named. We were both included. I telephoned my mother with the news and we bought a bottle of sweet wine to celebrate.

We were young and happy. It was warm. The wine was good, so the temptation offered by a nearby swimming pool was too great. We stripped and jumped in. Within a few minutes, an off-duty policeman arrived on the scene with his girlfriend and decided he was going to impress her by shouting and swearing at us.

A friend of mine, Lou van Rensburg, leaped out of the pool and asked the guy to leave us alone. The policeman hit him, and I ran in to hit the policeman. We had meant no harm at all, but the situation had spun out of control, and we dashed back to the hostel where we were staying. On the way, I ripped open my hand as I climbed over a barbed-wire fence. To our horror, the police arrived the next day – one of the guys left his identity card at the scene – but we weren't cautioned, just rattled.

My punishment was to compete at the Nuffield week, in Cape Town the following week, with stitches in my bowling hand. Obviously, my control was not what it might have been and I was severely punished by the batsmen in our second match, against the Border team. One Daryll Cullinan scored 88, including a huge six off my bowling. The future Test batsman seemed to have so much time. I felt inadequate. He was playing on a different level.

We had driven to Malmesbury for the Country Districts week, but we were flown back from Cape Town after the Nuffield week. It was my first flight; another landmark on the road of achievement I had set myself.

The athletics coach at Transvalia was Oubaas van Zyl, and he could not have worked harder to develop my athletics, but my performance was not improving. I had become bored by individual sport. I was galvanized and motivated by the spirit of team competition.

So I continued to play rugby but a broken ankle ruled me out of the 1984 Craven week and, while I was a regular member of the Transvalia first XV, a friend of mine, Drikus Lemmer, captained the side. The school never created much of an impression in the Administrators' Cup. We seemed cast as also-rans alongside larger Johannesburg schools.

I had had to work as a door-to-door salesman, selling various products including magic sponges and flycatchers, to supplement my pocket money. The more I saw the wealth in the world, the more determined I became to be successful.

My resolve was complete. Nothing would stand in my way and, from primary school, I was prepared literally to fight for my position. The days of needing my younger brother to protect me were over.

This was a conscious decision.

If I had to fight my way to success, then I would fight ...

Jan Steenkamp – I won't forget his name – followed me in to the toilet. We had both turned 13, and were newly arrived at Transvalia high school from primary school. He pushed me aside. I told him not to push me. He pushed me again. For almost the first time, I pushed back, and he fell, striking his head against the basin. His head was cut quite badly and there was blood on the floor.

Significantly, Jan's mother was a member of the parent body, so the deputy headmaster, Slang van Zyl, was quick to apportion guilt. Jan played the role of wounded victim perfectly, claiming not to remember anything as he cited dizzy spells and then managed to remember everything. Van Zyl initially said the school would hand me over to the police and press charges. If he wanted to scare me, he succeeded admirably. In the event, I received six lashes as a souvenir of my first fight – and my backside bled from the cuts.

News of the incident flashed around the school. I had started to earn the absolutely unwanted reputation as a 'fighter'.

The identical Kapp twins, known as the *Kappies*, were also in our year and, one day, they hung their drill blazers out of a classroom window. I decided to do the same with the brand-new blazer that my mother had recently bought me at great sacrifice. It was a fine blazer, of which I was proud.

One of the *Kappies* threw my blazer on the ground.

'Don't do that,' I said.

He walked towards me and head-butted me on the nose, leaving the middle of my face swollen and bleeding. Instinctively, I swung and struck him powerfully on the nose. His face was contorted with anger.

'Listen,' the enraged *Kappie* muttered in my ear, 'I will see you in the park after school, and we'll sort it out properly.'

I was not at all eager to fight in the park.

At break, the *Kappie* approached me again and said he would not be able to get to the park that afternoon; it would have to be tomorrow. I was delighted by the reprieve. My nose was still full of blood.

That night, I contemplated my options and, the next morning, the sight of my grotesquely swollen face made me more and more furious. The *Kappies* had heard about the Jan Steenkamp incident and, evidently, were trying to put me back in my place.

My first class the next morning was geography, and my desk was at the front of the room while the *Kappies* were sitting together at the back. Just before the teacher arrived, I walked to the back of the classroom, picked up a chair and hit one of the *Kappie* twins with it. I had struck him hard. His nose began to bleed. Momentarily, I felt triumphant.

'It wasn't me who hit you yesterday,' he stammered, as he tended to his wound. 'It was my brother.'

It couldn't be true. I had hit the wrong *Kappie*! After the class, the other *Kappie* told me the matter would not wait until after school. It would have to be sorted out behind the grandstand of the school rugby field during the first break. I manfully agreed. In truth, there was no option.

When I arrived at the appointed place, I found more than 80 boys had gathered to see the spectacle. Such fights were popular and, as *Kappie* and I squared up, the crowd formed a circle. They were shouting and yelling, but the bout didn't last long. I was lucky. I caught him with two early punches and he went down. He didn't really have the stomach for a fight and, to be honest, neither did I. Events had overwhelmed our better natures.

Nonetheless, the school was abuzz.

'Pienaar beat up both *Kappies* in the same day.'

Whether I wanted the reputation or not, I was now a fighter. Any rough boy who wanted to make his mark would now provoke me to prove himself. Of course, I strutted to maintain the image but it was a false one.

Minor scuffles peppered my years at Transvalia high school, but I did manage to avoid major incidents until my last year when I invited a girl from the nearby Vaal high school out on a date. Her name was Michele. I had had my hair cut according to the latest fashion, and I suppose I must have seemed quite a threatening figure to the local boys from Driehoek, a nearby rival school. They knew and resented me from the rugby field, despising me as a Transvalia *windgat* who was with an English-speaking girl.

Standing at the party, we suddenly found ourselves surrounded.

'Are you François Pienaar?'

I nodded.

One guy swung at me. I swung at him. We were in trouble. Another guy hit me from behind, another pulled a knife. Fortunately, the skirmish was broken up by some passers-by and the Driehoek boys scattered but Michele was left on the ground with her eye split open so badly you could almost see the white side of her eyeball. It was a gruesome sight.

'Who hit you?' I asked.

'You did,' she replied.

It turned out I had swung at one of our guys, missed him but connected with her. We went to hospital. I needed attention too because a bone was sticking out of the side of my right hand. Michele was soon fine, but the nurses stitched me up without giving me a tetanus injection (as I had not wanted to confess to being involved in a brawl) and, within a few days, my hand had swollen up alarmingly so I returned to hospital. As an eternal consequence, I have no knuckle in the small finger of my right hand.

My father told me I had done the right thing but the story only served to feed the rumour mill at school. Within a few days, the heroic tale of how I had fought off 20 Driehoek thugs had entered into legend.

Despite this reputation, I progressed through the school, passed all my exams and was appointed as a prefect – thanks to a lucky break on the day of the appointment. Drikus Lemmer and I had bunked off school that day and were swimming in the nearby river when we were caught by the headmaster's secretary. She took us back to school and said she wouldn't tell anyone we had been away. We were forever indebted to her.

She would probably say I was a rogue at school but I hope she would say I could be a 'loveable rogue' as well. I meant no harm. I passed my 'matric' exams at the end of the year and left Transvalia with, I hope, credit.

My father had changed jobs again, taking up new employment with the Highveld Steel company in Witbank. Since my parents had already moved, my brother Kobus and I stayed behind in the Vaal Triangle during our last months at Transvalia high school. I became a lodger with my friends, Danie and Gladys van Wyk, who were both extremely kind.

It was the end of 1984: I was not yet 18, and found myself at a loose end. I didn't have the money to go to university, and I was not excited either by the prospect of starting work or beginning compulsory military service. In the event, my parents agreed with my decision to attend an extra year at school to sit my matriculation exams again. I was still young, and I wanted to get better grades and secure a scholarship to university.

This was not in the tradition of our family, and I greatly appreciated the fact that my parents allowed me to continue my education when life would have been easier for them if I had gone out and started earning money. Not for the first time, or the last, they put my interests first, and I duly enrolled for just one year at the Patriot high school in Witbank.

The idea of becoming a lawyer had started to excite me, not simply for reasons of wanting to bring justice to the world. One of my friend's fathers was a lawyer, and he drove a large black Mercedes Benz. I was still chasing the same goal, still measuring my ambition in rand and cents.

The decision was made: my profession would be law.

My sports career also changed direction in Witbank. After showing such promise in 1984, my cricket began to drift and I failed to win selection to the Nuffield week team. I appeared to have hit my ceiling.

Meanwhile, rugby stepped powerfully to the fore. Patriot was not a recognized rugby school in the same way that Transvalia had been and, from being a face in the crowd at Transvalia, I became a larger fish in a relatively small pond. This was the boost I required. It is perfectly possible that, if I had not moved to Patriot, my rugby career would never have taken flight. Such is the unpredictability of school sport, such are the quirks of fate.

Playing in the trials, I tackled two guys into hospital, one with stitches to a head wound and another with concussion. I did not want to hurt anyone but it is a physical game. That is the way I wanted to play.

In an early match, we destroyed Witbank high school, the dominant English-speaking school in our area. Afrikaans schools such as ours used to enjoy playing English schools: we thought they were soft, and we invariably proved they were. I never lost a match against an English school.

My younger brother, Kobus, was also playing rugby, in fact emerging as a much stronger prospect than me. When he joined me in the Patriot 1st XV, I suggested to the coach he play at fly-half. That enabled us to pursue an excellent strategy where he would run the ball up the middle and, as a strong flanker, I would run off him. One memorable day we both played in the Patriot side that defeated the highly respected Middleburg HTS 9–6, winning the final of a rugby week and securing a rare Cup for our school.

On the back of these performances, I was selected to represent South Eastern Transvaal at the 1985 Craven week for provincial high school sides. That was the good news. The bad news was that the tournament would be staged in Witbank, so there would be no glamorous trip. We would be the host team, playing at home, staying at home.

Jaco Espag was named as my fellow flanker. He attended Witbank technical school and had become renowned as the school hero. In fact, a notable rivalry had developed between Jaco and myself in Witbank schools rugby. It became intense. I subsequently heard a rival school team in Witbank had pinned my photograph on the wall of their dressing room before a match against Patriot, and taken turns to spit at my image.

This antagonism towards me was probably explained by our family's recent arrival in the area and my physical approach on the field, but it soon spread to unreasonable proportions. On one occasion, before a major game, some youngsters threw a brick through our sitting-room window. Another time, the tyres on my father's car were let down.

Such was school rugby. It was a serious business.

I held my own course, with the result some people said I was arrogant. I would prefer to say I was self-assured. I know there can sometimes be a thin line between the two, and it did sometimes appear as if I stood apart.

Involuntarily, I became a topic of gossip.

There was a book of school laws at Patriot that laid down, among other things, how pupils should wear their hair. It clearly stated your hair should not touch your ears, so I cut my hair short at the sides but let it grow fashionably long and thick on top. The teachers told me to cut my hair, but I pointed out I was not infringing the rules, and they left me alone. In some ways, I enjoyed being different. Most boys at Patriot wore safari suits to school, but the fact was that I had always felt more comfortable in a jacket and tie. If my dress code earned me more attention, that was not a problem.

The headmaster at Patriot, Mr Welgemoed, seemed to understand where I was coming from. He often thanked me for my positive attitude to the school and my contribution to the improvement of the rugby team.

Craven week, I recognized, represented a huge opportunity. It has long been the foundation of South African rugby, the springboard from school into provincial age-group teams and on towards senior ranks. If you excelled during the week, you were set. If you failed, you sunk.

I had initially been named, ahead of Jaco Espag, as captain of the Witbank area trials side, but had been disturbed during a trial match when one of the teachers said he thought the captaincy would affect my play. We were playing to secure places in the South-Eastern Transvaal Craven week team and the message was clear: step down as captain or jeopardize your place. I was not going to risk irritating the selectors, so I asked not to be considered to lead the side and Espag was eventually named as captain. The teacher who warned me at the trial got what he wanted. I had just wanted to play.

As hosts, tradition demanded that we play the opening game and our opponents were announced as Western Province, a needle draw since the South Eastern Transvaal senior side had defeated the Province team in the 1984 Lion Cup, one of the greatest shocks for many years.

We lost the match, but there was some consolation in the words of Dr Danie Craven himself, president of the South African Rugby Board, who had watched and declared the two South Eastern Transvaal flankers impressed him more than anyone. However, I never had the opportunity to speak at any length with the greatest man in South Africa's rugby history before his death early in 1993. That will always be a regret.

Recovering well, we managed to win the remainder of our matches, and both Jaco Espag and I were named in the South African schools team announced at the end of the week. A young Natal schools fly-half called Joel Stransky had been selected in the national schools side of 1984, but he missed out in 1985. We would join forces ten years later.

The 1985 SA Schools XV played one fixture, against a South African Defence forces under-20 side, where I first found myself in opposition to a tall No. 8 from Northern Transvaal named Adriaan Richter.

My parents were obviously thrilled with my SA Schools cap, and I was pleased for them. I felt I had repaid them in part for the mornings when they drove me to practice or to a match, for the many days of sacrifice, even for the bricks sent flying though the front window and the flat tyres. My father and mother had never flinched in their support of my sport.

As a Nuffield week cricketer in 1984 and a Craven week rugby player in 1985, I was hopeful of securing a scholarship to university and it was the University of Potchefstroom who first made contact, offering me an annual bursary of R2,400 (£1200) which would cover all my tuition fees and maybe even pay for some of the other expenses associated with student life.

My personal preference, however, was for the University of Pretoria, where my girlfriend had already been awarded a place, but Tukkies could do no more than offer me an annual bursary of R700 (£350).

So I was heading to Potchefstroom when, out of the blue, the famous former Transvaal and Springbok player, Piet Malan, and RAU official Tap du Plessis arrived at my house. They wanted me to consider the Rand Afrikaans University in Johannesburg, and offered an annual bursary of R3,000 (£1500).

That was the deal.

By 1986, I was heading to RAU where I would study law ... and rugby. My steel foundations would, doubtless, stand me in good stead.

# CHAPTER TWO

# *Wild Days*

*I have learned more from my mistakes,*
*than from my successes*
Sir Harry Davy

South Africa is well equipped with universities, constructed in most of the major cities to groom the future. Rand Afrikaans University is one of the more modern institutions, constructed in concrete on the Witwatersrand ridge to the west of Johannesburg's central business district.

RAU may be relatively new, built on a golf course during the 1970s, but there is no lack of tradition or pride among its students.

This much was made abundantly clear upon my arrival in 1985. I had been placed in the Afslaan men's hostel; this surprised me since I knew most of the sportsmen were dispatched to Dromedaris. Nonetheless, my parents drove me to Johannesburg, my father pressed R100 (£50) into my hand as he wished me luck, and I braced myself for RAU.

*Welcome to Afslaan.*

Late afternoon on the first day, approximately 150 first-year students were summoned to a meeting in the hostel's mess hall. I knew no-one except for a farmer's son from Lichtenberg, a North-West province town, with whom I was sharing a room. We were nervous and apprehensive. Tales of initiation ceremonies in the hostels were rife, but nobody knew quite what to expect. I had not been well, spending two weeks in hospital with an acute virus, and had lost 12 kilograms in weight, but nothing was going to keep me away from the initiation.

So we waited, Afslaan's new intake.

The lights were flicked on and off. People started giggling.

Suddenly, the doors were flung open and unshaven guys, all smelling of alcohol, burst into the dining hall and started pushing people around. There was noise, aggression, bedlam, shouting, people being hit with cricket bats. I was pressed backwards by the crush, and dramatically pushed through a window.

Blood.

Broken glass.

Members of the House Committee took me to hospital to stitch up the wound in my back and, within an hour, I rejoined the initiation.

The essence of this ritual was to establish respect for second- and third-year students and to engender a shared pride in membership of Afslaan. The hostel was structured on a Roman model: with a *dictator* at the top, assisted by the *magistrum*, *quaestors*, *senators* and *mandators*. The authority system was rigorously laid down. For example, first years were instructed not to look *quaestors* in the eye, but to greet them while looking at the floor.

Next morning, we were woken at four o'clock and ordered to set off on a five-kilometre run. Thus began another 24 hours of shouting, and pushing, and orders and discipline. Sportsmen were expected to lead, so *quaestors* took special care to push you and harass you more eagerly.

Arriving back at the hostel, we were each given an egg, on which we were told to collect the signatures of all the *quaestors*. The clever first years kept their eggs in plastic bags while others, like me, simply put them in their pockets, where they were promptly broken during the next round of pushing and shouting. The initiation was relentless, but never cruel.

The hostel, set apart from the rest of the University, was divided into three areas: Upper Town, Central Town and Chain Valley. The tough students were reputed to stay in Chain Valley, from where you would walk across to the main campus, passing a sign which read 'You are leaving Chain

Valley alive, so thank your lucky stars'. At the centre of the hostel, there stood a statue of a woman, naked from the waist. This was known as *Uxor Aphrodite*, the last living virgin at Afslaan, and all the first-year students were compelled to greet the statue each and every morning.

*Good morning, Uxor Aphrodite.*

From the outside, the saga may seem childish but I believe the entire process served an important purpose. We were a group of people who had come together from a broad range of backgrounds and the trauma bonded us together as a unit. The value of an individual was zero. We were educated in the skills of relying on your colleagues and being relied upon.

I accepted the system, and enjoyed it. I met the challenge of greeting *quaestors* by memorizing their footwear. I will always remember how *quaestor* Peet Strauss wore flip-flops with tipex on his left toe. With my eyes gazing at the floor, that is all I would need to see before intoning solemnly: 'Good morning, quaestor Peet.' And so it went on: tradition demanded that we were made to wear special purple buttons on our blazers for more than six months.

In years to come, I would become a *quaestor* and perpetrate the same structure. We wanted membership of Afslaan to be something special, and it was special. Some guys could not cope with the discipline and the ritual, and they left to other hostels where they felt more comfortable. That was fine, but the overwhelming majority of us stayed, and loved it.

The last night of initiation was a social evening with the ladies. First years were compelled to comb their hair forward and to carry their toothpaste in one pocket and their deodorant spray in the other. We would then be told to dance while the most appalling music was played.

Yes, people were humiliated.

Yes, there was more shouting and pushing.

But we were becoming a unit. Adversity was breeding camaraderie. It was a useful lesson not only for rugby, but for life. Within two weeks, I felt as if I belonged at RAU. I was confident and assured … and careful to recall not only the names of the *quaestors* but also their preferred footwear.

The next challenge was Law first year.

I sat at the back of the lecture room. After all, I was from Witbank and would surely not be expected to sit in the front row and answer questions. We had been warned that Latin would prove the hardest element of the subject, and it was perhaps my sense of trepidation which led me to take my place at the first Latin class for those with surnames starting with any letter from A to N. It was only during the role call that I realized my mistake.

This was serious. I had to pass Latin. I had no spare money to pay for retakes, failure would mean the end of my university career and I had started by attending the wrong class. I sprinted to the room for those with surnames starting with a letter from O to Z, and quietly slipped in to take my place in the back row – sadly, not quite quietly enough.

'Good morning!'

It was the lecturer, Mr Basson. He had spotted me.

'What is your name?'

'François.'

'No, your name!'

'Pienaar.'

'Welcome, Mr Pienaar.'

From that undistinguished start, this young, clever lecturer took delight in driving me hard, aiming questions at me, and it was due to his interest that I ultimately took the exam and passed Latin with distinction.

Throughout my years at RAU, my primary challenge was to maintain my studies while giving my full commitment to rugby. The rugby, of course, had to take precedence. I could not afford to miss any training or matches for lectures or exams, so I put in place a system where, if I was to miss a lecture, I would arrange to borrow the notes of someone who was there.

It was usually a nuisance, and I often stayed up long after

midnight, copying notes, but that was my resolve. I wanted to secure my law degree, I wanted the security of a professional qualification and I was prepared to pay the price in terms of setting aside more exciting pastimes.

These were nominally amateur days for rugby union, when teams held training sessions in the evening and generally left the days free. The modern professional era now tends to demand a player's time from nine o'clock in the morning through until late afternoon, and the challenge of pursuing a rugby career and completing a degree at the same time has become much harder. I believe it can still be done, but only with the strongest resolve.

I completed B proc in four years and, in 1989, set about a further two-year course to complete my LLB. As my rugby commitments grew, so the task became greater. Many of my team-mates either allowed their studies to drift or took five or six years to complete their four-year course. For me, it was imperative to complete in four years because initially I was concerned about not being able to afford to stay longer.

Professor Sonnekus had earned a uniquely tough reputation at RAU, most notably for making absolutely zero allowance for sportsmen with other commitments. My course had reached a point where I could choose to sit either Private Law 4 or Private Law 5. Professor Sonnekus would take one of the classes. I heard a rumour he would take the latter.

So I selected Private Law 4.

I was wrong.

Sonnekus was named to take my class.

My heart sunk. I feared my chances of completing a degree were all but over. By this time, I was playing provincial rugby. Sonnekus held classes at 8 p.m., Transvaal trained at 8 p.m. There seemed no solution.

But I tried.

I needed to secure an average 50% mark during the semester tests to qualify for the final exams, and my chances were not helped when Sonnekus gave me zero for the midweek tests which I had been unable to write because of rugby practice. There was no opportunity to write the test later. Nonetheless, I kept my head down and, with luck, qualified for the exam, part of which would be oral. My time was booked for early morning, at 7.45 a.m.

Motivated by the challenge, I woke at five, ran through some last gasp revision, dressed and headed for Sonnekus' rooms on the seventh floor of A building. It would be an exaggeration to say I was feeling confident, but I was not shrinking from the challenge. I saw some friends outside the building and chatted for a while, having arrived 30 minutes early, I thought.

'François, where have you been?'

It was one of my classmates.

'Why?'

'Sonnekus is going crazy. You were supposed to be here at six forty-five.'

I was shattered. The idea that I had come all this way and would now fail the exam because I got the time wrong was too much to bear. I knocked on the Professor's door, breathless and desperate.

'Prof., I'm sorry. My car broke down,' I lied.

'Mr Pienaar, wait outside, please.'

It was just before 7.30 a.m. I waited until 12.30 p.m. that afternoon. Then, to my sublime relief, I was allowed to sit the test. The first question related to a subject where my knowledge was thin, but I recalled the advice of a fellow student, Chris Troskie, who had told me that whatever I do I should not say I have no idea. He had done that and Sonnekus had failed him. Instead, I started to flannel, saying I was nervous and rattled.

Sonnekus was accompanied by an outside examiner, who started to assist me, setting me at ease and helping me along. I managed some kind of answer and embarked upon probably the most gruelling 45 minutes of my life so far. At the end of it all, to my delight, I was told I had passed. It was maybe the toughest challenge of all. I had passed Sonnekus!

Rugby seemed straightforward by comparison.

My first year on the expansive RAU sports fields was occupied simply by the challenge of being selected for the Afslaan hostel team. Hostel rugby was grimly competitive and one of the most satisfying victories of my career unfolded when our unheralded Afslaan team defeated Dromedaris, nominally the most powerful sports hostel. There followed a party of note.

Progress was sustained to the University under-20 side, coached by Wim Hollander, and on to trials for the Transvaal provincial under-20 team. I was enjoying my rugby, settled at flank, tackling hard, running hard, feeling confident and assured. At the Transvaal under-20 trials, I rediscovered Jaco Espag, my teammate from Craven week now studying at Goudstad teachers' training college. We clicked back into our old pattern, and utterly dominated the afternoon – Jaco scored three tries and I scored two.

The consensus was that we would both be automatic selections for the provincial side but a problem loomed – Easter was beckoning and a group of us had planned to watch the national club championships in Durban, but the Transvaal under-20 side was now scheduled to hold a further trial on Easter Monday. In a dilemma, I telephoned Gerrie Germishuys, the convener and former Springbok wing.

'Obviously, I am keen to play in the team and I am prepared to cancel the trip to Durban if you need me at the trial,' I told him.

'Unfortunately,' he replied, 'you know you and Espag are in the side. We only want to sort out the centre pairing in any case.'

I said that didn't matter.

He responded by suggesting the Monday training was not important and repeated, cryptically, 'You already know you are in the side.' So I went to Durban, and watched Despatch win the club championships. The rugby was positive, the vibes were great and I really enjoyed the event.

The following Tuesday in Johannesburg, the Transvaal under-20 side was named. I was astonished to find I had been left out. Kenny van Rooyen, also from RAU, had been named on the side of the scrum. I quickly contacted the coach, Wim Hollander, who told me Gerrie Germishuys had informed the selection committee I had made myself unavailable.

Gerrie was from Goudstad, I was from RAU – there was intense rivalry between the two institutions and I suffered the consequences. It was my first brush with the kind of politics that besets rugby. Maybe he just wanted to teach me a lesson.

Almost every senior player has encountered some similarly perverted selection, some illogical incident at some stage of their career. It seems to go with the territory. Petty, small-minded politics has too often been the sad curse of South African rugby.

As the season wore on, I eventually earned my place in the provincial under-20 team and, happily, was able to make a strong contribution as RAU narrowly outlasted Goudstad to win the under-20 league.

The following year, 1987, I continued playing for RAU under-20 and Transvaal under-20, and moved forward a further step by winning selection for the South African under-20 team to play a touring team from England, known as the British Bulldogs. Coached by Jamie Salmon and captained by Andy Robinson, the touring team was older and stronger, and earned my respect during an intensely physical mini-Test at Loftus. They won, narrowly.

Fresh, young faces were starting to appear in teams around me. Pieter Hendriks, a dynamic wing, and Ian MacDonald, a powerful flank, were shining in the Transvaal under-20 team. We were flying around the country, playing in curtain-raisers to Currie Cup matches, having fun and, even in these dark days of amateurism, being paid R30 (£6), in cash, per game.

The money made a difference.

My bursary covered a little more than my tuition fees, so I was grateful when my father arranged part-time, holiday work for me at Highveld Steel in Witbank. It was rough work, cleaning the heavy equipment around the plant, working the drill to clear the refuse of the steel-making process, but the job earned me enough money to live a comfortable student life.

This arrangement continued every vacation for four years. I would get up early in the morning, clock in and then work for 12 hours. I would work for 16 hours on public holidays, to be sure of maximizing the double pay, and most years, this included the entire Christmas holiday. The conditions were often unbearably hot and I was invariably covered in dirt.

But I stuck at it. In some strange way, I think I wanted to prove to my father that I did not think I was something special by attending university and studying for a law degree. I wanted to show him that I could also put on a pair of dirty overalls and get the tough jobs done, just as he had all his life. And I wanted to show him, not by words but by actions.

*Enough money to live a normal student life.*

Some people might not consider my general behaviour as a student at RAU, beyond the studies and the rugby, as normal at all, but I hope it can be seen in the context of a young man who had emerged from an unfashionable part of the country and wanted to make his mark in Johannesburg. To stand back, to shrink from any challenge seemed to me, at that time, to be a mark of weakness – and I desperately wanted to be strong, wanted to be a winner, wanted to be someone who people respected and admired.

To some extent, I had achieved this goal at school by being prepared literally to fight for my status. The same would apply at university.

From 1986 through to the early 1990s, a Saturday ritual developed in which we would play rugby, shower, change and gather at Aligators, a bar not far from the RAU campus. Wayne Willemse, Louw Barnard, Peet Strauss, me and others were a group of students looking for a good time, and that resolve usually took us to Hillbrow, a cosmopolitan suburb north of downtown Johannesburg, renowned for its bars, its clubs, its buzz.

Hillbrow became our home on Saturday nights; we would then sleep most of Sunday, rising only to attend church in the evening. In Hillbrow, we would drink, and laugh and, more often than not, fight.

Fighting was part of the landscape, part of the deal. People went to the clubs, knowing what might happen, usually hoping it would happen. There was never an incident involving innocent bystanders. The fights were fought between consenting adults, young men who sought a challenge. Bouncers at the clubs and the police were other players in the game.

Saturday after Saturday, this became a way of life. In a sense, I was trapped by my reputation. People had heard I was a fighter, so they provoked me and, in order not to look a coward, I had to respond. Invariably, there was little more damage than a broken chair and a black eye.

But there were bad times, when the game turned sour.

One day…

I had temporarily split up with my girlfriend, Mirna Moller, and I felt restless, so I went to Afslaan to find some guys for a drink. Lou Barnard was sick in bed, with possible pneumonia. He initially said he did not want to go out, and I should have left him alone, but I pestered and pestered him until he agreed, and we started on the familiar circuit of bars and clubs.

By two o'clock in the morning, the two of us were sitting on a pavement outside the Fontana café in Hillbrow, minding our own business and eating an entire roast chicken with our fingers. Then, two guys walked past, making some unflattering remarks. Louw answered back. The guys stopped, looked at us. We looked at them. These were the signs. We all understood what was happening. Anyone could have chosen to back off. No-one did.

One of them went for Louw, the other came for me. I managed to force him down, punched him several times to the body and, in a surge of anger, grabbed his head and slammed it into the pavement. The sickening thud snapped me back to my senses. I panicked. I shouted to Louw that we should get out of there, and we ran up the street to the next block.

We disappeared into the darkness. I was certain I had killed him. He had not moved. There was blood. I was seized by fear. We waited and before long heard the sounds of an ambulance and police car pulling up in front of the café. Louw said we should get back to the hostel as quickly as possible. The problem was that his car was parked near the café.

Composing myself, I said that we should walk back to the scene as if we were nothing but innocent bystanders, calmly get into the car and drive off. I was trying to stay calm, but all the time the idea was bouncing around my head that I had killed the guy. What would happen then?

As we turned the corner, we noticed a group of people had gathered around where the guy had fallen. Unable to resist curiosity and showing some nerve, I joined the milling crowd and, peering between the people, saw, to my intense relief, the guy seemed to be all right. He was dazed and bloodied but there was no serious damage. I was lucky.

While he was being helped to his feet by two bystanders, he looked up, narrowed his eyes and recognized my face in the crowd.

'It was you who punched me,' he exclaimed, pointing in my direction.

'You were looking for trouble,' I replied.

A nervous pause.

'Don't worry, cousin,' he said. 'It was a good punch.'

Then he smiled, and was patched up by the medics. When they were left alone, Louw and I decided to give the other guys R10 (£2), which they promptly used to buy themselves a roast chicken.

It had been just another Saturday in Hillbrow.

Strangely, such experiences opened up new opportunities for me to earn some money and, classically turning from poacher to gamekeeper, I was eventually appointed to head the security team during the students' Rag Week celebrations. For five days, the entire campus essentially became a party and I accepted the well-remunerated challenge of ensuring top security with enthusiasm. As the drink flowed fast, we would usually be called upon to resolve two or three major fights each night. Our systems worked and I took pride in the successful execution of our plan.

Yet there were darks days here, too. The student tradition was to build decorated floats for the Rag parade through the streets of Johannesburg, and this chore would traditionally turn into an all-night party. At around one in the morning, I received a call on the walkie-talkie informing me of a fight. I rushed to the scene and found a guy who had passed out.

With his girlfriend in tears, I felt for his heart, found nothing and started mouth-to-mouth resuscitation, the procedure for which I had learned while at school. The guy then vomited red wine all over me and, when a doctor arrived, we started massaging his heart. But there was nothing we could do. He died, aged only 24.

When I had fetched a blanket and covered the body, the guy's father arrived on the scene. I told him he should not look at his son as he lay there, and the father landed a full punch on my jaw. Other people started shouting, but I was simply trying to keep everyone calm. The coroner's van arrived at around three in the morning and took the body away.

I felt numb.

My rugby career continued to develop apace with my appointment as captain of the RAU first team at the start of the 1988 season. It was a brave decision by coach Koos Ehlers since I was still only 21, but I wanted to prove him right as quickly as possible. Our first major match was the inter-varsity match against Tukkies, the University of Pretoria.

The entire University seemed to be involved in the event, from The Big Brag, a formal presentation of the XV in the main student auditorium on the Thursday night when we were made to feel like Hollywood superstars, right through to the match at the RAU stadium, packed with 18,000 students, on the Saturday. And we won comfortably on one of the happiest afternoons of my career.

It had been my first really big rugby occasion.

My first taste of top-class rugby before a large, boisterous crowd.

It tasted fantastic.

As ever, I was embroiled in RAU's ongoing struggle with Goudstad in the league but I was, by now, also playing for the Transvaal provincial B side, named the Rooibokke, and being asked to play for prestigious Invitation XVs such as the Quaggas. I was aware of increasing media coverage as well, but my general self-confidence was not especially high.

If anyone had sat me down during the course of 1988 and asked me if I thought I would play senior professional rugby, let alone international rugby, I would probably have answered no. I still had a long way to go. Some players burst into top rugby, whereas I was developing at a steady pace.

My progress was positive. Each year, I set goals which were realistic and achievable, taking care to look and learn along the way. My advice to young players has always been the same: in sport, consistent progress more often leads to longevity at the top of the game while the firefly who bursts spectacularly upon the scene tends to burn out.

Into 1989, I left the Afslaan hostel having reached the rank of *senator* and moved into one of the ideal bachelor apartments which the University set aside for promising sportsmen such as Kuifie van der Merwe, Hendrik Truter, Chris Kasselman, Warren McCann, athlete Karel Mouton and me.

The art of making money continued to be exciting. I worked as a barman at special events, and spotted an opportunity within the hostels when rumours that hostels would open bars on their premises came to nothing. I asked the Afslaan house committee if I could start a venture and run it. They had no objection and gave me the green light.

So I bought a cheap fridge and was given another by Louw Barnard, who became my partner in the enterprise. I secured a helpful liquor supplier in Melville, who would pass on the bargains of the week, and we started business in earnest, supplying alcohol to the guys in the hostel. Knowing students, and their habit of not carrying cash, we started a book in which a customer could run up an account and pay later. Whenever I needed money, I would chase down my debts on a Monday morning.

When the Springboks played Test matches, as they did against the International XV in 1989, we created a social event in the hostel, brought in some televisions and supplied the alcohol. It was a huge success.

This venture excited me. Making money was fun. After a year, I sold the business to the house committee as a going concern for R3,000 (£600).

Through the 1989 season, I continued to captain RAU and play for the Rooibokke, becoming familiar with the major stadiums in South African rugby and taking a greater interest in the major players of the day.

I had attended the Transvaal senior trials and been surprised by the levels of physical contact. It became clear to me that I would need to be much stronger to survive. Hours in the gym developing my upper body strength beckoned but Wahl Bartmann and Charles Pieterse were the incumbent first team flankers and they were very clearly in no mood to yield their position to the new youngster from RAU with the shock of fair hair.

The atmosphere was intimidating and no-one spoke to me although Dries Maritz, the veteran Vaal centre, did raise my spirits. When I tackled him solidly in the midfield, he responded by saying 'good tackle'. That was all, but it meant a lot to a youngster at his first trial.

As the weeks passed, the personalities of Transvaal rugby became increasingly familiar and, in particular, I was hugely impressed by Kevin de Klerk, a former Springbok lock, then a provincial selector. A physically huge man, he had gained a hard reputation on the rugby field. My friend, Louw Barnard, had once played lock against him and he told me how Kevin had addressed him as they approached the first lineout.

'All right, young man, this is how it will work,' Kevin said. 'My ball is my ball and we will talk about your ball.'

He was like an old bull, protecting his turf. Louw reckoned he would take up the challenge so he jumped for Kevin's first ball – and his lights went out very quickly. That was how the game was played.

Yet, despite this toughness on the field, Kevin de Klerk was the most elegant and gentle man off the field. He seemed to have got the balance just right, providing a model which I tried to emulate thereafter. In the years to come, I would always call him 'Oom Kevin'. I respected him.

On occasions, I would walk down to the RAU fields where Transvaal trained in the evenings and, keeping my distance to remain unseen, I would watch as Bartmann and Pieterse, the two flankers, set about the training runs up a hill. I would time their runs, assessing their performance.

The next day, when nobody was around, I would return to the fields and run the same hills, measuring my performance against theirs. I wanted to be as fit as them. I was growing hungry for success.

The 1989 season unfolded as a disappointment for Transvaal rugby. Louis Luyt, a self-made millionaire, had taken over as the Union president in 1984 and helped transform a perennially losing team into one which reached the Currie Cup Finals of 1986 and 1987, but both Finals were lost. Luyt was grimly determined to bring the Currie Cup back to Ellis Park and the turnover of both players and coaches became high as he hunted his goal. Poor results were invariably followed by crisis and new personnel.

Derek Minnie, a successful businessman, was coaching Transvaal in 1989 and, when it was clear that Western Province and Northern Transvaal would contest the Currie

Cup Final for a second successive year, he started to draft a few younger players into his first team squad.

Ian MacDonald was one of them, I was another.

Transvaal's season was effectively over, but I managed to perform well in home victories over Northern Free State and Eastern Province. My debut had passed as quickly as everyone said it would and, without going far out of their way, scrum-half Garth Wright and centre Martin Knoetze had helped me settle into the provincial team's environment.

The year ended with hope of better times ahead for Transvaal rugby, but the atmosphere was unpredictable and tense. Cheese van Tonder was another loose forward who had emerged in the provincial side, and I quickly found myself embroiled in another intense rivalry with a team-mate – we were both competing for the same place on the side of the scrum.

Cheese was reported to have said: 'If François Pienaar plays provincial rugby before me, then I will stop playing the game.'

When I heard this remark, it would be an understatement to say I was motivated to prove myself as a provincial player in 1990, and beyond.

The challenge was upon me.

# CHAPTER THREE

# *A Rugby Education*

Through more than 100 years of Transvaal rugby, young men had played their first match for the province and then faced an initiation ceremony. This was the tradition, their ritual admission to a select club.

Now it was my turn. The format of initiation had evolved over the years and by the early 1990s the ceremony was performed at a team meeting held after an away match. Thus, although I had made my Transvaal debut at the end of the 1989 season, my formal initiation had to wait until my first away match, at the start of the 1990 season. I respected the tradition, of course I did, but I found the experience to be degrading and humiliating.

We had played against Natal, and four of us were due to be initiated in the team room at our Durban hotel – Judex Burnett, Heinie Rietman, Cabous van der Westhuizen and me. We were stripped to our jockstraps, blindfolded and led into the room where our team-mates had gathered.

We were asked to stand on a chair and tell jokes, but no-one laughed. We were to be briefly humiliated. All the while we were instructed to rub butter into our hair, and to drink cans of beer. This was no problem but, then, each new player was told to lie on a table while the other 20 players poured beer over him and slapped his body as they sang the initiation song.

I can remember some of the Goudstad players in the Transvaal team taking full advantage of this opportunity to punish me. In their mind, I was the arrogant RAU captain and they wanted to teach me a lesson. I can still recall the look on their faces as they beat me. I was prepared to take it, and I did, but we were asked to perform other acts that night, acts which don't need to be detailed here, but which would degrade any man.

In the years that followed, these primitive rituals were abolished and replaced by a much shorter ceremony in which a trembling debutant would bend over a chair and be slapped on the backside by every member of the squad, usually once, sometimes twice. That may sound mild, but this was no slap and tickle. Powerful forwards, weighing 110 kilograms, would relish the invitation to pound their palms into soft flesh. Slight backline players would frequently be reduced to tears by the thundering barrage, and the bruising would often be spectacular, but they all recovered.

Legend suggests Springbok initiation ceremonies through the 1960s and 1970s were the most intense, the most brutal and the most unforgettable (in the worst sense of every word), but even these celebrated occasions were toned down during the 1990s. By general consent, we replaced the beating with the recitation of a Springbok Code of Honour.

The player would read out a pledge while keeping his right hand placed on the actual Springbok cap awarded to Dr Danie Craven on the occasion of his own debut for the national side in the 1930s. It is hard to overestimate the pride which every Springbok player feels for the jersey and it seems to me that a Code of Honour is a more appropriate measure of that pride than ten empty beer cans and a bruised body. It may have served a purpose in days gone by, but we had moved on.

Others may disagree, suggesting the ritual humiliation brought every player to the same level and effectively built team spirit. I can only say that was certainly not my personal experience. I don't believe I have ever forgotten the Goudstad players who gleefully battered my body black and blue back in 1990. Even now, I can recall their names. If that experience was supposed to build team spirit, then it had the opposite effect on me.

It is often supposed that any young player finds his second

season of provincial rugby the most difficult of his career. While many shine in their first year as an unknown quantity, it is true that many fade when opponents start devising strategies which counter their strengths and expose weaknesses. The mark of a genuine provincial player is one who can survive the attention, stay ahead of the pack and still make an impact at that level.

My second season at senior level, in 1990, would become distinctly uncomfortable, but it began in glorious fashion when I captained RAU to the national club championships, staged over the Easter weekend in Durban. As winners of the Pirates Grand Challenge, the Transvaal club competition, we were representing our province at the tournament. At stages, certain clubs had approached the prospect of Durban at Easter in holiday mode; others handled their players with rigid discipline.

Our attitude was different and, perhaps, ahead of its time. At the start of the tournament, I told the players we wanted to see them only at the training sessions and team meetings. The rest of the time was their own, but I did add they should resist alcohol and they should rest their legs for long periods. In aiming to win three matches in five days, we needed to retain all the energy we could.

The concept was to treat the players like adults, to leave most of the discipline to the players themselves and to focus on the rugby. This works for most professional teams today, and it worked for RAU in 1990.

We overwhelmed Villagers, champion club of the Western Province, in our opening match and won through to meet the University of Pretoria in the final. That afternoon at King's Park, our forwards dominated the set-pieces and rampaged in the loose while our backs picked all the fruits out wide. Our comfortable victory gave me intense pleasure. Tukkies had not enjoyed much success at the Club Championships over the years, but they remained one of the mighty, established clubs of South African rugby. It was a notable triumph for RAU, in the national spotlight, live on SABC television.

By the early hours of Tuesday morning, the celebrations had found their way to Durban's Marine Parade and I was drawn towards a group of players standing outside a restaurant. We were happy, relaxed and feeling playful. Someone passed me a cigarette, but it was obviously not a normal cigarette, and I duly inhaled my tentative first draw of marijuana, or *dagga* as South Africans say. There followed a frantic bout of coughing from deep within my lungs to ensure the first drag would be the last.

Victory at the 1990 Club Championships provided me with a valuable injection of self-confidence at a crucial stage of my career. We had won a major trophy, I had captained the side and I felt good about myself. Young players may swagger and saunter, but they are all uncertain and nervous on the inside. I was no different, and success so early in my career gave me the confidence to move forward in the game. I took from the happy scenes at King's Park the certain knowledge that I could succeed at the highest level.

Transvaal struggled through 1990. Derek Minnie was a knowledgeable and likeable coach, but we lost a couple of close matches and swiftly fell out of Currie Cup contention. I suffered an ankle injury that kept me out of action for six weeks midway through the season and two bold young flankers, Ian MacDonald and Cheese van Tonder, took advantage of my absence to seize a place in the provincial team. It was only with some difficulty that I battled back to displace Cheese as the season ended in a whimper.

As ever, a disappointing year prompted a change of coach and Minnie was replaced by Harry Viljoen, a former provincial scrum-half who had become a highly successful businessman in his own right. From the start, it was easy to understand why Harry had enjoyed so much success in every sphere of his life. He was driven by an infectious enthusiasm and an exciting willingness to dare and be different from the rest. He respected the past, but he was not imprisoned by traditions.

Harry Viljoen flung open the doors of Transvaal rugby, and fresh winds billowed through the corridors. It was an invigorating time. We prepared for the 1991 season not with a tough physical regime in Johannesburg, but with a carefully planned training camp at the coastal town of Hermanus. Suddenly, we were running on the beaches, training and having fun together.

Chris van Loggerenberg, a respected fitness expert, was appointed to lead a new, scientific, enjoyable exercise programme which had the players training at the Sports Connection gym, in Sandton, at 6 a.m. most mornings. It was professional and it was fun. Each performance was monitored, and we pushed ourselves to new levels of physical fitness.

The result was a memorable season. Transvaal played spectacular rugby during 1991, running the ball from our own line, dreaming and daring, hinting at a new game far removed from the attrition of the 1980s. For many years, South African rugby had been dominated by the power game: massive forwards trundling from set-piece to set-piece, driven on by fly-halves kicking the ball huge distances to grind down their opponents. This was the school of 'subdue and penetrate', the old dictum of Brigadier Buurman van Zyl, the legendary Northern Transvaal coach of the 1970s.

Harry envisaged a different, modern game, one where the fly-half attacked the advantage line and popped passes to team-mates on the burst. As a flanker, I felt liberated and exhilarated by the game plan. At the inspired suggestion of Ian MacDonald, we had started to play as open and blindside flankers rather than as the traditional No.6 and No.7. This was new ground for South African rugby, and the strategy was an immediate success.

The open side flank, fast and mobile, would go for the fly-half from the set-pieces – Harry called him a 'missile' – while the blindside flanker would be the damage man, the powerful physical barrier. People said MacDonald and I were the best flanks in the country that season, and we looked good because we were able to grow within the inspired strategy of a bold coach.

As praise for my performances increased, I became aware of special attention from the opposition: an elbow here, a face rubbed into the turf there. Nothing major, nothing to warrant a penalty, but enough to let me know that this was a man's game where nothing came easy.

Transvaal were drawn to play Eastern Province during the annual Test Union's day of 1991, and we prepared for an intensely physical match. A few weeks before, I had gained some knowledge of rugby in the Eastern Cape by playing for a Kohler Invitation XV. The invited Transvaal players were thrilled to be paid R1,000 (£200) each for the fixture, but we earned our money in a physical match that occasionally bordered on brutal.

That was fine. I didn't flinch from a physical contest. Early in the game against Eastern Province, a lineout was tapped back on our side. The referee blew his whistle to signal a scrum for a knock-on. Then, I felt this tremendous hammer blow to the side of my jaw. Armand du Preez, the EP lock forward, had delivered a completely unprovoked punch from behind.

I never lost consciousness but my jaw was hanging loose and blood was pouring everywhere. I immediately walked off the field and was able to push my tongue into my lower jaw. It was horrifying. I was angry, moved to tears of fury in the changing room by the sheer brutality of the attack. The incident had taken place so far from play, scarcely anyone had seen what happened. I recall our captain, Jannie Breedt, being unaware afterwards.

The specialist at the stadium's medical centre had decided I would need the operation that evening and one of the nurses offered me a lift to the hospital in her *bakkie*, which was fortunate because there was no-one else from either my team or the host union to help me. While I waited in the car park for the nurse to fetch the vehicle, the wound in my jaw dripped to such an extent that I left a gruesome pool of blood on the tarmac.

The operation to reconstruct my jawbone took three hours that night, and I awoke the next morning with a face which was grotesquely swollen and unthinkably painful.

So this was rugby?

You play the game.

You get assaulted from behind.

You are left on your own.

And you hitch a lift to hospital to have a major operation.

As I lay in the ward, I felt terribly disappointed in a game that could treat its players in such fashion. I had been seriously hurt and essentially left to look after myself.

Then, out of the blue, Toks van der Linde, playing prop for Free State, appeared in my ward and raised my spirits. His girlfriend had assisted me as I left the ground the previous night and he had just turned up to see how I was feeling. It was a remarkable gesture from someone whom I had not known very well. We were just two young rugby players, and he was probably aware that I had not been treated particularly well. At any rate, whatever the reason, he was there and I have never forgotten his gesture.

The RAU rugby administrators were appalled by the state of my face and they asked the Transvaal Rugby Union if they would consider taking any steps against Armand du Preez on my behalf. The lock forward had, after all, assaulted me from behind after the whistle was blown. The answer was 'no'. It appeared as though I was an expendable young player who had been punched, and the TRU was not prepared to make any waves on my behalf.

'It was a man's game... There was no point moaning ... Cowboys don't cry' – the clichés flowed. Du Preez escaped unscathed.

My sentence, as the victim, was a wired-up jaw and to be ruled out of rugby for seven weeks. Life was no easier when I returned to full fitness. No more than five minutes into my first match back, a club fixture for RAU, I was deliberately punched in exactly the place where I had broken my jaw.

Then, at a physical Transvaal trial match, organized a few days later, I was struck another blow on the jaw, this time by Ian Hattingh, the very player who had taken my place in the Transvaal team. Strangely, I was almost grateful for these deliberate blows because my ability to take them rebuilt my confidence. I developed a sincere respect for Ian Hattingh in years to come and we would become friends, at one with a hard game.

Week by week, I was learning to look after myself on the rugby field but the physical challenge was no easier away from the game. As a provincial rugby player with a growing reputation, I soon became a target for provocation whenever I walked into a bar – and, even in 1991, I was too young and naïve to keep out of trouble.

Transvaal had beaten Western Province at Newlands and, later that evening, we were gathered as a squad for our customary court session after an away match. The proceedings were abruptly disturbed by shouting in the adjacent hotel bar. Johan le Roux, the Transvaal prop, was there with some friends and some of us left the court to settle things down. We weren't looking for trouble, we were simply trying to resolve the trouble.

We found chaos with Johan in the middle of a mass brawl, but tempers were starting to cool when one guy came up to me from behind and cracked a beer bottle over my head. As I turned, he ran to the toilets but I followed him, cornered him in the Gents and hit him hard. I was angry, and sore. The stranger fell, unaware of what or who had struck him. James Small, Hendrik Truter and Harry Roberts were all standing around. I cleaned the cut above my ear and, after a few minutes, returned to the court session.

My head was spinning.

I knew matters had spiralled out of hand, but it was hard to understand where I had lost control. One of my friends, Johan le Roux, was involved in a bar fight and I went to try and calm things down; then I had retaliated against a complete stranger who hit me over the head with a bottle.

The following week, a lawyer's letter arrived at the Transvaal Rugby Union accusing Hendrik Truter and James Small of assaulting the man in the men's toilet. I was not even mentioned, but the guys didn't say a word and covered for me. In the end, the union agreed to pay around R7,000 (£1400) and the parties settled out of court. It had been a lucky escape although Louis Luyt did warn me about my behaviour, explaining I could not afford to react to any provocation. He was right. I had learned my lesson – almost.

Not quite.

One quiet evening the next year, in 1992, I went to a pub called Late Night Dukes in the Johannesburg suburb of Melville with a few team-mates: Chris Dirks, Hein Jordaan and Cabous van der Westhuizen. The era of fighting every Saturday night in Hillbrow was in my past. We were going to have a couple of drinks, relax a little, nothing dramatic.

Chris started talking to this girl, but we were very quiet when a group of guys approached us. One of them bit a chunk of glass out of his beer mug, and spat it on the floor. We didn't pay much attention. Then Chris' friend lost her earring and started searching for it on the floor.

'You bitch, you're vomiting on my shoes,' said the glass-eater.

'She's only looking for her earring,' I replied.

Thick-set and muscular with a powerful bull neck, he pushed me in the chest. He obviously meant business but I struck him with my right fist as hard as I could and he fell to the ground. As his friends carried him away, I noticed the blow had split open the skin on my knuckles, exposing the bare bone. It was clear I would need stitches in the wound.

As I headed for the exit, on my way to hospital, five or six of the group returned to the pub and were soon blocking my path.

'Come on, guys, I'm not looking for trouble,' I said.

'Well, you've found it,' one guy replied.

They piled in, knocking me to the ground, kicking me and punching me from head to toe. Cabous tried to help me, and was knocked out cold. The battering only stopped when one of my assailants warned his friends they would kill me unless they eased off. It had been five against one, and I was in a terrible state.

The staff at the JG Strydom hospital could not have been more kind as they repaired my face, chest and hand, but I was still extremely angry. I told them I was not drunk, and that I wanted them to call the police so I could lay charges against the people who had attacked me.

While I was receiving stitches to my hand, I looked up and saw the first guy I had hit arriving in the Accident and Emergency ward. I was consoled to see he had lost his front teeth, but then concerned to discover he had been escorted to hospital by the rest of the group.

They saw me.

'You haven't heard the end of this, Pienaar,' one shouted.

'We'll find you and kill you,' said another.

I said nothing and, my wounds tended, swiftly left the hospital by a side entrance. Two days later, with stitches in my nose and my left eye still swollen shut I was told that a group of 30 men had been hanging around Late Night Dukes looking for me, asking where I lived. The situation was becoming serious. I was clearly in trouble.

In some desperation, I called Calla Botha, a Transvaal lock forward whom I knew was somehow involved in the security forces. At that time, I did not know exactly what he did. At any rate, I told Calla what had happened and pleaded with him to help me. He said he would make a couple of calls, and, fortunately, I never heard any more of the matter.

When Louis Luyt, the Transvaal rugby president, heard of

the incident, he called me to his office and issued one final warning. If there was any more fighting, he said, he would sack me as the provincial captain. Mercifully, there was no mention of what had happened in the media.

I had been fortunate.

The lesson was straightforward.

I simply had to walk away from provocation.

Walk away.

Other players were subsequently involved in bar-room scuffles, most notably James Small two years later in Port Elizabeth. I had every sympathy with him when he was involved in a relatively innocuous incident and dropped from the 1994 Springbok tour to Britain as a result.

Late Night Dukes was the end. Thereafter, I walked away whenever a situation turned sour. Time and time again, I would abruptly leave a pub and sit alone in my hotel room in order to avoid confrontation; and, aside from one unpleasant skirmish in 1994 when the Rossouw brothers, Chris and Charles, helped me away from a Durban bar, I have not fought again.

It solves nothing.

My brother Kobus also lived hard through his student years, building himself up in the gym, enjoying a drink and working as a bouncer where he was expected never to shrink from any kind of physical challenge. There were Saturday nights in Johannesburg when I feared for his safety. I would lie awake in the early hours, waiting to hear the sound of his motorbike to know that he had returned home safely. The fighting life is not a life worth living. I hope my sons, Jean and Stephane, learn that more quickly than I did.

As the 1991 rugby season advanced, Harry Viljoen's Transvaal side continued to break records by playing consistently entertaining rugby. Hennie le Roux, our quick, creative fly-half, had arrived from the Eastern Cape and he played a central role in our expansive strategy. Pound for pound, he is one of the strongest players I have known, and he proved one of the first fly-halves with the physical presence to attack the advantage line.

Harry proved a tremendous motivator. He would put up a R500 (£100) bonus for the player who made the biggest tackle in a match. If you won that award, and claimed the Man of the Match prize as well, you could add R1,500 (£300) to the basic match fee of R600 (£120). This proved more than a decent incentive.

He also brought in Andre Roux as a team psychologist, another move which left the traditionalists gasping for air. Another time, he bought every member of the team a bomber jacket with their nickname embroidered on the back. Mine was 'White Hawk' – fortunately, the name never stuck. Harry's gift was to make everything fun: being part of the team was fun, training was fun, playing open rugby was fun; above all, winning was fun.

On the eve of South Africa's readmission to the international arena, this young Transvaal side was threatening the status quo. It seemed as if we were showing the way forward. Not everyone thought so. The old Springbok hierarchy were trapped in the mindset of 'subdue and penetrate'. At one function, I heard a national selector dismiss our running game as nothing more than 'candyfloss rugby. Change threatened him.

It swiftly became clear that much with South African rugby would have to change. Isolation had bred indiscipline and bad habits. We had been playing by our own rules, on and off the field; rules which the administrators had been making up as they went along.

In the first place, South African rugby was in flagrant breach of the International Board's laws relating to amateurism. In fact, these regulations were simply ignored. Everyone broke the laws, everyone knew everyone broke the laws and nobody seemed to care very much.

I had started to receive regular brown envelopes stuffed with R50 (£10) notes for invitation and provincial matches, and I was aware the Springboks had been paid the princely sum of R5,000 (£1000) each to play two matches against the South Sea Barbarians as far back as 1987, but the first hint of my earning potential only materialized when the Tukkies coach, James Stofberg, showed interest in taking me away from RAU and Transvaal to continue my career at the University of Pretoria and Northern Transvaal.

News of the Tukkies' offer reached the ears of Louis Luyt, and he swiftly invited me to lunch at the Touchdown restaurant, settled in the south stand at Ellis Park. It was the Transvaal president's favourite haunt, the scene of his negotiations with many players over the years.

'You're not going anywhere,' he told me, with typical bravado.

'OK.'

'How much are they offering?'

'Two thousand per month as a retainer plus match fees,' I replied.

'I'll match it,' he said.

'Fine,' I smiled. 'I'll stay.'

Precisely the same script would be followed four years later, though for slightly larger sums of money. We had not even asked for the menu, but the negotiations were complete and we enjoyed a relaxed lunch. I was happy with the result. The match fees would take my earnings above R4,000 (£800) per month. That seemed decent money for what remained essentially a part-time job.

At least, I was happy with the result until I discovered Pieter Hendriks and Ian MacDonald were already earning what Luyt had offered me. I learned the lesson well. A professional person is paid not as much as he is worth but as much as someone else is prepared to offer him. If Stofberg had not put his offer forward, I would not have had an increase from Transvaal. Leverage is everything: I would remember this fact four years later.

If semi-professionalism had spun out of control within

South African rugby, then it was also true that the use of substances, which would subsequently be banned, was widespread in the game.

From my early years in the RAU side and latterly with Transvaal, most of the players eagerly stretched out their hands when the team doctor passed round the small containers of pills before matches. There were the *rooietjies* (little red ones) and the *geeletjies* (little yellow ones). One lock forward of my acquaintance would not take the field without Reactivan, a pep pill which was subsequently banned elsewhere in the world.

No-one batted an eyelid. This was part of the game. I started taking the pills as everyone else did. In my experience, they helped you get through a hard 80 minutes if you were struggling with physical fitness, but they had little effect if you were in sound physical condition. Since I fell into the latter category, I increasingly declined the changing-room offer.

I do confess, however, that I grew accustomed to taking the pills after the game – some of us discovered they kept you wide awake, and that meant we could stay on the dance floor until the nightclub closed.

Through the 1991 season, however, I trained as hard as I had ever trained in my life. I was still working sporadic shifts at Highveld Steel, and I used to attend the gym with my brother, Kobus. We would do arcs and curls in a regime more suited to body-building than to rugby. It was fun, and we goaded each other to push ourselves to the limit.

The result was my upper body began to bulk alarmingly, and rumours started to do the rounds that I was taking steroids. This was not true, but that didn't worry anyone with a tale to tell. JJ van der Walt, the Northerns wing, was one who suggested Ian Macdonald and I must be taking something. I laughed the allegations away. One minute, the rumour mill was suggesting I was on drugs, the next minute I was supposed to be a homosexual.

At the end of the day, anyone in the limelight simply has to accept the fact that people will gossip about them, and most of that gossip is going to be unflattering or else it would not be interesting. It goes with the territory, and I was able to accept that from an early stage in my career.

Transvaal advanced majestically through the 1991 season, securing our place in the Currie Cup Final as winners of the group. Our opponents in the showpiece end-of-season occasion would be a Northern Transvaal side that had seemed out of contention until a series of odd results enabled them to scramble into the play-offs where they beat both Free State and Western Province. Thus, the Bulls earned their place in a final which would be played at Loftus Versfeld, in Pretoria, by virtue of the fact that the last final between the two provinces, in 1987, had been at Ellis Park.

Currie Cup Finals during international isolation were fantastically tense occasions, representing the highest available level of the game. Any player would count his career successful if he could play in one such match. The stadium was always packed to the rafters, tickets were hawked at many times the face value, the State President would more often than not lead the crowd in a thunderous rendition of the national anthem, 'Die Stem', and the rugby would be as hard and physical as any I have ever known.

The 1991 Currie Cup Final was no different. It was pre-viewed as a clash of styles: Northerns were marshalled by Naas Botha, epitomizing the traditional forward-orientated pattern of rugby, while we were portrayed as a young expansive team daring to adopt a new strategy.

It would be my first encounter with Botha, the dominant personality and player of his generation, and Harry Viljoen had given me the task of worrying the Northerns fly-half throughout the afternoon. I started well, charging down a kick inside the first 10 minutes but he soon began to control the game, taking advantage of a solid platform laid by his forwards.

Naas was a formidable player in his era whose unique kicking ability, with both feet, enabled him to dictate and win many matches. In this context, only Hugo Porta, the Argentine fly-half, could stand comparison. Of course, he benefited from a consistently strong pack of Northerns forwards but they also reaped the dividends of being driven forward by his kicking.

People often spoke about his speed, but that was generally only seen when he covered the field. That was his other legendary strength: an ability to read the game, to stay three steps ahead of the opposition.

It is extremely hard to say whether he would have been as effective in the modern era. The game has changed dramatically. Today Henry Honiball is admired as one of the top fly-halves in the world because of his outstanding defence and he hardly kicks the ball at all. Andrew Mehrtens is also highly rated; he kicks the ball as well as Naas did, although he is perhaps more willing to break and tackle his man.

In the end, I would suggest Naas was a rugby genius who would have adapted to the times and proved a match-winner in any era.

On the day of the 1991 Currie Cup Final, Naas Botha won again. Our preparations had been dominated by concern about the predicted sweltering heat in Pretoria. We practised at the hottest time of the day for a week prior to the match, hoping to acclimatize our bodies to the conditions. In the event, we simply exhausted ourselves. We arrived at Loftus with not much fuel left in the tank. Our hearts were willing, but our bodies wilted. The Northerns forwards ruthlessly ground out an advantage and Naas did the rest.

We were all desperately disappointed by the result although it seemed twice as hard to swallow for senior players such as Jannie Breedt who had lost finals in 1986 and 1987, and were nearing the end of their careers. At least we, as youngsters, would have other opportunities.

The Blue Bulls' victory celebrations were, tragically, cut short by news that Jan Lock, the Northerns prop, had collapsed after playing in the curtain raiser before the final, and died. I was attending the post-match function in a marquee on the Loftus B field when the announcement was made. I recall an immediate hush and, before long, everyone had gone home. Even the Currie Cup Final seemed irrelevant alongside that sort of news.

I had experienced death at a rugby field before. A spectator fell off the grandstand while I was playing for the RAU Under-20 side, and I rushed to give him mouth-to-mouth resuscitation. He was still alive when the ambulance arrived, but he subsequently suffered a heart attack and died. He turned out to be the father of one of the opposing team members.

Setting aside the disappointment of the final at Loftus, the Transvaal team was able to look back on 1991 with some satisfaction and forward to the 1992 season with confidence. We were playing the most devastating rugby in the country, and silverware was surely not far away.

Harry Viljoen sought to maintain the momentum from one year to the next by retaining the same format and the squad once again gathered for the pre-season training camp in Hermanus. It was during this week early in 1992 that Harry asked me if I would like to meet Kitch Christie, the former Northern Transvaal assistant coach. Kitch was on holiday with his family, and we met him and his son while they were fishing on the rocks near the harbour.

We spoke about rugby, but Kitch seemed more interested in helping his son prepare his fishing bait. That was fine. That was his priority, but my first meeting with this man who would play such an enormous role in my life was not particularly impressive. It was hello and goodbye.

As the 1992 season approached, it soon became clear the season would be the most exciting in decades. Nelson Mandela had been released from prison in 1990, an event which I had watched avidly at home in Westdene, unaware of the impact this man would have on my life, and his freedom and the repeal of all apartheid legislation combined with negotiated unification between the establishment South African Rugby Board and the anti-apartheid South African Rugby Union created the right circumstances for the Springboks to return to the international arena.

Two one-Test home series against the All Blacks and the world champion Wallabies were hastily arranged and, suddenly, there was more to play for than the Currie Cup and the North v South match. We were to be part of the world once again. The prospect was hugely exciting. As I watched much older players straining to retain their form and taste some of the official Test rugby which had been denied to them in their prime, I was keenly aware of being in the right place at the perfect age at the right time. I was lucky.

We had grown accustomed to isolation, to looking in upon ourselves and maybe overrating our players. At the start of 1992, there were possibly seven Springboks whom South Africans generally regarded as being the world's finest player in their position, yet they had never been truly tested. The challenges of this first season back would provide that long-awaited test.

Through the Springbok years in the wilderness, I had paid almost no attention at all to the World Cup tournaments staged in 1987 and 1991, and took very little note of the Five Nations championship. In fact, by 1992, I knew only the international superstars of the game by name. They had showed no interest in us, and I had shown equally little interest in them.

That was all about to change, and my sense of excitement grew when I was named among the 60 players asked to attend the first Springbok trials in many years. I started the week in the 'C' team, was named in the 'B' team for the second match and then, to my delight, was asked to captain the 'A' side in the final trial. Certain key players had withdrawn because of injury, and there seemed no likelihood at all that I would actually captain the Boks, but I was hopeful of being included in the squad at the very least.

Something went wrong. I am not sure what concerned John Williams, the national coach, but I was not only left out of the Bok squad to play the All Blacks and Australia, but I could not even find a place in the Junior Springbok team that played against the New Zealanders. With no explanation, no word of encouragement from anyone, I was left out in the cold.

I did, however, remain close enough to the 1992 Springboks to feel the massive excitement of their return to international action. Theo van Rensburg and I were sharing a house at RAU and he was named as fullback in the Bok team. When he came home with his green and gold formal gear and training kit, he would lay everything out and show me. I started to adore the feel and aura of Springbok rugby. I desperately wanted to be part of it.

Theo's inclusion in the squad meant, at the very least, that I was able to secure tickets for the Test matches against the All Blacks at Ellis Park on 15 August, and against Australia at Newlands a week later.

The decision to play the national anthem, *Die Stem,* before the New Zealand match may have been politically clumsy (it almost prompted the ANC to oppose the Test against Australia), but it remained an awe-inspiring couple of minutes. I know others saw an unacceptable degree of racial arrogance in the crowd's amazingly powerful singing, but I just saw a pride and a sense of relief that the years of isolation were coming to an end. I felt intensely proud to be a South African that day.

The Boks lost a high-scoring match narrowly, but Danie Gerber scored two tries in a team performance which served to sustain a general view that we had not fallen far behind world standards during isolation. With just a little luck, Naas Botha's side might even have won.

Six days later, I travelled to Cape Town with a group of

friends from RAU in excellent heart, convinced the New Zealand match had rid us of any rust and that the world champions would feel the full Springbok backlash at Newlands. On the eve of the Test, we dined at a wine estate where the staff intervened to prevent us removing a national flag from the entrance. We had intended to wave it from the stand. We were 'up' for the Test.

Sitting in the lower tier of the Jan Pickard Stand, in the rain which fell over Cape Town all afternoon, I trained my binoculars on Theo van Rensburg for most of a match dominated by Nick Farr-Jones' Australian side. Although the scores remained close for 70 minutes, the world champions proved to be more clinical than the All Blacks and far more ruthless.

Defeat by 26–3 did not properly reflect the balance of play, but it did abruptly awaken South African rugby to the fact that isolation had, in fact, left us a long way off the pace of world rugby. Our arrogance was unforgettably shattered on that sad and wet afternoon in Cape Town. I was desolate that evening, and needed to be dragged out to dinner.

However, I snapped to attention later when we happened to arrive at a nightclub at the same time as most of the celebrating Wallabies. I stood in the admiring crowd, and quietly watched the world champion rugby team walk by. The thought struck me that these men – Farr-Jones, Eales, Campese and the rest – were treated like Hollywood movie stars, hailed wherever they went. I was exhilarated by the sight, thrilled by the mood and style, motivated beyond description to reach that level of the game.

Through 1992, my immediate challenge was to negotiate a Transvaal season that became more complex than anyone had expected. The subtext was the growing assertion among the province's administrators, most notably Dr Luyt, that senior players needed to be replaced. The argument ran that they had had their chance to win the Currie Cup, and failed.

Jannie Breedt, the outstanding Transvaal captain since

1986, seemed to be standing first in the firing line, and I was increasingly being touted as the man to lead the side in his place. Such speculation damaged the morale of the side and affected my approach, not least because I knew in my heart that I was not quite ready to take on the mantle of captaincy.

Early in June, at Luyt's insistence, I was named captain of a Transvaal side which still included Jannie Breedt. I had protested to the Transvaal Rugby Union president that I was not ready for the elevation, but he told me to trust him and to take my chance when it was presented.

Nonetheless, the atmosphere could not have been more uncomfortable. Harry Viljoen appeared not to agree with the move and would typically spend more time discussing tactics with Jannie than me – and I could hardly blame him. Jannie should have remained captain.

This impossible situation was tolerated for four matches before I told Luyt emphatically that I did not want to captain Transvaal at that stage. At first he was furious. His plan had not worked, and he blamed Harry and Jannie for undermining me, but it was not their fault.

Jannie Breedt had become a legend within Transvaal rugby, and we had got along well ever since I joined the provincial squad, despite the fact I had effectively replaced his friend, Wahl Bartmann. We shared an occasional interest in gambling and Transvaal's away trips would often be enlivened by games of cards with stakes starting at R10 (£2). Whenever possible, Jannie and I would visit illegal casinos starting to appear around the country. Blackjack was his game, and I was content to look and learn.

With Jannie reinstated as captain, the team found new momentum and proceeded on a steady course towards a second successive appearance in the Currie Cup Final, this time against Natal at Ellis Park. By coincidence, the final would be Breedt's 100th match as the Transvaal captain. After no fewer than three losing finals, surely the gods would smile on him now.

Sadly, the gods had other plans. Inspired by captain Bartmann, Natal won another tight final 14–13. Not for the first time in their careers, Breedt and Viljoen needed to be content with second place when, by any measure, they had deserved to clinch the elusive golden trophy.

Harry Viljoen resigned as Transvaal coach immediately after the game and Jannie Breedt soon announced he would seek a new challenge in Italy. Despite their heroic efforts, the Currie Cup had still not returned to Ellis Park and Dr Luyt had lost patience.

The coach and captain were gone, but the 1992 season was still not finished. The knockout Lion Cup competition was scheduled to be played at the end of the year and the draw took Transvaal to play Western Transvaal in Potchefstroom with no-one other than Luyt, himself, as caretaker coach, and me as the captain. Luyt had briefly coached the team before, appearing at the training sessions in a tracksuit and happily offering the forwards the benefit of his opinions on how to win the ball in the lineout. A former Springbok triallist, he had been a formidable lock during his playing days. The media invariably scoffed at his efforts, but the players weren't laughing. They respected what he had to say, listened and set about the task at hand.

On the morning of the match in Potchefstroom, we met in his room at the Algro hotel and enthusiastically discussed the future. I genuinely liked Louis Luyt, respected him for his wisdom and business acumen. He appeared to like me as well, showing real compassion for me as a young captain whom he desperately hoped would succeed where others had failed. I left his room hugely encouraged for the future. He was backing me.

We duly defeated Western Transvaal, advancing towards a semi-final against Northern Transvaal at Ellis Park. Luyt handled the training during the week before the match but the newspapers were starting to speculate that a new Transvaal coach would be named without delay.

The team had gathered at a Johannesburg hotel before the match with Northerns. We were changed into our tracksuits, almost ready to leave for the stadium when Luyt suddenly strode into the team room.

'Gentlemen,' the TRU president said, with a smile which indicated he had emerged from a convivial lunch. 'This is your new coach.'

There were only three hours until the kick-off of a major semi-final.

'This is Kitch Christie.'

# CHAPTER FOUR

# 'Arguably the finest provincial team in the world'

*I am the greatest, I said that even before I knew I was.*
*Don't tell me I can't do something.*
*Don't tell me it's impossible.*
*Don't tell me I'm not the greatest.*
*I'm the double greatest*
Muhammad Ali

Kitch Christie had had no involvement with any provincial rugby since resigning as Northern Transvaal assistant coach after the Blue Bulls' Currie Cup Final defeat against Natal in 1990. Now, on the day of the 1992 Lion Cup semi-final, he had agreed to coach Transvaal over a happy lunch with Louis Luyt and had immediately been taken to meet the team.

There were only three hours until kick-off.

It was a bizarre occasion. We, the players, sat and looked at this man standing before us. It was the first time I had seen him since our conversation on the rocks at Hermanus. What would he say? What would he do?

Kitch introduced himself and Ray Mordt, the former Springbok wing who had been appointed as the assistant coach. He then picked up some chalk and turned to the blackboard. Incredibly, he was going to hit the ground running. No small talk.

'How do you play Northern Transvaal?' he barked. 'Come on, how, how, how? How should any team play Northern Transvaal?'

Silence.

The players were stunned. Kitch moved on.

'You play on the left-hand side of the pitch. Why? Why? Why?'

Silence.

'You play on the left-hand side because you force them to throw in to the lineouts and tap with their weaker hand. Their control will be bad and you will be able to regain possession. It's simple. Think about it.'

Silence.

We had never heard such theories, but we would learn this was classic Kitch Christie. He looked at the game in a totally original manner, and offered views which seemed at first bizarre and irrational but which gained greater credibility on closer inspection. He was on a roll.

'And watch out for Gerbrand Grobler. He's magic, very dangerous on the ball. You must keep possession away from him and play on the left side of the field. That is how you will beat Northerns tonight.'

The new coach had spoken for no more than ten minutes, but he had been businesslike and concise. We had listened carefully. That night, we did defeat Northerns in the rain, and we did kick heavily on the left side and they did struggle to control their own lineout ball.

Through the following week, we became better acquainted with Kitch and Ray Mordt as they guided us through training ahead of the Lion Cup Final against Free State and, again thriving in wet conditions, we won another tight match to finish the year with a trophy.

Louis Luyt, Kitch Christie and I would joke for some years about who should take the credit for that Lion Cup victory. Wherever the credit lay, the win marked the start of a wonderful relationship between the three of us. We trusted and respected each other, even liked each other, and began to forge the most successful period in the history of Transvaal rugby.

It was Rod McQueen, then the Queensland coach, who suggested at the end of 1993 that Transvaal were 'arguably the finest provincial team in the world'. We appreciated the compliment.

The trail of success may have started with the 1992 Lion Cup but the true foundations of the province's progress were laid during the squad's close season tour to Europe at the end of that year. At first sight, the trip appeared no more than a consolation holiday for those of us who had not been selected for the Springbok tour to France and England.

I was once again desperately disappointed to have been omitted, and found myself competing at a low-key sevens tournament in Swaziland on the weekend when Naas Botha led South Africa in their first overseas Test match for 11 years, against France in Lyon. The tournament was suspended while the Test match was being played, enabling everyone to watch on television. I decided to play a round of golf instead, alone.

It turned out to be an introspective afternoon. I asked myself why I was not good enough to play Springbok rugby, which weaknesses I would have to address, and set down my goals and ambitions; all the while, these thoughts were punctuated by cheers from the packed hotel rooms rolling out over the course each time South Africa scored. And every time I heard a cheer, I told myself that is where I wanted to be, playing for the Boks. The idea of representing my country on the rugby field had always excited me, but from that afternoon on the golf course in Swaziland, it became an obsession.

For now, my focus remained on the Transvaal tour to Europe, the first overseas trip of my life. We arrived in London on the Thursday before South Africa's Test against England at Twickenham with a squad which was missing nine regular players. Kitch Christie didn't seem to mind because the absence of the stars gave him an excellent opportunity to discover whether he had any depth or quality in his new squad. For him, this six-match tour was of crucial importance: he was getting to know us, and I saw him taking care to observe the guys not just during matches or training, but on the bus and on the plane, everywhere. He was obviously a different kind of coach.

It must be said that Lappies Labuschagne, our lugubrious lock, did not make the most favourable first impression on the new coach. Together with prop forward Bongo van der Merwe, Lappies had been enjoying a couple of glasses of red wine during the flight to London before he staggered down the aisle to where Kitch, on the brink of falling asleep, was sitting.

'Don't worry, Kitchie,' slurred Lappies, 'we're going to stuff them when we get on the field and, afterwards, we'll stuff them in the bar!'

Kitch glared at the lock. The lock slunk back to his seat. I don't recall any other player ever using the name 'Kitchie'. At the first training session in London, the new coach told us emphatically that the players would either call him 'Mr Christie' or 'Coach', but never 'Kitch' or 'Kitchie'.

And that was that. He drew the line, and no-one crossed it. Discipline and respect lay at the core of his coaching regime.

We watched the Test at Twickenham, growing excited as the Boks led at half-time but trooping away sadly after England took control in the second half and ran out convincing winners. South Africa's fourth defeat in five Tests since readmission provided the clearest possible indication of how much work lay ahead before we could claim to stand among the world's best.

Speaking to some of the players afterwards, it became clear the team was not playing as a unit. The Springboks from Transvaal appeared to be generally disgruntled within a national squad coached by John Williams, from Northerns, and captained by Naas Botha, also from Northerns. Provincialism had grown so intense during isolation that the resulting divisions and mistrust would hamper national performances for at least three years.

As the Boks returned home, the Transvaal tour began in earnest and Kitch Christie set to work. We soon discovered he was not too proud to invite other respected coaches to lead a training session. Alex Evans, the intuitive former Wallaby coach who was involved with Cardiff at the time, appeared on two occasions and taught us new rucking techniques.

Kitch also instilled new customs: at seven o'clock in the morning after any match, the squad was instructed to gather for an 8–10 kilometre run. This was another Christie innovation, and would become known as 'Doc's run' because it would be planned and led by Dr Frans Verster, team doctor to Transvaal and South Africa ever since readmission. I still don't know whether the coach wanted us to sweat out any alcohol that might have been drunk the previous night, or whether this was a fitness drill, but I suspect his primary aim was to introduce an element of discipline for the sake of it.

Beyond all these traits, Kitch's greatest gift was to let his players know that he believed in them. From these early days, he made it clear to me that I was his captain, that he trusted me, that he would support me and that he felt proud to be associated with me. These powerful sentiments, though expressed discreetly, offered me the absolute assurance I needed to take the Transvaal captaincy from Jannie Breedt and to lead the team forward. Everything I became in the game arose from this early, absolute vote of confidence.

We lost our opening match against Gloucester at Kingsholm, despite Jaco Louw's try in the opening moments. Many players underperformed but Chris Dirks achieved the unwanted distinction of being awarded only 25% in the coach's post-match assessment of the players' performances. It was the lowest percentage score Kitch ever gave. He was furious.

'There are only four players in this team who are good enough to play Currie Cup rugby,' he told me after the game.

We did, however, pull ourselves together to win the remaining five matches on tour. Bridgend offered a physical challenge as their lock punched both our fly-half and scrum-half within the first ten minutes, but I responded in kind and triggered a mass brawl. At one stage, Kobus Wiese was surrounded by five Welshmen.

Such a hard-fought victory prompted an enthusiastic celebration, and two players – Jeremy Thomson and Steve Jacobs – only returned to the team hotel in the early hours of the morning. The coach had stressed that the bus would leave the hotel promptly at 7 a.m., so Jeremy and Steve had decided to remain in their clothes and sleep on the floor propped up between their suitcases. Their plan was that they would be woken by the wake-up call and would walk directly down to the lobby and on to the bus.

I had arrived at the bus by twenty to seven, determined not to be late and upset a coach who had shown himself to be serious on punctuality but by seven there was still no sign of either Jeremy or Steve. Kitch was becoming angry. I dashed to their room and banged on the door. They had missed their call and eventually arrived 20 minutes late. The coach fumed.

Jeremy, however, had hardly slept and he promptly fell asleep on the back seat of the bus. We were travelling through traffic and the former Natal centre soon slid off the seat and was lying in the gangway of the bus. Each time the driver put his foot on the brakes, he slid further and further forward, still fast asleep, still wearing his Transvaal blazer, looking terrible.

Before long, he slid to a point where he was lying directly beside the coach's front-row seat. As ever on cue, Jeremy woke up and said 'Good morning, coachie'. Kitch stared at him. Immediately, I could see this would become a problem. By the time we had arrived at the airport, the coach was adamant that Thomson and Jacobs should immediately be sent home to South Africa.

I pleaded with him to be lenient, explaining he was blowing the issue out of proportion and prompting a drama where none were needed. At one stage, Steve Jacobs became irritated, complaining that he was being treated like a child, but Kitch simply wanted the players to understand that discipline was crucial. 'Be on the bus at seven o'clock' meant 'be on the bus at seven o'clock', not a minute later, certainly not 20 minutes later.

After an hour of animated discussions, the coach was persuaded to let the players remain on tour and they travelled with us to Venice where we won a tough match against Padua, Rudolf Straeuli's club at the time. We enjoyed site-seeing in the city of canals, and I swiftly learned two words of Italian: *va bene* which means 'go well' and *swatchero* which means 'son-in-law' as in 'Look coach, there goes Jeremy Thomson, your future *swatchero.*'

Kitch was determined to be a disciplinarian, but he rarely lost his sense of humour. There was a time for being tough, but there was also a time to laugh. He relied on instinct to get the timing right. By the end of the tour, he was still saying he thought only four of the squad were good enough to play Currie Cup rugby.

The 1993 season heralded a new competition, the Super-10 involving the ten strongest provincial teams in the southern hemisphere. The challenge prompted an official return to serious training in January, no more than three weeks after the team had returned from Europe. We had started an era when players would perform like professionals and be paid like amateurs.

It was in my nature to address this anomaly by exploring ways in which we, as players, could supplement our income. The most obvious vehicle was to launch a Players' Trust. This had been done with some success in Northern Transvaal, and I had the time to tackle such an enterprise.

Having completed my law degree, I received several invitations from law firms to take my articles but I declined them all because my commitments to rugby would not have permitted me to give enough time to law. When the companies said that didn't matter, promising I could just come and go as I liked, I sensed they wanted me purely for public relations reasons and that was not going to help me in the long run. If I was going to pursue law, I wanted to do so properly and on my legal merits.

So I focused on conceiving the Transvaal Players' Trust, which would raise income from the province's generally affluent support base. My starting point was the 320 executive box-holders at Ellis Park stadium. I calculated if I could persuade each box-holder to sponsor every try we scored for R50 (£10), we could raise sums which would dwarf the R800 (£160) match fees paid out, in cash, by the union. In return for this financial support, we, as players, would make personal appearances in their boxes after home matches.

For a further R5,000 (£1000), a company could join Club 1000, and book two appearances by the entire team. These were early days: the whole side for sale at the rate of only R2,500 (£500) per appearance! Within five seasons, many companies would happily pay R20,000 (£4000) to secure an appearance by just one leading player. We had no idea of our true market value.

These were my basic ideas, and it seemed their time had come when the players began to grow restless about the lack of financial reward for their efforts. In my absence, they met with Louis Luyt to discuss match fees for the new season. The meeting did not go well, and the players only succeeded in negotiating themselves a net reduction in match fees. Luyt had systematically destroyed their arguments, attacking anyone who stepped forward.

Against this background, I called the players together and made a full proposal for the establishment of a Players' Trust. I told them I was prepared to run the trust but on the basis that I would take a 20% commission on everything. The response was overwhelmingly positive. I was offering them a new source of income. I explained I would need the guys to make a few appearances, and I wanted their clear approval.

And I got their clear approval.

Through the weeks that followed, I started working from a small office at Ellis Park and spent every available hour arranging visits to box-holders, inviting them to sponsor us for R50 (£10) per try. The owner of the Touchdown restaurant, Melitza Borek, was the first to sign along the dotted line; she would become a close friend and the Touchdown restaurant at Ellis Park would become my regular haunt. Not every sale proved so simple.

This was hard work because people had already paid heavily for their box and they were now being asked to find even more money, but I stuck to the task and must have made more than 75 presentations.

My head was full of business concepts. When it was confirmed the 1995 Rugby World Cup would be hosted in South Africa, I conceived a plan whereby each box-holder would be asked to make available two seats in their box for the World Cup Final at Ellis Park. Armed with those 640 match tickets, we wanted to compile and sell a complete package tour for overseas visitors which would include trips to Sun City and a game park. All profits would find their way to the Transvaal Players' Trust. This scheme did not materialize as planned, but this was the way I was starting to think.

As the season advanced, I accepted the onerous responsibility of arranging player appearances after home matches. Sometimes the guys would forget, and it would usually be me who had to fill in at the last minute. When the letters of complaint arrived, it would be me who would have to respond and apologize to the box-holder. Yet the money started to flow into the Trust. Other ventures were planned: the Reebok Kloof vineyard had gone bust, and Kitch Christie helped me secure fine wine at a cheap price. We would design our own Transvaal labels and sell the bottles.

The Trust's primary negotiation took place with Dr Luyt, and we managed to secure substantial cash bonuses if the team was successful. We would receive R250,000 (£50,000) if we won the Super-10, another R200,000 (£40,000) if we won the

Currie Cup and a further R50,000 (£10,000) for retaining the Lion Cup. The season ran its course, the team won and the Trust swelled.

By the end of its first year, the Transvaal Players' Trust had reaped in excess of R650,000 (£150,000), and the funds were to be distributed on the basis of how many shares each player had earned. It had been agreed that one share would be awarded to each player per match played, with half a share being awarded to substitutes who had sat on the bench.

At the start of the meeting to allocate payments, I was asked if I was planning to take 20% commission on the full R650,000 (£150,000).

'Yes, that's what we agreed at the start,' I replied.

'Well, we think you can take 20% on the money you raised, but that you should not take a commission on the win bonuses received from the union. Those were won by the team as a whole, not just by you.'

I was shocked and amazed. The players had clearly been discussing the issue in my absence. Pieter Hendriks and Kobus Wiese were doing most of the talking, which was ironic because they had been vocal in their initial approval of my commission, but they held their position. I understood the logic of their view, but it did not match our original agreement.

I stated my case. 'There would have been no win bonuses if we had not created this Trust, and it was me who put the Trust together,' I argued. 'Luyt only made those payments because we had created a vehicle which could receive them, and it was me who built that vehicle.'

Another meeting was called. The difference was becoming a dispute, the atmosphere was turning distinctly unpleasant, the discussions became emotional and damaging to team spirit. In the end, I told the players I would relinquish the 20% commission, but I said I felt this was unfair and asked to be released from any responsibility for the Trust in future.

I was hurt by what had happened. Even now, I can sympathize with all sides of the argument, but my perspective was that I had worked for the Trust on the basis of an approved commission, and I was bitterly disappointed that the commission payable to me should have been withheld in a manner which somehow cast me as a villain trying to take the players' money.

The saga taught me two lessons: the first was that the smell of money affects rugby players, like everyone else – some become jealous, others turn nasty; and the second was that, where players are involved, the issues of money and playing affairs should always be kept apart. With the benefit of hindsight, the seed of the conflict was my dual role as the players' agent on the one hand, taking my commission, and on the other hand their team captain, striving to build team spirit. It was ultimately impossible to perform both roles properly.

This issue did not, however, impair the development of the Transvaal rugby team of 1993 into one of the happiest 'families' I have known. Money was generally kept to one side while we embarked upon a winning streak of irresistible rugby, exhilarating occasions and many happy days.

This was the secret of our success: we were a family. That may sound trite and superficial, but I have played in many rugby teams and very few can have claimed to be family. Perhaps this quality can be most easily explained by saying we, as players, enjoyed each other's company. When we arrived at the training ground, we were genuinely happy to see each other. When we criticized each other, we learned to take the criticism in good heart. There were no airs and graces, no pouting, no sulking, no whispering. When we travelled, we laughed. We felt a sense of belonging.

Most teams, in sport or business, are thrown together. They celebrate when they are successful, but they do not truly stand together in every deed and in every thought. They are transient groups with a shared goal, whereas we felt as though we truly belonged together. It might not be an exaggeration to say that, through 1993, we genuinely loved being with each other.

The foundation of the family was laid in sweat, and the man

who called the shots in demanding our physical commitment was the team coach. Kitch Christie did not worry at all with modern kinetic theory. He was content to drive his team through the same exercises which had taxed rugby players for most of the past hundred years: push-ups, sit-ups, bench-steps. Worst of all, we would be instructed to hold dumb-bells weighing 5 or 10 kilograms, and be asked to lie down, stand up, lie down, stand up etc. until the sweat literally poured from every pore of our bodies.

As we neared the pain threshold, we bonded. This was Kitch Christie's way. We trained as a team and suffered as a team, and the training sessions became fun as we goaded the coach into pushing us harder.

'Give me thirty push-ups,' he would ask.

'Thirty?' we would shout, in unison. 'Why thirty? We can do sixty.'

And we would do sixty, counting each push like a band of army recruits at drill; and Kitch would smile – he loved the family. He would tell us over and again that we needed to be the fittest rugby side in the world. 'In life, you must be damn good at something, and constantly so,' he liked to say, and he was determined that our physical condition would be nothing less than 'damn good'.

He was also eager the squad should train and play in the best possible conditions, so he set about building a new training complex at the Wanderers rugby club field which would comprise our own gym and changing rooms on the ground floor and a brand new clubhouse for the Wanderers rugby section on the first floor. It would be a win-win situation. He wanted nobody to feel short-changed.

Upholding his Scottish heritage, he did prove extremely conservative during the building process, negotiating the best possible deal on every nail and screw. Where he could borrow, he borrowed. Where he could barter, he bartered. The Union were paying for everything, but he allocated every rand and cent as if it were coming from his own wallet.

By the end of the year, we had the finest training facility in the land, a far cry from the wood huts and ramshackle showers which Transvaal players had found at their training facilities until the 1980s.

The season was launched with the M-Net Nite series, scheduled as a warm-up tournament ahead of the Super-10, and the event was provided with some glamour by the participation of the Harlequins club, from London. There was, however, little glamorous about the way in which Wade Dooley, the England international lock forward, stamped on one of our forward's head or, indeed, about the way in which our prop, Heinrich Rodgers, took revenge by delivering a ramrod punch to Dooley's jaw. That's the game.

Our tight five dominated the match, boosted by the decision of hooker Uli Schmidt to play for Transvaal after sensing he was no longer required in Pretoria where he had become one of the legendary personalities of Northern Transvaal rugby. He was one of no fewer than seven players who joined our ranks from Pretoria, following Kitch Christie down the M1 from the capital city, but these were not casual, cold-hearted mercenaries. They joined Transvaal in body and spirit, and were never less than wholehearted.

We eventually shared the M-Net series title, content to draw the Final with Northern Transvaal, and the stars of the tournament were judged by general consensus to have been our two young centres, Japie Mulder and Hennie Wiggett. They had played with unquenchable enthusiasm and genuine talent, darting into gaps on attack, relishing every midfield hit on defence. If ever two youngsters seemed well-starred, it was this pair.

Not long afterwards, Hennie Wiggett visited the Lanseria air show and was involved in a motor accident on the way home. As soon as I heard the news, I rushed to visit him in hospital at Olivedale. Hennie was being treated in intensive care, out of danger but evidently in a serious condition. His shoulder was extensively damaged and it soon became clear that his rugby career would be brought to a sudden conclusion.

As I stood by his bed, strangely, he kept apologizing to me.

'I'm sorry,' he said. 'I'm so sorry.'

So was I, so were we all. Hennie pulled through, recovered from all his injuries and accepted his appalling luck manfully, but we will never know what he might have achieved on the rugby field.

We were well prepared for the inaugural Super-10 but, nonetheless, grateful for the benefits of a competition draw which enabled us to launch our challenge with two matches at home. North Harbour and Waikato travelled from New Zealand to Johannesburg, and were defeated 39–13 and 30–15 respectively at Ellis Park. It would later be claimed that New Zealand teams did not take the Super-10 seriously at this stage, which was strange because we had been told they took every match seriously.

As we crossed the Indian Ocean, we did so in the knowledge that victory away to New South Wales would be sufficient to win the group and secure a place in the final.

Dr Luyt travelled with the team, cutting a benevolent and supportive figure among the players. We respected him and liked him, and he played an integral role within what had become an extremely happy squad. He joined us in Sydney and sat with us on the coach journey to train at the Concorde Oval, venue for our match against New South Wales. The ground had hosted major games during the 1987 World Cup, but it was tiny.

Luyt and I sat in the front row of seats and laughed as we surveyed the scene. We could actually see buses passing by at one end of the ground. 'And they say *we* will have difficulties hosting a World Cup,' we scoffed.

As we changed into our boots, the groundsman approached and, in classic rugby fashion, informed us that we would not be allowed to train on the field. Of course, we were outraged. Dr Luyt promised he would never allow a New South Wales team to train at Ellis Park, Kitch muttered and cussed at the groundsman's intransigence and we bathed in outrage.

The New South Wales match would present our first major challenge of the season and, the night before the game, I gathered the team together for a team-building exercise which I had read about. Standing at the front of the room with a flip chart, I wrote the names of all the players on the board and, calling each individual's name in turn, asked the entire squad to shout out exactly what they thought about each of their team-mates.

'Pieter Hendriks,' I said.

'He's electrifying,' someone shouted.

'He scores tries out of nothing,' another said.

I wrote all these remarks on the flip chart. We proceeded through the team … Uli Schmidt? 'I'd rather play on the same side than against him.' Ian MacDonald? 'Fearsome, always gives 110% for the team.' My goal was to boost the team's confidence. Daily routines often leave very little time for any praise to be given; and people are rarely told how much they are appreciated and admired by their team-mates. I was determined our players should know their standing, and that they would carry the sense of confidence forward into the game. As the praise flowed, I could sense players starting to sit up in their seats. The session was having its desired effect.

Kitch and I had planned to throw everything at New South Wales in the opening 15 minutes in search of an early score to set a positive tone for the match, and we were delighted by our opening move.

The home side kicked off, I managed to win the ball. We recycled and carried the ball up the middle of the field. The ball popped back again, Japie Mulder had a bash but New South Wales robbed him in the tackle. Thumping into the rucks, we regained possession. Uli Schmidt took the ball on. We recycled cleanly, whipping the ball wide with an overlap and waiting calmly on the wing to score in the corner … Uli Schmidt.

After the conversion, we led 7–0. Deon Lotter, our 35-year-old loose forward, produced a memorable display at the heart of a defensive action that resisted the home team's second-half pressure. We emerged with a 10–3 win, my first major overseas achievement as Transvaal captain. Our success had helped restore some lustre to the reputation of South African rugby.

We returned home to contest the Super 10 Final at Ellis Park against an Auckland side that included All Black superstars such as Sean Fitzpatrick, Michael Jones, Zinzan Brooke and others. But we were not fazed. The coach developed a game plan which involved moving the ball around to wear down an Auckland pack unaccustomed to playing at altitude.

The hero of a happy afternoon proved to be Uli Schmidt. He had said his primary motive in joining Transvaal had been to play in a provincial side coached by Kitch Christie, and I had admired him from the moment he arrived at his first training session. He was not a man to speak when there was not much to say, but, if there was something to say, he said it.

And I listened. I was so hyped up for the Super 10 Final, I had played the opening 15 minutes in almost maniacal fashion, charging around the field, making tackle after tackle. During a break in play, Uli simply approached me and said quietly in my ear: 'Relax, you're playing too hard.'

'Too hard?' I thought. This was a Super 10 Final! But I later reflected on the wisdom of his words. It is foolhardy to hurl your body into every ruck and maul – it is more important to be selective and remain on your feet. This advice, at a critical moment, has stayed with me throughout my career.

Uli is a remarkable man in many respects. The son of Louis Schmidt, the man who inspired the Blue Bull nickname on account of his handlebar moustache, he took the change of province comfortably in his stride and made a huge contribution to the Transvaal team with a well-chosen word here or a piece of advice there. He seemed to have an uncanny sense of how the game should be played although, as he once told me, this did not translate into a capacity for captaincy.

'You are blessed to be a captain,' he said. 'You have all the qualities. I would like to have been a captain, but I was not blessed.' I am not sure I agreed with him, but I was moved by his humble approach and grateful for the wholehearted support he gave me through 1993.

Tales of his amazing physical endurance had passed into the legend of South African rugby, and his aggressive approach to the game had often provoked controversy. I don't believe Uli ever set out to hurt anyone, but he did seek physically to dominate every member of the opposition. If he could hurt you as he ran through your tackle, he would do so. He was magnificently physical but the essence of his greatness was perhaps his ability to go not to where the ball was but to where the ball was going.

He had been badly treated towards the end of his career at Loftus Versfeld and I think he was spurred by a determination to prove wrong the Northerns selectors who had dismissed him as over the hill. When he scored two tries in the inaugural Super-10 Final, most observers were of the opinion that this achievement represented an eloquent statement.

Uli's second try had brought the stadium to its feet. I received the ball from Hennie le Roux in the inside centre and was able to break clean up to the Auckland 22-metre line. We rucked and recycled with precision, Hennie took possession again and the ball was whipped wide to Uli, once again on the wing. One cavalier sidestep and he was crashing over the line.

'Ul-i! Uli-i! Ul-i!' Ellis Park chanted its approval in unison.

Auckland did fight back and, in fact, were leading with 15 minutes to play, but I sensed the momentum was on our side. Japie Mulder engineered a great break, but was ankle-tapped. We rucked, I collected the ball and set off for the line. Michael Jones stood in front of me, but I dipped my shoulder and took him with me on my way to scoring the winning try.

Earlier in the game, Jones had seemed alarmed by the sheer physical intensity of our performance: 'Just play rugby,' he had told me at a lineout. 'Don't play the man.' I had great respect for the All Black flank. This sort of confrontation, in the midst of a bruising match, is the rich essence of rugby union. It is hard, it is wonderful.

And we won, crowned champions of the southern hemisphere. Thus my first encounter with Sean Fitzpatrick ended on a victorious note. The All Black and Auckland captain was, however, a notable opponent who I would grow to know and respect through the next three seasons.

I have always found him to be an inscrutable character, wearing the same expression in victory as he does in defeat. He seems a sincere person and he always behaved in a gentlemanly manner, but we never really found the right moment to talk much away from the field. The pressures of modern rugby have evaporated the camaraderie of the game.

In fact, Sean did most of his talking on the field ... and, often, to the referee. South African supporters were frustrated by his antics, but I used to admire the skill with which he managed the referee in an important match. This ability was of real value to his side, and it was something which I envied.

If decisions went against my side, I would retreat ten metres, put my hands on my head and look fed up. Bruce Gardner, my friend, would say my body language sent bad radar signals to the referee which would invariably illicit a negative response, but that would be how I felt at the time.

Sean was much more clever. If the referee gave an indifferent decision against his team, he would smile, put his arm around the official's shoulders and start chatting to him as if to say: 'Don't worry, you've made a mistake. It happens.' He had a special aura about him, and he played the referee in a way which can only be described as highly intelligent. Beyond all this, of course, he must be rated among the great All Black forwards and captains.

Buoyed by success in the Super-10, we returned to the domestic Currie Cup and Lion Cup competitions with new confidence, approaching every game, certain of our ability to win. Success began to breed success and Kitch Christie was content to keep the pot boiling, cleverly adjusting the personnel or strategy where necessary.

The coach, however, had had his own problems as well for he had been managing lymphatic cancer for nearly 13 years but his condition deteriorated alarmingly before the Lion Cup Final. He was hospitalized and, for a while, his life appeared to be threatened. I visited him in hospital and was shocked to see him in such poor, haggard condition.

'You look terrible, coachie,' I said bluntly.

'What do you mean? I'm fine,' he replied.

I shook my head.

'If you want to see something bad,' he said firmly, 'just take a walk through the children's cancer ward next door. I have already had one hell of a life. Those kids haven't had anything yet.'

He was right, of course, and as I left, he told me quietly, 'Don't worry, cappie, you know I will never stop fighting.'

And he did fight so that, three weeks later, he was back at the helm. By then, we had added the Lion Cup trophy to the Ellis Park cabinet. Kitch had watched the final against Natal in hospital and, during the television interview that followed the match, I had dedicated the victory to him. He told me later he had been moved to tears. We were growing very close, relating to each other more like a father and son than a coach and captain.

In the coach's absence, I relied heavily on Ray Mordt and Uli Schmidt to prepare the team. Just an hour before kick-off in the Lion Cup Final against Natal, I had begun to despair at the lack of atmosphere within the team. I had run through our set moves, to no response. I had given what I thought was a stirring team talk, to no response. In 90% of matches, you can tell whether the team is going to perform by the mood immediately before the match. If ever we looked a beaten side, it was this particular afternoon.

I approached Uli Schmidt in the changing room.

'Uli, you must help me here. Something is wrong. Do anything you can to get the guys focused for the game.'

With that, I left to warm up myself. When I returned 15 minutes later, it seemed as if Uli had pushed a switch in the tight five. They were snorting, up for the game, and we produced a compelling, winning performance. Much has been said and written about the mental preparation of sports teams, but often the task hinges on an instinct to say the right thing at the right time.

As Saturday followed Saturday, the team spirit remained sky-high and we continued to play enterprising, winning rugby. We were a happy squad. Kobus Wiese and Balie Swart, close friends since their schooldays in Paarl, played an integral role in our team not just because they both performed to international standards on the field but also because it was they who were generally to be found cracking jokes and raising a laugh.

During training, they would sometimes resemble a double act. Balie would shout at Kobus during the scrummaging, and Kobus would shout back if Balie failed to provide adequate support during the lineout drills. Christiaan Scholtz, the centre, could hardly believe his eyes during the first weeks after his arrival from Cape Town, and was moved to wonder out loud whether Kobus and Balie actually were friends at all.

Friday nights before home matches would typically be spent attending a team *braai* at Dr Luyt's house, and we generally ate out as a team after the match as well, usually at a steakhouse where Dr Luyt picked up the bill. We wanted to spend time together. This was the key.

Uncommonly in the era of amateur rugby, the province had settled on a structure with which all parties felt absolutely comfortable. Dr Luyt was the boss, a man whose word was law but who was generally regarded, within the province, as a benign dictator with the players' interests at heart. He, at least, had long ago given up on the charade of amateurism.

Kitch Christie and Ray Mordt combined perfectly as the coaching team with the former providing wisdom while the latter supplied energy. The coach also played a vital extended role as a kind of liaison between his players and the union. If there was a dispute of any kind, Kitch would speak to the player, then to the union and a solution was found.

Finally, I was fortunate to lead a squad which remained in a positive state of mind throughout the year and which also offered a veritable wealth of natural rugby talent. We became a truly powerful XV.

The front row of Balie Swart, Uli Schmidt and Heinrich Rodgers or Johan le Roux were mightily supported by locks Kobus Wiese and Hannes Strydom, forming a tight five of such relentless power that we, in the back row, hardly needed to scrum at all. The super-fit Ian MacDonald and myself, as flankers, combined effectively both in the loose and the tight phases while either Deon Lotter or Rudolf Straeuli brought a mature rugby brain, rare intelligence and selfless courage to the position of No. 8.

Of the eight first-choice forwards, three were already Springboks and five would become Boks within a year. By any measure, the Transvaal pack had developed into a unit of genuine international quality.

Johan Roux emerged as a scrum-half with an ability to read and control the game, while I developed an almost telepathic relationship with Hennie le Roux, our fly-half. I was able to drive up the midfield and almost sense when Hennie would appear on my shoulder to collect a pop pass – and he would not appear at half pace, but at full pace.

Japie Mulder was a naturally gifted centre, a great tackler and as fast as anyone over 10 metres, one of the finest players of his generation. His upper body strength was remarkable but, freakishly, to the great amusement of his friends, he struggled to execute any dips at the gym. On one occasion, he was bet R100 (£20) to complete four, and he failed.

Bernard Fourie, a reliable, solid and strong presence throughout the campaign, held his place as Mulder's midfield partner; and Pieter Hendriks soon established his golden reputation on the wing. His greatest quality was amazing acceleration which enabled him to power past defenders. It was an exhilarating experience to run in support and watch him burst clear.

Theo van Rensburg started the season at full-back, but was injured during the Springbok tour to Australia and replaced by Gavin Johnson, who Kitch Christie plucked from the backwaters of Pretoria club rugby where he was playing for Harlequins. His keen eye for a break, his ability to play flyhalf and his remarkable goal-kicking consistency soon earned Gavin the appropriate nickname 'Magic'.

Simply to recall the Transvaal team of 1993 excites me. With quality from numbers 1 to 21, we bonded as a unit and played outstanding rugby throughout the season. While an under-strength team did lose a couple of games when the Springboks were overseas, the fact remained that, when at full strength, we had put together an unbeaten season.

A notably satisfying dimension to our game had been our new-found ability to destroy lesser teams. The coach told us repeatedly: 'Whenever we play a bad side, we make sure we make them look bad.' One day, playing against South-Eastern Transvaal, we were relentless, compiling more than 116 points before the referee blew with 10 minutes to play.

And yet Transvaal had still not won the Currie Cup outright since 1972 and we were eagerly aware that, without seizing that prize, the season would still be regarded as having been a failure. As Natal secured second place in the final table, the prospect of a Natal versus Transvaal Currie Cup Final at the Stadium, King's Park in Durban became a reality.

The fates conspired to produce a rich plot. Harry Viljoen had guided Transvaal to the 1991 and 1992 Finals, losing both, and he now reached his third successive final, this time as the new coach of Natal. I still counted him among my friends and it was some consolation to know that, by the end of the match, at least one of us would have ended the losing streak.

Kitch Christie planned our preparations meticulously and bravely flew in the face of tradition when he decided the squad would not travel to Durban until the morning of the match. The players would spend the night before the Currie Cup Final, sleeping in their own beds at home.

This was classic Christie: ignore the customs, look at a situation, trust your instincts and make a logical decision. He did not want us to be panicked by the big match atmosphere in Durban, and he was eager that we avoid the crush and inconvenience of a busy hotel. So we stayed at home and the guys were able to relax in their most familiar environment.

I won't forget the vibe and buzz when the players met at the airport in Johannesburg at seven o'clock that Saturday morning. Their eyes were alive with the excitement and opportunity of the day. Supporters milled around, and wished us luck, but the guys were happy and focused.

We arrived in Durban and spent a couple of hours at the Royal hotel before making our way to the ground. The importance of the match was clear in every face. Japie Mulder had turned pale with nerves and Pieter Hendriks, who starts spitting when he is nervous, was salivating a pool. Ian MacDonald looked grim. We arrived at the ground, in silence.

As captain, I had learned to be sensitive to the moods and vibes of the team at all times. The guys were nervous – that was fine, but I needed to say the right things and act in the right way to ensure the nerves kept us on edge and never started to inhibit our instincts. It was a fine balance.

Uli Schmidt, drawing on his personal experience of winning Currie Cup Finals in a Northern Transvaal jersey, was ready to help. Arriving in the King's Park changing room, he took care to set down his kit on the bench between Hendriks and Mulder. Apparently without a care in the world, eyes glinting, he looked at the youngsters and asked if they had seen the referee.

'What?' asked Mulder, disturbed from his dread.

'Has the ref been here,' Uli repeated, 'to send the points?'

It had been a running joke throughout the season that some opposing teams would rather send us the two points than take a beating on the field. Uli was smiling like a small boy. Japie laughed. The ice had been broken, the mood was right, Kitch grinned, we were ready.

So were Natal. We hardly touched the ball in the first 20 minutes, and were content to meet the home side's physical challenge. We threw bodies at them, they threw bodies at us in a truly ferocious struggle.

Gavin Johnson kicked an early penalty but then allowed a punt to spin off his foot. The Durban crowd were laughing at him, but the strength of this Transvaal team was that nobody panicked, least of all Gavin, nobody sighed or complained. We resolutely got on with the task at hand.

As the second half drew on, and with the scores still tight, I sensed we had drawn Natal's strongest punch and the match was now there for us to take. Natal centre Dick Muir then made a break and I moved in to make the tackle, but only collided with his hip and took a blow to the head. I was knocked out cold, and lay still as I was removed to the touchline by medical staff. Kitch Christie walked from the stand to see me.

'Coachie, coachie,' I gasped wildly, losing my mind, 'this is not in the game plan. I must not leave the field. I've got to stay on.'

Before the game, the coach and I had planned that Deon Lotter would leave the field after 10 minutes of the second half, to be replaced by Rudolf Straeuli. In my delirium, I was becoming confused.

'Cappie, you must come off,' the coach said.

'No, coachie, you don't understand. The game plan is that Deon must come off. I must stay on.'

That was not an option. Ian MacDonald assumed the captaincy, and set about playing perhaps the game of his life, appearing as a tremendously influential figure wherever the ball was to be won.

As the Currie Cup Final moved down to the wire, Johan Roux took the ball and once again displayed his supreme kicking skills by delivering a neat punt into 'the box' with such precision that Cabous van der Westhuizen could not reach the ball before it bounced. In the twinkling of an eye, the bounce fell kindly for Uli Schmidt, and he scored in the right-hand corner.

It was a moment of intense pleasure. The veteran hooker had scored vital tries in the Super-10 Final, had motivated the team before the Lion Cup Final and was now scoring the decisive try in the Currie Cup Final. The extent of his contribution to our side could hardly be overestimated.

At the final whistle, Kobus Wiese sunk to his knees and stretched his immense arms up to the skies, in thanks that our prayers had been answered. The 21–15 scoreline represented the end of a long quest for Transvaal and Louis Luyt, in particular. He had finally secured the Currie Cup and he wore a broad smile for several weeks after victory at King's Park.

The 1993 season had finished on the highest of highs and the annual squad photograph was taken with no fewer than four trophies standing before us. It had been an unforgettable year for Transvaal rugby.

It would probably have been unreasonable to expect the 1994 season to match the emotional intensity and drama of the previous year, but we did remain the dominant provincial team in South Africa.

Our Super 10 campaign, however, proved a disappointment. We found ourselves at a disadvantage by having to start our programme with two away games, and were defeated by Queensland in Brisbane. They had played well, generally outmuscled us up front and we had lost our way, but Kitch Christie was absolutely furious with me after the match.

'What's the matter?' I asked. He disliked losing as much as I did, but I had never seen him so angry and restless after the game.

'Do you know why we lost?' he barked.

*Left:* As a two-year-old outside the family home in Vanderbijlpark.

*Below:* A family holiday on the beach with younger brothers Kobus (left) and baby Deon.

*Above:* Patriot High School first XV in 1985, with Kobus in the back row, second from right. With my brother as fly-half and me as flanker, we were an irresistible combination.

*Left:* On graduation day at Rand Afrikaans University in 1989, alongside my proud parents.

*Above:* Fail to plan and plan to fail – Kitch Christie and I spent many hours plotting our challenge for the 1995 World Cup, although Kitch doesn't seem too impressed with my suggestion during a break in training.

*Below:* Theo van Rensburg's late penalty had bounced off the crossbar, and we had lost the second Test against France, and my first series as Bok captain in 1993. Dutifully, Springbok coach Ian McIntosh and I congratulate Olivier Roumat in the French dressing room.

*Above:* Ian McIntosh appointed me as Springbok captain when he took over as coach, and never enjoyed either the luck or support that he deserved, eventually being sacked after the 1994 tour to New Zealand.

*Left:* With Transvaal moments away from a first Currie Cup final victory in 21 years, concussion forced me to leave the field at Kings Park – Dr Frans Verster, right, looks concerned.

*Below:* With concussion subsiding, I was still able to drink from the Currie Cup of glory with Japie Mulder after beating Natal at Kings Park in 1993.

*Left:* Uli Schmidt, in action against Argentina at Ellis Park in 1994, played a major role in our success both with Transvaal and South Africa, but injury cruelly denied him of a place in the World Cup squad.

*Above:* After the shock defeat in the first Test, we recovered to square the series against England at Newlands in 1994 – here, I'm looking to get rid of the ball as Will Carling, Rob Andrew and Phil de Glanville close in.

*Left:* Johan le Roux was unfairly vilified following the incident with Sean Fitzpatrick at Eden Park in 1994, and I have regretted ever since my failure to stand up more strongly for him when I had the chance.

*Below:* Kobus Wiese provides me with moral support during our 1994 Currie Cup final win over Free State

Celebrating the greatest prize in South African rugby, after defeating Free State in the 1994 Currie Cup final at Springbok Park – from left, Hennie le Roux, Kobus Wiese, Johan Roux, me, Pieter Hendriks, Charles Rossouw and Ian Hattingh.

*Left:* Prince Charles was the guest of honour at our tour match against Llanelli at Stradey Park in 1994, and Kitch Christie is tuned in to our conversation.

*Right:* We were determined to finish 1995 unbeaten, and our comprehensive victory over England at Twickenham was sealed by Chester Williams' second half try.

*Below:* The 1994 tour to the British Isles established crucial confidence ahead of the World Cup, and Japie Mulder barged over for one of our five tries against Scotland at Murrayfield.

*Left:* The entire country was mobilised in support of the Boks during the 1995 Rugby World Cup although some did persist in waving the old flag – but they were free to do so.

*Above:* Kitch Christie was determined that we would be the fittest team in the World Cup, and we paid for our success in sweat on the practice ground – every moment of rest was greatly appreciated.

*Left:* Chester was back – recovered from injury, he scored four tries in the World Cup quarter-final against Western Samoa at Ellis Park.

*Left:* James Dalton's World Cup is over – referee David McHugh delivers his verdict, sending off the Springbok hooker in Port Elizabeth with Gareth Rees, the captain of Canada, standing by.

*Right:* Joel Stransky scored the clinching try in the opening match against Australia, bursting over from short range after a planned move at the back of the scrum.

*Right:* With referee Derek Bevan delaying the World Cup semi-final kick off by 90 minutes, staff at a drenched Kings Park set about brushing the water away.

*Left:* The World Cup semi-final against France was played in appalling conditions, but it was played – here Japie Mulder gets to grips with Thierry Lacroix.

*Right:* The Springbok team selected for the 1995 World Cup final at Ellis Park – 21 privileged South Africans.

*Left:* The threat of Jonah Lomu dominated the days before the World Cup final, but our guys were queuing up to tackle him every time he touched the ball – here Joost van der Westhuizen beats Ruben Kruger to the man.

*Below:* The ball is on its way, and Joel Stransky's winning dropgoal in the 1995 Rugby World Cup final has been struck – I had actually called a blind side move but Joel seized his moment magnificently, despite the close attention of Andrew Mehrtens.

*Left:* No greater moment, 24 June 1995 – the President thanked me for what the team had done for the country. 'No, sir, thank you for what you have done for the country,' I replied.

'Why?'

'Because of you,' he snapped. 'You forgot about the team and played for yourself. You were not making the right decisions. You had a bad game.'

'But I thought I played well.'

'You did play well. That's not the point. And that's not enough. If you are to captain the side, you must always consider the side, not just yourself. I need you to be concentrating on the strategy as well.'

I was quiet, silent. His criticism was acute and direct, and all the more hurtful because, the more I thought about, the more I realized he was right. In 1994, too many players, including me, believed we only had to turn up to win any match. We were just not hungry to win after the trophy glut of 1993. Kitch Christie, on the other hand, remained as resolute as ever. This difference in mental approach yielded some tension between coach and players.

We travelled from Brisbane to New Zealand for another awkward away match, against North Harbour. Stung by the criticism of my coach, I produced a performance that earned the Man-of-the-Match award, but we lost 19–6. Two away defeats destroyed our campaign almost before it had begun. Queensland finished as winners of our group, and moved on to defeat Natal in the final.

Broken down by the prolonged absence of top players for the home series against England and the long Springbok tour to New Zealand, we were unable to gain much momentum in domestic competition and Transvaal soon gained a reputation of being the 'Houdini' of South African rugby.

There is no doubt we were arrogant. It was almost as if the match was more exciting for us if we let the opponents get ahead and then tried to turn the match around in the last quarter. Time and again, we fell behind only for Uli Schmidt, Hennie le Roux or Kobus Wiese to make a break, or for someone to produce a moment of magic and bring the game back in our favour.

At times, the coach would be missing up to 15 first-choice players and he would take great delight in scouring club rugby in the province to discover an otherwise unknown player who could do a job for him at provincial level. Kitch Christie's achievements in making the most of limited resources during this period attracted little praise but were remarkable nonetheless.

Playing against Free State at Ellis Park, we took this bad habit to quite ridiculous proportions. The visitors led 22–0 at one stage but there was still time for us to get our act together and win the match.

Long before October, Transvaal had booked what started to feel like an appointed place in the Currie Cup Final for the fourth successive season, on this occasion to play Free State at Springbok Park cricket stadium. By then, Kitch Christie had moved on to a greater Springbok challenge and been succeeded as provincial coach by Ray Mordt, a man who had successfully transferred the enthusiasm and talent of his distinguished playing career to his contribution as head coach. Continuity was assured.

On a hot day in Bloemfontein, on an unsuitable rock-hard surface off which the ball would often bounce three metres, we possessed too much heavy artillery for a skilful Free State side and won the final 56–33. We were growing happily accustomed to jubilant trophy scenes, and the triumphant smiles again spread across our faces at Springbok Park.

Gerbrand Grobler was smiling, too. The talented Northerns full-back had joined Transvaal earlier in the season and played a starring role in the final, most memorably kissing the ball as he ran through to score our sixth try of the day. He was an effervescent character who I had essentially dismissed as too cocky for his own good when he first arrived in the squad, but we grew to know each other and became close friends. He played golf to a handicap of 12 and was never, ever known to lose a ball in the rough, no matter how many eyebrows were raised afterwards in the bar.

Five weeks after the Currie Cup Final, we would hear the awful news that Gerbrand had been killed in a road accident north of Pretoria. A talented sportsman who played both cricket and rugby to provincial level, he became just another victim of South Africa's dangerous roads.

Thus, Transvaal's 1994 campaign ended in sadness.

It had, however, been a remarkable period of two years during which the perennial bridesmaids of South African rugby had suddenly discovered how to win, and the trophies had arrived in a torrent.

The finest provincial team in the world? In 1993... probably.

# CHAPTER FIVE

# *In at the Deep End*

*People are always blaming circumstances for
what they are. I do not believe in circumstances.
The people who get on in the world are the people who
get up and look for the circumstances they want, and,
if they cannot find them, make them.*
George Bernard Shaw

John Williams, the coach, was predictably culled as the first victim of the Springboks' humbling readmission to world rugby. Such was the pride, and perhaps arrogance, of Springbok rugby, it almost seemed unthinkable that a national coach could lose Tests against the All Blacks, the Wallabies, France and England, against one win over the French, and survive.

The reality, recognized by the players at the time, was that Williams should not have been held responsible for an overblown re-entry to Test match rugby. What other country would have had the nerve to stage their emergence after eight years in isolation by scheduling back-to-back Tests against Australia and New Zealand, and embarking upon an uncompromising tour to play Tests against France and England?

Williams, an assured coach and respected man, was sacrificed, yet history should record that his teams performed well under impossible circumstances.

The 1993 season seemed to bring the opportunity of a new dawn in South African rugby. Dr Danie Craven, president of the South African Rugby Board since 1956, passed away during January and Naas Botha successfully bowed out at the top, announcing his retirement from the game after the Test match against England at Twickenham. As these hugely admired pillars of the past moved aside, new faces would be brought forward.

Ian McIntosh was appointed as the new Springbok coach, a decision remarkable not only for the fact that he was not himself a former Springbok, but also for the fact that he was English-speaking and from Zimbabwe. In the past, either fact would have disqualified him from contention.

Times had changed. This was 1993 and, as coach of a Natal side that had won the Currie Cup in 1990 and 1992, McIntosh was appointed because he was the best man for the job. I was pleased. He possessed all the right credentials and enjoyed the players' respect.

His first task was to name a 21-man squad for two home Tests against France in June 1993. Transvaal had won the inaugural Super-10 competition, and my captaincy and personal form seemed to be top of the media pops. As the rumour mill stepped up a gear, I was told one day that I would be named in the squad, the next day that I would be captain and the day after that I was going to be left out altogether. I was trying not to read newspapers, but there was no escaping the situation or the excitement.

McIntosh's first Springbok squad was announced on a Saturday night. Transvaal had won earlier in the day and the players were milling around the changing room, waiting to hear the news. Suddenly, it happened. Twenty-one names were announced, but I heard only one … François Pienaar.

The sensation of such moments has been described many times, but I can only recall an enormous sense of relief. I had realized what seemed to be the overriding ambition of my life: to be a Springbok. The nerves, the concern and the fear that I would never achieve that goal, that my life would somehow be a failure, literally seemed to melt away.

I was sharing a house with Theo van Rensburg and Japie Mulder at the time, and we held a double celebration because Theo had been included in the squad as well. The telephone rang all weekend. My mother and father visited us on the

Sunday, bursting with pride and excitement. I even read the newspapers, soaking up speculation how no captain had been named and how the choice lay between me and Tiaan Strauss, the Western Province captain.

The issue largely passed me by. My total focus had been on earning a place in the squad, and I genuinely did not mind about the captaincy. In fact, I recall hoping I would not lead the side so I would be able to concentrate on my own performance and adjust to the pace of Test rugby.

There had been no trials and no time for any training camp. We would gather, practise four of five times and then take on France at King's Park. Not for the first time during the early years after readmission, the Bok coach and players found their chances severely diminished by the sheer lack of thought and basic planning in arrangements for the national side. We knew nothing of each other, we knew nothing of Test rugby.

When the Bok squad gathered at the Beverley Hills hotel in Umhlanga Rocks, north of Durban, it became clear to everyone that the captaincy issue would have to be swiftly resolved. Ian McIntosh had said nothing to me, Tiaan appeared to be relaxed about the issue. We set off for training at King's Park on our first full day together and arrived to find crowds of journalists and TV crews at the main field, apparently expecting an announcement.

I knew nothing.

'François? Tiaan? Would you come over here.'

The players were warming up, but the coach had called the two of us to one side, alone and yet in full sight of both the players and media.

'I have had a difficult decision to make,' McIntosh said, 'but I would like François to captain the team on Saturday.'

My first thought was for Tiaan. He shook my hand, and congratulated me, but I could see he was extremely disappointed.

Having barely coped with the idea of making my debut for

South Africa, I was now challenged by the task of captaining the team on my debut. I knew I could count on the support of Transvaal players in the squad, but I was not at all certain how other, older players would react to the appointment of such a young captain. I was aware of possible resentment.

My head spun through most of the training session, trying to take in the significance of what had happened. Media interviews followed for almost an hour afterwards. Strangers shook my hand like old friends. I felt as though part of me, part of my life had been claimed as public property.

McIntosh and I were in the same boat. We had both been appointed to launch a new era and we were both aware of still influential personalities who questioned our ability. We appeared to be in positions of power but, without positive results – and quickly – we knew we would be vulnerable. I am certain it was this element of shared fate which brought us together.

We trained hard through an unavoidably frantic build-up to the Test, rehearsing set moves, getting to know each other, and I made arrangements for my parents to fly to Durban for the Test – their first ever flight – and I set aside time to spend with them on the Thursday evening.

Mercedes had become a sponsor of the South African Rugby Football Union and loaned three cars for the use of the team while in Durban. To my poorly concealed delight, one of these was allocated for use by the captain. If the position did bring largely unwanted responsibility, it was also true that the perks of the job were not bad. So, that excited Thursday, I dressed in my new Springbok tracksuit and drove the Mercedes to my parents. In my mind, there could have been no more powerful symbols of success.

We spent a happy hour together, as they snapped photographs of me in my tracksuit. Events had surpassed my wildest dreams.

The coach's game plan was to run the ball up the middle of the field, using Tiaan Strauss to play off the centres, with the aim of creating situations where our forwards would be running on to their backs and our backs would be running on to their forwards. This made sense to me. I respected McIntosh and would have implemented any game plan he wanted. Our calls were christened with a startling lack of imagination, 'Green' and 'Gold'.

Expectations were running wild, and my hands were literally dripping wet with sweat as the kick-off neared. People had warned me my Springbok debut would pass in a flash, but they were wrong. With the noise and colour, the match seemed to pass twice as quickly as a flash.

Midway through the first half, Alain Penaud, the French fly-half, set off on a run from a scrum. I was moving across to cover, when he jinked off his left foot and headed for the blindside. I was almost caught, but managed to change direction and tackle him into the advertising hoarding. I had received a shock. He had almost got past me, and he would have scored.

'Come on, François,' I told myself angrily. 'Stay awake. You must play these matches with your eyes open, not just with passion.'

An exciting Test match was ultimately drawn 20–20, although my view was that the French should have won. We had survived against a better side purely by virtue of our guts and commitment, a spirit exemplified by a superb performance from Uli Schmidt, but the draw did not fool us into any false dawn. As players and coaching staff, we knew we were a young side at the start of a steep learning curve; we knew we lacked the experience to be consistently successful and we understood that experience would most probably have to be bought by some defeats along the way.

We prepared carefully for the second Test, to be played under lights at Ellis Park a week later, but the occasion was overwhelmed by tragedy. The day before the match, we learned that Cameron Oliver, the Transvaal fly-half, had been killed in a road accident on his way home from Sun City, and the shock was doubled on the morning of the Test when news reached us that Stef Nel, the Transvaal scrum-half, had also died in the accident. Both men had been due to play in the main curtain-raiser, and now they were gone.

Their Transvaal team-mates stood quietly around the team room, talking quietly, glazed. Personally, I found it hard to generate any excitement or enthusiasm for the match. Indeed, I was so dumbfounded and distracted by this news that I only realized upon reaching the changing room at Ellis Park that I had left my boots in my room at the hotel. Two bike riders from the Flying Squad were dispatched to fetch the boots, completing the round trip in 25 minutes.

We held a minute's silence before the match and performed very well under the circumstances. Tiaan had sparked our momentum with a powerful surge upfield, we poured over him, whipped the ball wide and scored a try in the corner. We dominated long passages of play and generally appeared to be the better side, but the French kept taking their chances, ever hanging in the game and another Test came down to the last seconds.

By that time, Uli Schmidt had had enough. Steadily frustrated by our inability to translate domination into points, he became increasingly physical and opened up a cut above the eye of Laurent Cabannes, the French flanker. Uli's eyes were on fire. The prospect of losing another Test upset him so profoundly that he lost control. That was how much Springbok rugby meant to him; it meant everything.

France were leading 18–17 into the 81st minute, and it was left to Theo van Rensburg to line up a penalty from 40 metres which would win the game and the series. He connected sweetly but the ball rebounded off the crossbar and we lost. I was disappointed, but not shattered. The news from the road to Sun City earlier in the day set everything in perspective.

In at the deep end, we would remain at the deep end. Six days after the second Test against France at Ellis Park, this wide-eyed Springbok squad was setting off on a full tour of Australia, including three Test matches against the world champion Wallabies.

The first challenge of this first extended tour after readmission was to establish excellent public relations and we were exhaustively briefed on the importance of behaving well off the field. Certainly the appointment of the genial former Springbok wing, Jannie Engelbrecht, as the team manager gave the Springbok squad a far more friendly face. Ebrahim Patel, the new SARFU president, also seemed well-placed to establish and maintain a kinder, more conciliatory tone and approach.

As captain, I needed to project a confident and happy mood, and the most effective means of achieving this aim was to smile. I smiled, and smiled, and smiled again. My spoken English was not bad, but it was not as fluent as I wanted and there were times, in answering media questions, when my brain clicked into Afrikaans and I was lost for words. In that sort of difficulty, I would invariably smile, and the moment would pass.

We arrived in Perth, anticipating a media barrage of issues relating to racism, professionalism and drugs. These were the three sticks used to beat us, but the management team handled the grilling competently. The opening press conference of the tour was scheduled for eight o'clock in the morning but still drew a room full of media. We seemed to be news.

The players observed this new public relations campaign with some cynicism, generally adopting an aggressive attitude towards an overseas media who, it seemed to us, were too quick to reach judgements against us and our country. We believed they did not understand South Africa, and we were tired of having to apologize for everything. Once and for all, we wanted to be able to play rugby and leave everything else behind.

The 1993 Springbok tour of Australia unfolded as the most enjoyable tour of my career. We would only be genuinely challenged in five of the 13 matches on tour (three Tests and the fixtures against New South Wales and Queensland) which gave the overall trip a much lighter feel than, say, a visit to New Zealand which offers blood and thunder twice a week.

We enjoyed the climate and the hospitality of the local people, both of which tended to remind us of home. After eight weeks in Australia, most of us concluded it was a country where we could happily live.

After an opening fortnight of comfortable victories and new try-scoring records, we were brought down to earth by defeat against New South Wales in Sydney, the same city where we would play the first Test a week later. We had not played badly, and our confidence remained intact because defeat had been caused not by any lack of skill but by an odd lack of physical resolution, and we were confident of putting that right against the Wallabies. Strangely, defeat set the right tone for our Test preparations.

On the Sunday after losing to New South Wales, the squad took a boat trip on Sydney harbour, a memorably positive occasion. The setting was great, and the mood was outstanding as the players started to sing together. In my experience, rugby tours can hinge as much on positive team events away from the action as they can on team selection or strategy. Man management is everything, and it was almost possible to say this particular boat trip made the tour.

The coach seemed happy and relaxed. In less than three weeks, I had quickly developed a profound respect for Ian McIntosh, not least because his coaching was based on a passionate love for the game. He was evidently a student of rugby not because he thought it could make him rich or famous but because he truly loved the game. It was his hobby and his life. His passion for the game engaged all emotions, with the result that he was not slow to criticize referees, but his crimes – if they were crimes at all – were crimes of passion and, as such, could be easily forgiven.

'Mac', as we knew him, was no cold man revelling in the prestige and status of the position. That meant nothing to him. He could not have coached a local school team with any less enthusiasm than he coached the Boks for his paramount concern was for the game and for his players.

The series against the Wallabies represented a special challenge for him because so much of his rugby philosophy had been founded on the open and flexible Australian approach to the game. The 1984 Wallabies had begun to play a game where forwards handled and ran like backs – he loved that. He also sought power and speed, and imagination.

'It looks like we're underdogs,' the coach said to me after reading the newspapers one morning during the week before the first Test. 'That suits me down to the ground. What about you?'

He was grinning broadly, his eyes alive. No reply was necessary. Our mood remained up-beat as the game drew near. We trained hard, but with an excitement born of eager anticipation not fear. Perhaps this ideal mental state was born of our status as complete outsiders: we had not won a series since readmission; they were the world champions. Whatever the reason, when we finally arrived at the stadium on match night, we were on fire.

It was to be my first overseas Test, and my head was full of thoughts of millions of South Africans getting up early on a cold winter morning, preparing a pot of coffee and sitting down to watch the match on television, exactly as I had done with my own father 12 years before when the Springboks played in New Zealand. I felt part of evolving history. I felt good.

The Wallabies were stunned by our onslaught. Early in the match, I called a planned move from a scrum where the scrum-half darts on the blind side before passing back inside to me. I would draw the No. 8 before popping the ball to the winger bursting through at speed. Every element of the move clicked with perfection, and we sent James Small in the clear. He beat two defenders and scored a truly memorable try.

As I moved to congratulate him, he gave me a hug and said, 'That was your try.' But he was wrong. It had been his try, worked out on the training field and executed with aplomb on the night, and it struck the first blow in what finished as a well-deserved 19–12 victory.

We had to defend frantically in the closing stages and I cut my head open while making a tackle in cover defence by the right-hand corner but the whistle sounded moments later and the celebrations started for what, beyond any doubt, had been our finest performance since readmission.

Perhaps the most satisfying dimension of the triumph for me, as a still inexperienced captain, was the manner in which those squad members who had not been on the field so obviously shared in our delight. We had worked hard at breaking down the barriers of provincialism and, as I stood beside the team bus talking to a thrilled Ruben Kruger, one of our reserves, about how much he had enjoyed watching the game from the stands, I was starting to feel that we could again blend as a national team, united in thought and deed.

The morning after the Sydney Test, I was able to gain some first-hand exposure of the finished article: a complete international rugby captain. I had been asked to take part in a television sports discussion programme early on a bright Sunday morning, and arrived at the studios at 7 a.m., which was no small achievement after the celebrations the night before.

Nick Farr-Jones, the Wallaby captain, was already there. Setting aside the disappointment of the previous night, he congratulated me warmly. As the show ran on, Nick could not have been more kind and eloquent in conceding we had deserved to win. He had offered me an impeccable lesson in how any captain should behave in defeat; it was a lesson which I hoped I would not require too often, but it was one which I would not forget.

Our tour caravan moved on to Brisbane where we were to play the full Queensland provincial team ahead of the second Test at Ballymore. We won 17–3 in a match memorable for one of the most aggressive performances that I have ever witnessed in rugby. Garrick Morgan, the home side's lock, began charging into every ruck and maul screaming 'Hit the ******s, hit the ******s!' The referee tried his hardest to control him but we were taken aback by a display that epitomized the spirit and aggression of Australian rugby.

We knew Morgan's breast-bursting determination would be matched by the Australian team in the second Test. Partly because we knew of the whirlwind awaiting us, partly because we were threatened at our team hotel by a noisy handful of demonstrators, partly on account of the ruthlessly warm weather, we failed to settle comfortably in Brisbane.

During one training session, the coach had seen someone standing almost 500 metres away from the field, watching us train. 'Mac' had heard tales of how the Australians tended to spy on opposition training sessions, and two of our technical staff were dispatched to 'fix' this person because we thought he might be filming our practices for the Wallabies. I felt we were becoming rattled and irrational.

A combination of all these factors proved too much for what remained a young, raw Springbok team, and we were defeated at Ballymore much more emphatically than the 28–20 scoreline suggested. Ilie Tabua, the Wallaby flank, had produced one of the finest individual performances I had ever seen. Joel Stransky scored a fine breakaway try which flattered us, and James Small was sent off for swearing at the referee, Ed Morrison. I had not been close to the confrontation, but felt the punishment of being sent off in the Springbok jersey outweighed James' outburst. He was emotional, not malicious in any sense.

Defeat turned the heat on 'Mac' and myself. We were desperate to win the series, even with a young team that was learning fast in the extrovert and enthusiastic environment of Australia. We met Mal Maninga, the Australian rugby league superstar reputed to be earning Aus $2m per year, and we all swooned at the idea of becoming fully-fledged professional rugby players before too long; we visited the Australian Institute of Sport and yearned for a day when South African sport could also benefit from such a dynamic, forward-thinking structure; and we even visited the Great Barrier reef on a high-powered catamaran.

Happy holidays.

However, we lost the third and final Test 19–12 in Sydney, largely because we were inexperienced and, as a result, our minds were on the trip home, on seeing our families again. It had been the longest period abroad for most of the players and homesickness had set in. We had actually packed our suitcases before we even left the hotel for the ground, and we were on the flight home three hours after the final whistle.

Of course, we had tried everything, and James Small and Henry Honiball almost contrived to score a try beneath the posts in the closing stages, but we scarcely deserved to draw the Test and thus leave the series squared. In simple terms, the Wallabies had outplayed us because we lacked the experience and vigour to compete at the very highest level.

Victory in the first Test had given us a glimpse at the pinnacle of world rugby and it was almost as if we had gasped for air and returned to the base camp by losing the next two Tests and the series 2–1. I was disappointed to have lost, but I could see the positive dimension of the tour. We had played better than against France, we had shown we were only two or three scores away from the world champions and were, I felt, closing fast.

I felt certain the core of this Springbok team would gather experience and would learn to live and thrive in the rarefied atmosphere at the top of the rugby world. We possessed the talent and the will to succeed: with those two qualities, no goal could ever be considered beyond our reach.

The 1993 season concluded with an ostensibly easier Springbok tour to Argentina where, we hoped, we would continue to develop as a team in the more positive context of two Test victories over the Pumas – we were not disappointed by a narrow 29–26 victory in the first Test and a more emphatic 52–23 win in the second international a week later.

Our progress on the field was now satisfactory, but it was the squad's morale away from the rugby that developed most swiftly in Argentina. Great teams are not constructed only on the training field, but in every circumstance where the squad can grow together as a group of people who genuinely care about each other and enjoy each other's company.

We had been told during the flight that there were seven women to every man in the city of Buenos Aires, a statistic, accurate or not, guaranteed to win the attention of any rugby squad in the world. What we did find was a bustling city of 18 million people where opulent skyscrapers stand beside the most appalling slums and where the traffic flows in eight lanes.

Madonna, the pop icon, happened to be staying at a hotel just across the street from us and several of the players took their places in the mob of fans that was enthusiastically keeping a 24-hour watch outside her fifth floor bedroom window through every day and every night. Every time the curtains moved, the crowd would start cheering and chanting.

Members of our squad would come back to our hotel and tell us what had happened, and we would talk, and laugh, and be together and grow as a squad. It was important for the Springbok squad to be a family, to be enthusiastic about the game and happy together. We wanted to hear laughter from the team room and I wanted to feel a powerful vibe on the team bus.

We didn't want silence, nor did I want cliques, I didn't want the Transvaal players going to watch a movie, the Northerns guys going shopping and the Free Staters staying in their rooms. That was not the way of a family, that was the way of a divided team ready to play indifferent rugby.

When I heard a group of players had visited a flea market, ended up in a typical bar and spent the rest of the night talking, laughing and even crying about a recent tragedy in one of their lives, I was encouraged. That was a step forward in the process by which we would become a family and by which we would become a consistently winning squad. Rugby is a game like few others where it is absolutely necessary for players to perform for each other, support each other and back each other – we needed to like each other, and to do that, we needed to get to know each other.

In Argentina, in 1993, we started to behave as a group, never more so than at Tucuman when we became involved in one of the most brutal brawls in the history of South African international rugby. The midweek side set out to play basic rugby against the club team but encountered the most physical and hostile reception. Our physiotherapist, Evan Speechly watched the match from the touchline, where he would be on hand to treat injuries, but he had to fetch his wet suit because the crowd was spitting at him, and it was not only the adults but also the children who were behaving so badly.

The initial forward exchanges were of such ferocity that a fight seemed inevitable, and it duly erupted in amazing style, involving all 30 players on the field. Tiaan Strauss controlled the Springbok team magnificently that night – he led by example. Even sitting in the stand, I became so angry that, at one stage, I wanted to call our players off the field, and was only restrained by the coach. Keith Andrews, the personable Western Province prop, stood his ground manfully throughout while full-back Chris Dirks threw a punch and broke his hand.

No-one could pretend Tucuman was good for rugby. It was not, but I knew it had been excellent for the Springboks. We had been challenged as a squad and we had responded as a squad. In umpteen relaxed moments over the coming years, we would recall Tucuman with excitement.

We fought together and played together, one night joining more than 3,000 people at a fancy dress ball in Buenos Aires. There was little drinking, a great deal of dancing and a wonderful atmosphere until about 3 a.m. when the music suddenly stopped. With most of the South Africans anticipating a police raid, we were amazed to see two enormous television screens slowly extend to dominate the hall. The clubbers collected their drinks, sat down in disciplined rows and prepared to watch a live satellite broadcast of a soccer match between Argentina and Australia in Melbourne.

The organization was impressive, but the crowd's reaction when Diego Maradona first appeared on screen needed to be seen to be believed. I had never witnessed such adulation of an individual sportsman, and scarcely ever heard such a thunderous roar, all in a nightclub.

So the squad returned to South Africa with two Test victories and a host of happy memories. Ian McIntosh seemed happy with the progress being made, although he was a coach who never completely escaped criticism. He demanded basic levels of discipline, but he was the sort of personable coach who would not rule out having a drink with the players if he felt the moment was right. I heard some people say he became over-friendly with the players during the tour to Argentina, but such remarks were wholly unfair. 'Mac' was well liked by his players – and well respected.

I think our relationship had developed as well. The 1993 season had not been an easy year for either of us: we had started slowly against France, enjoyed some wonderful highs on tour to Australia and finished on a winning note against Argentina. I don't think it would be unfair to say that, under the new Bok coach, we had transformed a disparate group of individuals into a squad that cared about each other.

The question foremost in my mind was whether this progress could be sustained throughout the six months between November 1993 and June 1994 when the Springbok squad would not gather, would not speak to each other, would not effectively exist. This is the eternal challenge of creating spirit in a national side – the long stretches of complete inactivity.

It was, of course, worse than inactivity because, during that time apart, we would be squaring up to each other in the Super-10, the Currie Cup and the Lion Cup competitions. It was fine for me to develop common ground with Ruben Kruger outside the team bus in Sydney, but he would then be cast as my bitter opponent when Transvaal played Northerns.

The ideal situation would have been for the squad to gather ahead of the first Test against England at Loftus Versfeld on 4 June 1994, in precisely the same frame of mind as that in which they left Argentina. Life is not ideal. Within two hours of assembling at the Centurion hotel, it almost felt as if we would have to start building morale from scratch.

The guys were cool and, worst of all, we were complacent because the English touring team had lost no fewer than five of their matches on tour. They appeared as lambs to the slaughter in a Test, scheduled to take place barely two months after our country's first democratic general election and only four weeks after Nelson Mandela's inauguration as president.

'Guys, don't think this is going to be an easy match.'

Ian McIntosh's words dissolved into thin air.

The faces in the team room gazed back at him as if to say 'Well, he's got to say that, hasn't he?' There was nothing to be done, nothing to shake them from their conviction that England would be trounced by a Springbok team at full strength. I understood their logic. Transvaal had defeated the tourists emphatically, producing one of our most exhilarating displays and reducing the international side to mere shadows, but we should have known England would have more to offer in the Test match.

All our training sessions lacked the conviction, purpose and intensity that is required before a Test and, as 'Mac' grew concerned, I sensed players looking at him in wonder. By Thursday, even I had started to think he was overreacting. Perhaps this was an ordinary side. Maybe we should relax and enjoy what was going to be a day of celebration for the nation, and Springbok rugby. President Mandela was to attend the match. Everybody was going to party.

Bring on the lambs!

We eventually ran onto the field at Loftus in our tracksuits because we were aware the pre-match celebrations, the introduction of the teams to the new President, the three national anthems (two for us, one for them) and other ceremonies could take as long as 15 minutes. So we stood in a line to be formally introduced to our new president. I was tense, and maybe seemed distant and detached as I shook President Mandela's hand, but the mood and the atmosphere was all wrong. We were celebrating before the match had even begun. In our heads, of course, the match was won.

'Relax, François,' someone smiled to me.

Relax!

Bring on the lambs!

After 17 minutes, the lambs were leading 20–0. Penalty kick, converted try; penalty kick, converted try. Boom, boom, boom, boom. We were caught stone cold, and we were gone. The afternoon unfolded as, beyond any doubt at all, the most humiliating and embarrassing day of my rugby life.

Each time we gathered under our posts during that disastrous opening quarter, I looked at the guys and implored them to keep their concentration. I was furious. I looked into the eyes of the players, and I could see they were not there, not in any fit state to take on the challenge of a hard international match.

We fought back, of course, and created a couple of opportunities to get right back into contention, but Rob

Andrew capably continued to translate the shared resolve and passion of the England team into points and, by the end of a dizzy afternoon in Pretoria, we had lost 32–15. We were outplayed.

The atmosphere in the changing room was worse than at any funeral I have ever attended. A Springbok team in defeat is never less than desolate: men sit silent among the steaming kit and despair. No-one talks, and nobody catches anyone else's eye, the room full of 20-odd people sitting on their own, struggling to come to terms with the reality of defeat.

At Loftus on 4 June 1994, there were tears as well. We had started with such high hopes, and we had been humiliated. We had learned a tough lesson in the toughest way: underestimate anyone at your peril. We knew we had let people down, and we knew we had under-performed.

Yet someone called Boland Coetzee took it upon himself to tell us. The former Springbok, who became almost as renowned for his services to the media as he was for his abilities on the rugby field, waded in to the post-match recriminations and told journalists after the disaster in Pretoria that my team didn't 'deserve to wear the Springbok jersey'.

It was a ludicrous, appalling remark to make about players who may have failed to win, but had not failed to try their best. I have never met Boland Coetzee, but I do know true Springboks do not speak about other Springboks in such a way.

Five guys were dropped from the team chosen to seek revenge in the second Test against England at Newlands a week later, and I felt personally responsible for their fate. I played no role in the selection process at all, but I would have liked the opportunity to have taken the same XV who had lost at Loftus and put things right at Newlands to prove the critics wrong. That would have been my preference, but five players were left out. I felt we had let those players down.

Our preparations during the week before the second Test

were as intense as any I have known. There was less laughter than usual, less jokes in the team bus: we were, in every sense, grimly resolved.

Ian McIntosh and I pinpointed a primary need to be physical, to tackle and drive the English with every ounce of bulk and power at our disposal, and our training sessions reflected this strategy. I actually broke my nose during a driving practice on the Tuesday before the game, but completed the training session and never momentarily considered missing the Test. We had been stung at Loftus, and the entire squad set their hearts and minds on squaring the series. We were cross, bloody-minded, angry, grumpy. We would not be denied, and a broken nose seemed simply irrelevant.

We would not be denied. From the moment we executed a planned move close to the English line and sent Hennie le Roux over for the try, I was secure in the knowledge that we would win. Ian MacDonald produced a great performance in the loose, but the team was tight, strong and disciplined, and the 27–9 victory soothed some of the pain.

And yet the Test match yielded other situations and problems. Midway through the second half, we had kicked long and deep into the England dead ball area. They dotted down for the 22-metre drop-out but James Small got in the way of the kicker and conceded a penalty.

'Come on, James, get back,' I shouted.

'**** off,' came the reply.

I could not believe what I had heard. I stared at him, and I could see in his reaction that he knew I was furious. James has always been an emotional player, and he has always said things on the field which should not be taken too seriously, in fact should be left on the field. But this was different. I was his captain and he had told me to **** off during a match.

As the match ran it's course, I boiled. We were winning the game, and yet I was unable to derive any pleasure from the situation at all because one of my most senior and respected players had sworn at me. The final whistle sounded, but I did not even raise my hands in the air. I simply ran off the field to the privacy of the changing room where I would deal with James.

As the players started arriving in the changing room, celebrating the win, Ian McIntosh was pulling me to one side and instructing me to deal with the matter in a calm and rational way. On reflection, I was extremely grateful for his intervention. I was furious at the time.

Ultimately, I took our unique wing to one side and explained he would never again swear at me on the field. The matter was closed.

The England team returned home with the comfort of a drawn series in South Africa, and the Springboks were soon heading west for a first full tour to New Zealand in 13 seasons. One of the most intense rivalries in the rugby world would be renewed through a three-Test series, and I felt privileged to be leading the Springboks in such an historic adventure. I never lost sight of my good fortune to be involved with the national rugby team through one of the most exciting periods in it's 104-year history.

In our own minds, the 1994 tour to New Zealand would be nothing less than make-or-break for our young Springbok squad. We had come together at the start of 1993 under Ian McIntosh and made satisfying progress through the year, but our inability to beat England at home had raised doubts and the South African public were demanding that the 'learning curve' which they had heard so much about should start producing decent results against respected opposition. They were tired of being told we were an emerging side.

Patience was wearing thin, in the grandstands and in the President's suite where Dr Louis Luyt had become the fourth president of SARFU in the space of 16 months. The country demanded that a strong Springbok squad be in place when the country hosted the Rugby World Cup in 1995, scarcely ten months later, and we were left in little doubt that failure in New Zealand would prompt changes. We were playing for our futures – in New Zealand, of all places. Only the 1937 Springbok squad, of all previous South African sides, had managed to win a series on New Zealand soil, yet this was our challenge in 1994. We would face consistently physical and tough rugby in consistently difficult conditions. We would be tested and tested again, and were exhilarated by the prospect.

Our first sight of New Zealand could not have been more enticing, with an opening fixture at Taupo but from there we travelled to Invercargill and to sub-zero temperatures. To South Africans spoilt by constantly fine weather, it soon appeared New Zealand is a country of outstanding natural beauty with the only drawback being that the weather, on most days, makes it extremely difficult to observe any of the natural beauty.

The changing rooms at the ground in Wellington were not, however, an object of natural beauty. Preparing for our first major challenge of the tour against the local team, we were amazed to see the low standard of facilities at what was a Test venue. My first reaction to Athletic Park was to consider what a stupid place it was to put a rugby field, in a location where the lie of the land ensured the wind would howl all day long. The total environment for the players seemed hard and without frills, much like the game itself. In New Zealand, rugby prides itself on the value attached to being physical, being brave. These are the qualities that make their rugby great.

We had started our tour, playing hard, disciplined rugby, generally to the satisfaction of the coach, and we were leading Wellington with less than ten minutes to play when I struck my head against a knee while tackling one of their centres. I was knocked out like a light; not just for a minute or so, but for almost an hour after the game.

Evan Speechly and Dr Frans Verster, our team physiotherapist and doctor respectively, were subsequently criticized for the manner in which they had helped me stagger from the field when a stretcher might perhaps have been more appropriate, but they had been under instructions to disguise any concussion. That condition carried an automatic three-week suspension from all rugby, and the first Test was only seven days away.

I wanted to play in the first Test and, if necessary, we would deny that I had been concussed. If I felt OK, I would play in the Test. Foolishly, I felt as though I should not be restricted at this critical stage of my career by medical restrictions drawn up by people who didn't understand rugby – or, at least, did not understand the overwhelming desire of this Springbok captain to lead his team in the first Test of the series against the All Blacks.

That evening, hours after being concussed, I fulfilled an obligation to speak at a dinner attended by 250 lawyers and, was reliably told later that I had performed well. The team captain is always allocated a room on his own, but our doctor, Frans Verster, arranged for Hennie le Roux to sleep in my room that night and to check on my condition at two-hourly intervals.

When I woke the next morning, however, I could recall nothing of the banquet the previous evening, nothing at all, and I started to realize the scale of the risks when anyone strives to minimize concussion.

But I wanted to play, and Ian McIntosh wanted me to play. Journalists were suggesting in the newspapers that I had been concussed in the match against Wellington, but we maintained I was only a little shaken, and I duly changed and joined the team at training on the Monday before the first Test, scheduled to be played at Carisbrook in Dunedin.

I started to sprint during the warm-up, and immediately felt as though my head would explode with the pain. The agony was indescribable, and I returned to the changing room. The coach followed. We both knew there was no escape from reality: I would not be able to play. Tiaan Strauss was named as captain and No. 8, with Rudolf Straeuli summoned as flank.

In such situations, the injured captain must withdraw. I made myself available to offer advice if required, but the Test became Tiaan's show, and I retreated to the shadows and watched from the stands. Notwithstanding my injury, the team's confidence was high. We had played impressive rugby on tour, winning all our matches. Meanwhile, the All Blacks had been defeated by two Tests to nil in a home series against France and it seemed as though we might just have caught them at a weak moment.

The day of the Test dawned cold and wet, but the sense of occasion was every bit as intense as it is before international matches in South Africa. My girlfriend, Nerine Winter, and her parents were following the tour, and we spent the morning of the match enjoying the excitement and atmosphere as eager New Zealanders arrived from all over the country in cars covered with snow. It was fun, but I would rather be playing.

I found the experience of watching from the stands to be excruciating, all the more so when we were defeated 22–14 in a match which we could have won. The team had been well prepared and we set about the All Blacks with relish from the start, but we had wasted too many scoring opportunities. On several occasions, players dashed for the line and were held short with team-mates better placed outside them. Such errors generally prove to be decisive in Tests between New Zealand and South Africa, where the line between victory and defeat can be so perilously thin.

The tour was set back on the rails by an encouraging win over Waikato but we knew we would reach the point-of-no-return at the second Test, to be played in the wind tunnel at Athletic Park, Wellington. Nothing other than a victory would keep alive our hopes of winning the series, and I set my mind to preparing the team as well as any team had been prepared.

I was not interested in the history and the statistics, which so favoured the All Blacks. My only concern was the sure knowledge that, at our best, we could beat this still vulnerable New Zealand side. My task was to ensure the players were prepared to be at their best on the day.

Inspiration arrived in a CD, sent from South Africa. Hannes Strydom, the Transvaal lock forward, had been ruled out of the tour by injury but his mind was firmly with us and he took the trouble to dispatch the CD to me with a note which said: 'Listen to Track 12'. It turned out to be 'Something Inside So Strong', a song recorded by the Flying Pickets. The lyrics immediately struck a chord with me, and David van der Sandt, covering the tour for SABC TV News, generously assisted me by editing visual material of the players to the music. The result was an explosive montage.

*There's something inside so strong,*
*I know that I can make it,*
*Though you're doing me wrong, so wrong*
*You thought that my pride was gone, oh no*
*There's something inside so strong,*
*Something inside so strong.*

*Brothers and sisters,*
*When they insist we're not good enough*
*Well, we know better.*
*Just look' em in the eyes and say*
*'We're gonna do it anyway,*
*We're gonna do it anyway'.*

We showed the music video to the players during a team talk on the Friday before the match, and I was amazed by the reaction of the players. I could see they were moved, in fact psyched out of their minds, and I decided to make arrangements for a television and video recorder to be placed in our changing room at Athletics Park, Wellington. We played the piece again, just 15 minutes before kick-off. I have always believed in the power of music, and that team was incredibly motivated when they took the field.

With hindsight, we may have been too psyched-up, may have used up too much nervous energy in the changing room. Once again, we did not capitalize on several scoring chances and, after trailing 10–6 at the break, conceded a penalty in the second half and were defeated 13–6. There were several incidents when the match might have turned in our direction, but the pass went forward, the referee gave them the ball, the ball was knocked on, an All Black tapped an ankle ... something happened. At the end of the game, however, we were comprehensively beaten.

I was desperately disappointed and started to wonder whether the series defeat would signal the end of my Springbok career. I felt I had personally played well, but captains are judged by the performance of the teams they lead and the simple statistics were that in five series since taking over the captaincy of the national team, I had lost three, drawn one and only won against Argentina. Those were the bare facts.

I spent some time with the coach that evening, both of us wondering what we needed to do to turn the narrow defeats into narrow victories. Maybe it was a question of confidence, perhaps it was purely a question of luck. I felt genuinely disappointed for 'Mac'. He seemed down.

At various stages of the tour, he had given me the impression that he felt frustrated by the outdated system in which the Springbok coach was just one of six national selectors, creating a situation where he could not be sure of getting the squad he wanted. It seemed very unfair that a coach should be judged by the performance of a team picked by someone else.

In years to come, at the insistence of Kitch Christie, the Springbok coach would become virtually a sole selector with two advisers. Ian McIntosh would have greatly appreciated working under such a system.

Very early in the morning after the second Test defeat in Wellington, a new controversy erupted which would at once sweep the rugby to the back of every mind and destroy the equilibrium of the entire tour. The ringing phone in my room woke me some time around half-past one.

'François, it's Jannie Engelbrecht speaking. We have a problem. Can you come to my room immediately?'

I dressed and arrived to find the tour management huddled around the television, watching what I recognized to be a tape of the Test.

'Watch this,' the stern-faced team manager told me.

I saw Sean Fitzpatrick on the fringes of a maul, and I saw Johan le Roux, our prop, challenge him and apparently bite him on the ear. The incident was replayed again. I could see this was, indeed, a problem.

'These pictures are being broadcast all over the world,' Engelbrecht said, 'and people are expecting us to do something about it.'

My instinct was to say Johan had been provoked, and that the incident had not been as serious as the footage seemed. There was hardly any blood on Fitzpatrick. As bites go, it was hardly in the Dracula class.

'But we have to do something,' Engelbrecht insisted.

After some discussion, we all decided that Johan would be sent home. I did not agree with the decision and, to my eternal regret, I did not disagree with the decision either. With hindsight, I can clearly see we should not have been pressurized into taking any action at that time. The disciplinary process should have been allowed to take its course, but I was still disappointed by the Test defeat, still distracted, not thinking clearly.

It would be the only occasion during my career when, under similar circumstances, I failed to support the player in my team. At a time when what seemed the entire world was against him, I should have backed Johan. It was not so much a matter of right and wrong as a matter of loyalty.

So the decision was made and, we thought, the tour would go on. We had scheduled a boat trip for the entire squad on the day after the second Test but, scandalously, we left Johan le Roux behind. It was by far the worst decision I have ever made as a captain on tour. Others told him to stay, but I should have insisted that he join the rest of the squad.

The players naturally noticed his absence and the atmosphere on the boat quickly turned sour and morose. The issue was destroying team spirit, ruining the tour. Players felt one of their number had been sold out by a team management running at the beck and call of the media.

In effect, we had left Johan to the wolves. The fact that he had been so clearly condemned by his own side and countrymen effectively gave the New Zealand disciplinary tribunal a free hand to deal with him as they liked. Their judgement was to ban him from rugby for 17 months – a punishment that was ridiculously out of proportion to any offence he committed.

Humiliation after humiliation had been heaped on Johan: he had been forced to arrange his own legal defence and been afforded no assistance by management in advance of his hearing and, afterwards, he was denied the right to wear his Springbok blazer on the flight home. Johan's reaction to the saga was to remark ruefully: 'In South African rugby, it's dog eat dog.'

The tour did move on but I will never forget the sight of Johan le Roux standing outside the team hotel as our bus pulled away. He was wearing a blue and orange checked jersey. I won't ever forget the sight, because I knew we had not stood by him when we should have stood by him and I knew that, as his captain, I should have done more to help him. Months later, I found an opportunity to reflect on the course of events with Johan le Roux and I asked if he would forgive me. I still don't know if he has forgiven me.

The combination of the second Test defeat and the 'ear-biting' furore knocked the stiffing out of the tour and left most of the players looking forward to nothing so much as the flight home. Everything that had seemed so fun and positive now seemed so negative. I understood how they felt.

When Louis Luyt suggested in a newspaper interview that both the team manager and the coach were 'history', all spirit and morale appeared to evaporate. Everyone became more concerned with their own survival in the wreckage of the tour than what happened with the team.

In almost complete adversity, the players responded with the sort of guts and courage which I have always expected from Springboks. A meeting was held without the team management where we discussed our sentiments following the sacrifice of Johan le Roux, and came to a conclusion that we should pull together for one final effort in the third Test.

It might have been academic to the result of the series, but we wanted to leave New Zealand with our heads held high, and I think we did. The Test at Eden Park, Auckland, was drawn 18–18 but, even the All Black supporters appeared to agree, was a match which we deserved to win. Yet again, we had wasted chances, conceded foolish penalties and enjoyed no luck.

Our situation was neatly captured by a crucial incident late in the game. Leading 18–15 with little time left, we had seemed to have the match under control when Brendan Venter, our centre, moved across to execute a tackle in cover defence. As he ran, Sean Fitzpatrick tugged irritatingly at his jersey. Brendan saw red, swung a wild fist that failed to connect and the wily All Black captain had successfully 'won' the penalty. These were the ways and means of international rugby that we had yet to learn.

The 1994 Springboks returned home from New Zealand to the sort of public debate and controversy which follows any major defeat. Ian McIntosh was the primary scapegoat and was sacked as coach. He learned of his fate in the media – nobody had even bothered to call him.

Jannie Engelbrecht was also dismissed as team manager, but

he was not prepared to lie down before the will of Louis Luyt and generated enough popular support to force the SARFU president to change his mind.

Beyond the personal misfortune, my greatest sadness was that the tour was generally perceived throughout South Africa to have been a failure of which we should have felt only shame. This seemed to me to be a harsh judgement on a tour in which we had lost only three matches.

In reality, much had been achieved. It would subsequently become clear that the spirit launched by the players before the third Test in Auckland would lay the foundation for the greatest Springbok triumph of all.

# CHAPTER SIX

# *World Champions*

*'Come to the edge,' he said.*
*'We are afraid,' they replied.*
*'Come to the edge,' he said.*
*They came. He pushed them, and they flew.*
Guillaume Apollinaire

I an McIntosh did not deserve to be dismissed after the 1994 tour to New Zealand. A decent and knowledgeable man, he had taken a young, emerging Springbok squad to Australia and New Zealand in consecutive seasons and had narrowly lost both series when both might have been won.

A pass here, a kick there – the margins were tiny, and yet he was cast as a failure at a time when many people, most notably the players, knew how close he had come to achieving all his goals.

Dr Louis Luyt and his SARFU Executive ran out of patience with the young team on a learning curve, and dismissed the coach. The fates decreed others would reap the benefits of McIntosh's work when players, who he had nurtured into Test rugby, matured to rule the rugby world.

I felt desperately sad for 'Mac', but the mere players had no say in the decision-making process and were certainly not expected either to ask any questions or express any views. We were pawns in the game. Players were expected to play the game, and never to reason why or how. It seemed to me that, at the very least, we should have been consulted.

The disappointment of McIntosh's departure was, however, partially tempered in my mind by the news that Kitch Christie would be appointed in his place. We had worked as coach and captain of Transvaal through 1993 and 1994, winning seven trophies, and we had grown uncommonly fond of each other to the point where I was working with Kitch in setting up a trading company. Together in work and in rugby, we would spend hour after hour together, talking, laughing, trusting … and I was enthused by the prospect of applying Transvaal's winning formula to the Springboks.

'Congratulations, coach.'

I had telephoned him, immediately upon hearing the news.

'Yes, but I feel sorry for Nelie,' he replied.

This response was typical of the man. At a moment that represented the crowning achievement of his rugby career, Kitch Christie's foremost thoughts were not for himself but for another person. It is not widely known that Nelie Smith, Springbok coach in 1980 and 1981, was in contention to coach the Boks through to the 1995 Rugby World Cup, but had withdrawn because his wife was ill. He preferred to look after her.

But Kitch Christie knew. 'That shows what sort of person Nelie is,' he said. 'You must respect that kind of selflessness and devotion.'

He continued: 'Now, cappie, do you think we can do this job? Can we win the World Cup? Have we got the right players?'

Before I could respond, he was giving the answers himself. He was in the process of convincing himself. My role was simply to listen. 'We have to get the guys fit,' he went on. 'That was the problem in New Zealand, we were tiring in the second half; and we must get the management structures right. We must start believing in ourselves. We must be a family. There's a lot to do, but this is an ambulance job, cappie. There's no time to waste.'

I told him I thought we were fit in New Zealand, that it was more of an incredible opportunity than an ambulance job, and I stressed that we did have the talent to develop into a World Cup-winning side. I sensed Kitch was exhilarated by the task ahead. He was in his element.

In naming the squad for his first training camp, the new coach dropped no fewer than 18 of the 36 players who had represented South Africa on tour to New Zealand. I was not consulted in this selection, and I had stressed to Kitch that I did not want to be consulted in any selection. That was his job. It was my role to lead and motivate the team I was given.

Privately, I felt Kitch's initial selection was harsh, particularly in view of our performance in the third Test against the All Blacks, but I never questioned his judgement and it was perhaps to be expected that a new broom would sweep clean. He was eager to make his mark from the outset, and he seized another chance when two established players, Andre Joubert and James Small, missed their flight to Johannesburg from Durban and arrived late for training. Both men were dropped from the squad. The players gasped in unison.

The waters soon calmed, but the new coach had demonstrated in the most dramatic manner that he demanded high levels of discipline. He did not seek the players' approval, he wanted their respect – and, above all, he wanted them to respect the game.

Kitch's forthright strategy was launched against a background of simmering discontent around the country, with people grumbling the national side had somehow been taken over by a Transvaal Mafia. Dr Louis Luyt was president of both SARFU and the TRU, I captained both teams and Kitch Christie, at first, wanted to coach both sides. They said the Springbok jersey should be redesigned to feature a broad red horizontal stripe.

The coach quickly realized he could not hope to motivate players from other provinces at national level and plot against them at provincial level the next weekend, so he swiftly resigned as Transvaal coach. But the perception of Vaal domination remained and was reinforced when many of the techniques, methods and habits that had worked successfully for Transvaal in 1993 and 1994 were swiftly introduced to the Springbok squad.

Both Kitch and myself wanted to be sensitive to the pain of

players and officials from the Western Province and Natal who seemed to feel somehow dispossessed, but it was inevitable that the strongest provincial team through the past two seasons would strongly influence the Boks.

Our priority was to win matches, not friends.

Two home Tests against a young Argentine side in September 1994 represented a more comfortable baptism for the new Springbok coach than either of his immediate successors had enjoyed, and his team played bright, open rugby to win both games by 20 points. Our performance in the first Test at Ellis Park carried more conviction than our efforts in the second Test in Port Elizabeth, but the overriding impression was that the national side had settled smoothly within a new coaching environment.

The post-series headlines were, however, dominated not by rugby but by a saga which had unfolded during the night after the international in Port Elizabeth. Most of the players had set off to celebrate the victory, and the sought-after James Small found his way to a nightclub not far from our hotel. It later transpired a woman had pinched his backside triggering an incident that developed into an untidy brawl and a slanging match outside the club.

Kitch regarded the incident as a blatant breach of discipline, deciding James should be declared ineligible for the Springbok squad to tour Britain. I spoke up for the player, explaining how we can be provoked in nightclubs by guys performing for their friends and how difficult it can be to keep in control of the situation, but these pleas fell on deaf ears.

James was left out of the squad, and I was subsequently disappointed to learn he felt I had contributed to the decision. In fact, I had defended him because I understood his situation – I had been there myself, but Kitch was resolved to make an example of James just as he had made an example of Jeremy Thomson and Steve Jacobs when he was appointed as Transvaal coach. It was his way, and nobody could dissuade him.

The 1994 Springbok tour to Wales, Scotland and Ireland had taken on the status of a 13-match trial in which the new coach would determine which players he could count on for the 1995 World Cup challenge.

Kitch took care to ensure everyone was aware of the process: nobody could be sure of their place and nobody had been ruled out. He would not be intimidated or impressed by reputations – the rules applied to everyone, and he took a chance to show what he meant on the morning after the opening match of the tour, a narrow victory over Cardiff in driving rain.

The squad had been instructed to gather in the car park of the hotel at 7 a.m. for 'Doc's run', another Transvaal custom which had been transplanted to the Springbok camp. The 13 Transvaal players in the 30-man squad knew the importance of being punctual for this appointment, but Tiaan Strauss was not familiar with the coach's resolve to enforce discipline. By five past seven, the tour vice-captain had still not appeared for the run.

At ten past seven, Tiaan finally emerged from the hotel; the coach was furious, pacing up and down in the car park.

'OK, bend over,' Kitch said, staring at Tiaan.

'What?'

'I said bend over. You're late.'

The Western Province captain stared at the coach with a combination of shock and absolute disgust. He was wearing only his running shorts and now he was being asked to bend over. His punishment for being late would be a slap on the backside from each member of the squad, not in the privacy of a team meeting but right there in the hotel car park.

I stood, silent, watching the confrontation. This would prove a crucial moment in Kitch's career as Springbok coach. Would his discipline prevail, or would he fail to exert control over the national team? In his mind, there was only one outcome. Unmoving, he stared down the player.

Tiaan turned away, and somebody held him up on their shoulders as the players took their turns to slap him on the backside. It may be accurate to say the relationship between the two men never recovered, but Kitch wanted to make clear in the strongest possible terms that no-one would be exempted from team discipline, not even the most senior players.

The incident sparked loose speculation that Tiaan and I had proved incompatible, not only as loose forwards in the same team but also as men, and that Kitch was working on my behalf to undermine him.

This was not true. I admired Tiaan both as a courageous player, and also as a person, but the fact is that he did lose his place in the Test team, largely because a bout of flu made him unavailable for the first three matches on tour. During that period, Kitch settled upon a loose trio comprising Ruben Kruger, Rudolf Straeuli and me. He felt that, with Ruben and myself as flanks, he needed a tall No. 8 like Rudolf to win possession at the back of the lineouts. Thus, Tiaan found himself out of the frame. Such things happen in every sport. It was ridiculous to suggest any kind of plot.

The first phase of the tour comprised matches against the top four club teams in Wales and the Wales A side, and almost immediately became characterized by hysterical media claims that we were a dirty and cynical team. Isolated incidents, such as Kobus Wiese rucking on someone's back at Newport and Uli Schmidt running over a Llanelli player, were blown out of all proportion, and reported as virtual acts of war.

We sensed an orchestrated campaign to intimidate us into changing our strategy. We may have been paranoid, but the 1994 Springboks were not dirty. Kitch did want us physically to dominate our opposition and we wanted to be strong in the tackles and fierce in the rucks, but stamping and gouging were never part of our plans. There is a difference between being hard and being dirty, we knew that.

Faced by such an onslaught, we resolved to maintain our physical, but fair, approach on the field and to be as accommodating and polite to the media as possible.

Edward Griffiths, a former Sports Editor of the *Sunday*

*Times* in South Africa, had been appointed as our media liaison officer, and he created an organized environment which transmitted a positive image in the media while making relatively few demands on the players. I had not met him before, and found him to be straightforward, innovative and decisive in all his dealings.

When the tour match against Neath erupted into a prolonged brawl, it was Edward who, immediately after the game, gathered Kitch Christie, Jannie Engelbrecht and me to discuss how we would approach the media. He had taken the trouble to watch the match on television, rather than from the stand, and was in a position to inform us that video evidence suggested the trouble had been started by a Neath player. That was the line we would all take, and the result was better coverage than we probably deserved.

This new professional approach to media management made my life on tour substantially easier. Where the incessant requests for interviews had filled up my day in the past, now the flow was calmly controlled and sustained within agreed limits. I started to enjoy dealing with the press.

We managed to win our first four matches in Wales, despite the hostile crowds at most venues, and we arrived to play Swansea on what dawned as the first sunny day of the tour. The fixture against the Welsh champions had been previewed as the toughest match on the schedule outside the Tests, and the contest remained tight for 30 minutes.

Then, as we prepared to feed the ball into a scrum near our own line, I called a back row move where we would run the ball up the middle and keep possession, but Hennie le Roux, our fly-half on the day, seemed to have other ideas. He appeared uncomfortable as I made the call.

'What's the problem?' I asked.

'Give us the ball,' he shouted, smiling.

So we gave them the ball, and Hennie threw a long, extravagant pass to Chester Williams on the wing. He slipped his man, chipped ahead and the 80-metre move was rounded off by Andre Joubert scoring beneath the posts. When the full-back converted his own try, we edged ahead 12–7.

The floodgates opened and, by full time, we had won an astonishing match 78–7. It was true we had been favoured by every bounce but we had also played thrilling rugby and the players deserved to hear an emotional standing ovation ringing in their ears as they left the field. After the criticism that followed the New Zealand tour, this was chicken soup for our souls. I could almost feel a sense of confidence returning to the squad.

My own performance in Swansea had been hampered by an aching knee injury which I had resigned myself to carrying throughout the tour, and which Kitch and I had decided to keep secret. That was my burden. So the rest of the team hit Swansea and celebrated in style, while I remained in my hotel room, holding an ice pack to my swollen knee.

It must have been after two o'clock in the morning when I was woken by the hotel's fire alarm. I rushed out of my room to discover a furious Jannie Engelbrecht, the team manager, striding down the corridor with nothing more than a towel wrapped around his waist. He was heading in the direction of the room being shared by Uli Schmidt and Rudolf Straeuli where, it transpired, a variety of fireworks, rockets and crackers had been let off.

It was Guy Fawkes Day, and the two close friends had decided to mark the occasion in traditional style, inside their hotel room. Damage to curtains, bed spreads and carpets amounted to £800, and a bill was raised by the hotel management the following morning.

I suggested the entire squad should contribute towards a Disaster Fund, and this was duly achieved with contributions of around £25 per man. The response was encouraging because no-one complained, as they might have done, that Uli and Rudolf should pay the account themselves. The players had stood together, and paid together, as a squad, showing the first green shoots of the sort of remarkable team spirit that would carry us through the tour of Britain and on towards the World Cup. Every team needs incidents such as this to spur development.

We travelled north to Scotland and reached the point where, on every tour, morale is threatened – the time when the Test team is announced. It is then that 15 players become euphoric and practise even harder and the other 15 players start counting the days until they go home. It was a consolation that, in 1994, this inevitable and painful division would took place in the most beautiful of surroundings, at Peebles in the Border country.

Once the names had been called, the euphoric Test team set about a physical session with vigour and excitement while the crestfallen midweek team headed out to a muddy back field. There they half-heartedly prepared for a midweek match against the Scotland A side, a fixture that was lost to a late drop goal in the incessant rain at Melrose.

Victories in Glasgow and Aberdeen put the tour back on course, and the Test team set about preparations for the international against Scotland at Murrayfield. The match represented something of an emotional homecoming for Kitch Christie, who had spent his teenage years at school in Edinburgh, and the coach was eager to point out the landmarks around the city. For their part, the players were keen to mock his enthusiasm.

'Look, there's the Forth Bridge!' the coach exclaimed.

'It's amazing!' Kobus Wiese replied.

'A wonder of the world!' Balie Swart added.

And the squad would laugh. At least, most of the Transvaal players in the squad laughed, and a few others, but it had become clear to me that the provincial divisions within the Springbok camp remained strong. Any morning, I would arrive at breakfast and find the Free State players sitting together at one table, the Northerns guys at another and then see three tables full of the Transvaal players. It was not a healthy situation, one which would have to be resolved if we were to realize our potential at the World Cup.

We approached the Test against Scotland with apprehension. These were still amateur days when neither the All Blacks, Wallabies nor Springboks could approach an away Test against one of the home unions with the kind of casual confidence that would become prevalent in later years. We knew the Scots would field a physical pack of forwards and incisive backs, all wrapped up in a formidable team spirit when playing at Murrayfield. As the Springboks stood in line, listening to, and enjoying, the superb mass singing of 'Flower of Scotland', we fully appreciated the size of the challenge.

The day unfolded as a landmark in one man's career. Joost van der Westhuizen scored two tries and established himself among the world's top scrum-halves. He had struggled to establish himself in the Springbok team through 1993 and 1994, and a consensus had developed that Johan Roux presented a more consistent option for the World Cup.

But Johan missed the tour to Britain through injury, and Joost seized his chance at Murrayfield. I had spent some time with him, at his request, in Napier during the tour to New Zealand earlier in the year, and we had spoken about his game and the areas where he needed to improve. He had been receptive, worked hard and reaped the rewards. Joost may occasionally, to the opposition, appear cocky on the field, as scrum-halves invariably do, but this often gives him the edge over opponents. Off the field, his nature is respectful and willing. He would become a genuinely great Springbok.

Uli Schmidt had already attained that status, and he presided over what proved to be an infamous Springbok court session that followed the 34–10 victory over Scotland at Murrayfield.

'The next case is a particularly awkward one,' said Uli, sitting at the main table as the squad sat, hushed, around the perimeter of the conference room in the hotel. 'Please stand up, Mr Christie.'

The coach seemed surprised. He preferred to maintain a low profile at such events, but he was being required to stand in the dock. Uli declared he had received alarming evidence and unfolded a piece of paper.

'Mr Christie, I have a betting slip here and it refers to a bet which you placed almost one year ago. Mr Christie, it seems to me that you bet the sum of R100 (£20) that the Springboks would lose to Scotland at Murrayfield. This is not the kind of behaviour which this squad expects from its coach.'

Kitch was aghast and, amid his embarrassment and general laughter, he was fined £50 for 'treachery'. He had placed the bet in jest with his friend, Bruce Gardner, before his appointment as coach, but the comfortable way in which he accepted his 'sentence' was important – even if the Scotsman in him winced at the thought of dipping his hands in his wallet.

He wanted us to be a disciplined side and he was prepared to exercise that discipline over any member of the squad, at any time. He also wanted us to respect him as a coach, but not to be over-familiar with him as a man. He was resolved to maintain an appropriate distance. And yet, despite all this, he was able to laugh at himself in front of the squad and to accept teasing on the bus in the spirit it was intended without appearing remotely threatened. Kitch proved the most genuine and steadfast of leaders.

Having enjoyed Scotland tremendously, we returned to Wales and won a midweek match against Pontypridd before contemplating the second major challenge of the tour, the international against Wales at Cardiff.

If Joost van der Westhuizen had stepped forward at Murrayfield, then it was Rudolf Straeuli and Chester Williams who enhanced their growing reputations by scoring decisive tries at the Arms Park. Rudolf had opened our account with a storming blindside burst, and Chester dashed to the line on the outside, finally putting us beyond Wales' reach with 15 minutes of a competitive match remaining.

Chester had joined the Springbok squad towards the end of 1993, and worked hard to address a weakness under the high ball to the point where it became one of his strengths. Quiet by nature, he seemed to come alive with a rugby ball in his hands and, as he jogged back to halfway after scoring the crucial try against Wales, I gave him a grateful bear hug. Like Joost, he had emerged as a Springbok of genuine international class.

The atmosphere within the stadium in Cardiff ranked alongside any I have experienced at any stage of my career. The 1990s may have become a traumatic and disappointing period for Welsh rugby, but the raw passion of the crowd in Cardiff needs to be sensed to be believed. As the teams lined up to sing 'Cwm Rhondda' before the game, the thousands packed in the grandstands started to sing – not to shout like soccer fans but to sing like a choir. I recall feeling goose-pimples rise on my arms as the cavernous stadium reverberated to this most beautiful and passionate sound.

The tour concluded with a week in Ireland, distinguished by a sparkling victory over Combined Provinces in Belfast and a closing fixture against the Barbarians at Lansdowne Road, in Dublin. At my suggestion, we had scarcely trained through the week, concentrating on touch rugby and resolving to play a traditional open, expansive game against the famed Baa-baas.

Unfortunately the club itself appeared more concerned with chalking up a prestigious victory to sustain their position within the game. Thus, while we played Barbarian rugby, the Barbarians unusually pursued a 10-man pattern and won the match.

The defeat was, however, irrelevant to our overall plan. Kitch Christie and I laughed our way through the final press conference of the tour, safe in the knowledge that we had laid a reasonable foundation for the World Cup. There was still a long way to go, but we were on track. I spent Christmas of 1994 in Cape Town, contemplating the challenges ahead.

First among these, I needed to repair the damage to my knee and return to full fitness as soon as possible. An orthroscopy was duly performed in January, but it very soon became clear that I would miss most of the Super-10 competition. I had been warned by doctors not to rush my return to action, but the period of recovery became slow and frustrating.

By the middle of March, I was still not close to match fit and was becoming concerned. The Rugby World Cup was 10 weeks away and people started to speculate whether I would be ready. Karel Mouton, an 800-metre athlete and a friend of mine at RAU, was aware of my problem and suggested that I visit a kinesiologist called Ron Holder, who, Karel said, helped athletes overcome injuries by cutting up telephone directories and putting them in the heels of their shoes. It seemed a long shot, but I was willing to try.

So I knocked on the door of a house in Parkview, Johannesburg, and was met by a man who resembled Demis Roussos, the Greek singer. Large, friendly, with black hair and a black beard, Ron Holder welcomed me in and asked me to lie down on his physiotherapy bench.

He began to manipulate my feet. When he pressed a spot in my left foot, my left hand suddenly felt numb. It was remarkable, and frightening, but it soon became evident to me that this man had been granted a special gift for understanding and healing the human body.

The gentle probing and pushing continued, until he asked me whether I had injured my ankle recently. That was uncanny because I had turned on my ankle during the previous Currie Cup season. Then, just as Karel had said, Ron took a telephone directory and cut out a chunk to place in my shoe. It was his conviction that the majority of sports injuries were caused by an imbalance of some kind, and the makeshift 'wedge' of directory would serve to correct that imbalance and expedite the swiftest possible return to full fitness. In the days to come, we would call the treatment 'wheel-balancing'.

Within four days, I was sprinting, raring to go. Quite amazing.

Meanwhile, Transvaal had progressed to the Super-10

Final and, even though I had declared myself available for selection, it was decided to retain the same team for the final against Queensland that had beaten Otago in the semi-final. I knew that Rudolf Straeuli, my replacement as captain, was keen to take forward an unchanged side. I was disappointed at the time. This was an important match and I would like to have played. But, in retrospect, I can see the correct decision was made and Transvaal were unfortunate to lose in the final.

There were, however, no time for recriminations over the decision. South Africa was gearing itself to host the Rugby World Cup and, as the Springbok captain, I found myself drawn into the marketing whirl.

During February, a group of Springboks had been invited to Cape Town to film a television advertisement for Lion Lager, our team sponsors, in which we ran through various places – an urban centre, a beach, a township, a field, a rural lane – receiving the good wishes of all South Africans. The day of filming was enjoyable, particularly in the township, where Chester Williams proved tremendously popular among the people watching us film. But I was surprised how many black people seemed to recognize me. The profile of the tournament would extend rugby's traditional frontiers.

I was also asked to participate in what was originally conceived as a World Cup-orientated television advertisement for Black Steers, but the proposed scripts which arrived from the advertising agency had little to do with rugby. I was asked to choose from one of three drafts, all of which appeared heavily laden with sexual innuendo. That sort of thing is permissible for actors, but for rugby players...

After some consideration, I selected an advertisement which adapted a scene from the film *When Harry met Sally* in which Meg Ryan's character is having dinner in a restaurant with a man played by Billy Crystal, when she starts to experience an orgasm. An elderly woman sitting at an adjacent table watches the gasping and tells a waiter, 'I'll have what she's having.' My initial response was that the advertisement would be a bit of fun.

I was being asked to play the Billy Crystal role and my only task was to look surprised as my dinner companion's performance unfolds. We gathered at the Black Steers restaurant in Rivonia, Johannesburg for filming, and I almost fell of my chair during the first take. Looking surprised was no problem at all. I was taken aback by the attractive actress and the realistic manner in which she played her part, not just the first time but in all the 22 takes that followed. Within a couple of hours, I was feeling exhausted. I can only imagine how she felt.

The advertisement hit the airwaves at the start of May, and instantly sparked controversy. I was strongly criticized by various people for participating in something which they believed to be less than tasteful. Others told me how much they enjoyed the advertisement. With hindsight, I don't regret my role. The advertisement was conceived as fun and light-hearted, and screened late at night. It harmed nobody.

Certain elements within South African rugby, of course, were unable to resist the temptation to climb on the bandwagon of criticism. It had become clear to me that, as the World Cup drew near, such people were resolved to criticise me and the team whenever and wherever possible.

We suspected this was motivated by jealousy. The 1995 Springboks would have the opportunity to play in the Rugby World Cup, something so many others had been denied by Springbok isolation in 1987 and 1991. This fact alone established us as a target for slings and arrows.

Some of the media comment was venomous, but Kitch Christie did not seem distressed by such developments at all. On the contrary, the pragmatic coach believed the criticism would sharpen our resolve; he knew we would be strong enough to withstand any kind of onslaught.

We were strong because we were organized. The Springbok squad had been immeasurably strengthened by the appointment of Morne du Plessis as team manager. The hugely popular former Springbok and Western Province captain had been restricted to the periphery of the game since his retirement, but he was recalled at a time of need and he proved equal to the moment, bringing dignity and integrity to the position.

Indeed, the point should not be lost that it was Louis Luyt, himself, often at his own insistence, who had gathered together such an impressive Springbok management team ahead of the World Cup.

He had called Kitch Christie out of the coaching wilderness in 1992 to guide Transvaal and had then supported his elevation to the national position in 1994; he had recalled Morne du Plessis to rugby after 15 years' absence; and he had also driven the appointment of the energetic Edward Griffiths to the new post of SARFU chief executive officer.

Together, these three sat and planned every detail of the team's preparations: the hotels, the training sessions, the warm-up matches, the announcement of the squad, the press conferences. Matters were discussed openly, decided by consensus, finalized and communicated.

Such clear and sensitive leadership served not only to reassure the players and insulate them from outside criticism, but also to give them true confidence in a happy, professional and decent management. 'Fail to plan, and plan to fail' runs the old cliché. The Springboks of 1995 were aware of the pitfalls, and I think we planned exceptionally well.

The Western Samoa World Cup side were brought to Ellis Park as the opposition in our primary warm-up Test, and they were overwhelmed by the best performance from a Springbok backline since isolation. The 60–8 victory was full of imaginative, open rugby, and duly applauded; although the next stage of our preparations would present a sterner test.

The coach had said he wanted to see how we would react to pressure, so he arranged matches against Western Province at

Newlands and, a week later, against Natal at King's Park. With the local crowds supporting the local teams against the Springboks, the atmosphere crackled.

Defeat in either match might have proved disastrous to team morale on the eve of the World Cup, but Kitch's characteristically audacious gamble paid off when a late Joel Stransky drop goal gave us the victory in Cape Town (after which I prophetically told the press we could 'always rely on Joel when we're in trouble') and we won by a couple of points in Durban.

We had not played particularly well and the media reviews tended to be unflattering, but the simple fact of the victories gave the 26 players, as selected, confidence that we had deserved our selection. Nonetheless, the experience of being booed in a Springbok jersey at Newlands had jarred the senses. National unity seemed a distant dream.

Naas Botha, reincarnated as a television pundit with Supersport and a columnist with the Sunday newspaper, *Rapport*, led the criticism. He had never had a decent word to say about me during my whole career and, while I admired him as one of the finest players of all time, that did not give him the right to snipe at me incessantly. I may be wrong, but his hostility appeared to start when I took over from him as Springbok captain.

Most of the journalists sang from Naas' song sheet. Balie Swart arrived in Cape Town for the Western Province match to read that he was not fit for provincial rugby let alone a World Cup. The report concluded by saying Balie would be the weak link in the Springbok scrum.

A general consensus seemed to be reached that we would be lucky to reach the semi-finals. Everyone talked about the resurgent All Blacks or the Wallabies, unbeaten for 12 months, as potential winners of the Webb Ellis trophy. Subsequent events would cloud the memories, but the fact was that scarcely any of our compatriots gave us a chance.

The World Cup squad had been announced live to the nation on the main SABC evening news, and the omission of Tiaan

Strauss prompted the sharpest response. I did feel desperately sad for a man who had represented South Africa since readmission but would now miss the greatest occasion in any career. I wanted to telephone him and commiserate, but I was uncertain whether he would have appreciated the gesture at that stage.

I was also terribly disappointed for Ian MacDonald, my 'partner' from Transvaal, Gary Teichmann and Pieter Hendriks, all of whom were among the unlucky ones to be left out of the squad, but the coach had made up his mind. That was his job. I played no role at all in team selection.

Their desolation contrasted cruelly with the boyish excitement among the 26 players who gathered at the team hotel in Cape Town. I doubt whether any squad can ever have approached a World Cup with such anticipation as the first Springboks ever to contest the showpiece event. Live on television, each player strode into the room as Morne du Plessis read out his name and, before long, the World Cup Springboks were posed behind a three-metre sign that read ONE TEAM, ONE COUNTRY.

This would be our motto for the World Cup although it did seem at the time to be more of a goal than a reality. It would be our challenge to bring the concept to life. Would the country really unite behind our team? I hoped so. Whatever lay ahead, the players were up for the challenge.

The tournament drew nearer and the pressure grew on all the players, but it took the greatest toll on Chester Williams. As the only coloured player in the squad, the marketing men had decided that his smiling face would be the face of the tournament. South African Airlines, one of the event sponsors, ensured his picture was spread across every luggage trolley of every airport in the country, across billboards and magazines, everywhere. 'The waiting is over', read the caption. He was the most mobbed and cheered player at every function, held high as a symbol of the new South Africa, a totem of the rainbow nation.

But Chester had damaged a hamstring during the Test match against Western Samoa, and the injury was not responding to treatment. Finally, one week before the World Cup, he decided to withdraw from the squad, as his hamstring had not sufficiently healed in four weeks. The marketing men had lost their superstar, and we had lost a world-class wing. Chester's sad despair, however, prompted a recall for Pieter Hendriks.

I suffered a further scare when I pulled a hamstring days before the tournament. Every player wants to feel 100% fit as they approach a major challenge, but the reality of this contact sport is that very few rugby players, at least among the forwards, ever feel 100% fit. We battle on as best we can. The idea of withdrawing from the squad was anathema, so I ensured news of my injury did not reach the newspapers. Then I searched for Ron Holder, the only man who could return me to full fitness in time.

My fiancée, Nerine Winter, contacted Ron in London, asked him if he could come to South Africa immediately and reported back that he had other commitments and would not be able to travel. But she knew how critical the situation had become and sent another facsimile, imploring Ron to change his plans and get on a flight to Johannesburg.

Ron subsequently told me how he read the fax but could still see no way of rearranging his schedule. The same afternoon, he was travelling on the London Underground when he saw a poster advertising Supporters' trips to the World Cup in South Africa, and the poster showed a photograph of me leading out the Springboks. On the spur of that particular moment, he decided he would take the train to Heathrow Airport and try to get on a flight to Johannesburg that night. If the flights were full, at least he would be able to tell me he had tried. If he could get a place, he would travel.

This remarkable man had no luggage, just his credit card and a calm sense that the fates would determine his destination – home or Johannesburg. Arriving at the SAA reservations desk, he discovered there was still one free seat on the flight to South Africa. He promptly purchased his ticket and was treating me in Johannesburg less than 16 hours later.

Once again, his gifted hands managed my swift return to fitness and the decision was taken that he would join the Springbok medical staff for the entire tournament. It was an inspired move, subsequently justified by the low number of injuries the squad suffered during a physically punishing month. Ron Holder was the ace in our pack, the guru in our midst.

The days ticked away until the evening when, with great excitement and relief, the Springbok squad finally assembled at our team hotel in Cape Town, the Eastern Boulevard Holiday Inn. It was 18 May 1995, the waiting was over, our Rugby World Cup was underway.

We were welcomed in the hotel foyer by happy music, dancing and champagne cocktails. Amid the rousing strains of 'Shosholoza', smiles spread over every face. For the first time in a month, this group of players started to feel as if there was a nation out there, urging them to win. I have rarely known such a rush of exhilaration and, as I surveyed the happy scene, I considered we might just have a decent chance of winning this tournament.

The tournament was to be officially opened at a grand lunch attended by all 16 squads and the media, hosted at the Groot Constantia wine estate, nestling beneath Table Mountain. Morne du Plessis was resolved that, as the home nation, we should arrive early and position ourselves at the entrance to welcome the other squads. It was an entirely appropriate gesture that struck exactly the right note and we duly performed the task, even if I could sense some players were uncomfortable as genial hosts.

James Dalton, Rudolf Straeuli and Japie Mulder, for example, prefer to look rough, tough and unconcerned in the presence of opposing teams. That was their habit, and their greetings were more dutiful than warm. I managed to smile and shake every other guest by the hand, but it was hard to avoid an air of boxers greeting each other before a bout.

We were keen to be friendly, and we wanted to be polite but there was no escaping the fact that the people we were greeting were the people who stood between us and without doubt the greatest achievement of our lives. I was quietly pleased with the simmering aggression within our side, because it showed we were not there for the good times, but to win.

An occasion which might have been spectacular beneath blue skies and bright sunshine was instead marked by thunderous clouds and persistent rain; and, as aperitifs were served in the giant marquee, the 16 captains of the competing sides were asked to gather in an adjacent building where they would pose together for photographs with the Webb Ellis trophy.

As I headed towards an increasingly muddy path, it happened that Michael Lynagh, the captain of Australia, was at my shoulder and we walked down the path together. Suddenly, I felt awkward and shy.

'So, er, how was your flight?' I asked.

'Fine.'

'And have you settled into your hotel?'

'Yup, no problem.'

The thought struck me that I must have cut a confident figure, as I stood and welcomed the leading players of the world to the formal launch of the Rugby World Cup in South Africa when, in reality, I was consumed by nerves and wonder at the size and stature of the occasion.

We walked a few more paces, but I had run out of questions and, in the midst of my embarrassment, I noticed Adriaan Rossouw, the elder brother of Chris Rossouw, our hooker, walking nearby. Mumbling and ill at ease, I excused myself from Michael Lynagh and hurried over to greet Adriaan, who was carrying his child on his shoulders and, I shall never forget, was wearing typically eccentric red laces in his shoes. As Adriaan and I spoke, I managed to compose myself before heading on to the room where the 16 captains were gathered.

'François, as host captain, would you sit at the front?'

The photographer's voice hit me from behind and, caught in a smiling trance, I sat in the middle of the front row. Placed on a small table in front of me stood the gleaming, gold Webb Ellis trophy. I had seen it at a function in Edinburgh while on tour to Scotland the previous year, but this was the first time I had sat within touching distance of the ultimate prize.

I stared at the trophy. I could almost see my reflection in the polished gold, and I wondered what would be required to win this Cup, to be standing with this Cup in my hands at Ellis Park on 24 June. I sat and stared, almost oblivious to everything else. I could not take my eyes off the Cup.

As lunch was served, there was not much talking at any of the three tables where the Springboks were seated. We were all arching our necks to see past people, gazing around the room to recognize the great players of the world. Above all, we were eager to check out Jonah Lomu, the new All Black sensation. We had heard about his devastating performance at their trials, but we had not seen anything of him during our tour to New Zealand in 1994. There was no argument. He did look an awesome figure.

We had arranged to train within the secure and private surroundings of the Silvermine military base, adjacent to Pollsmoor prison, in advance of our crucial opening match against Australia, and our preparations soon assumed an awesome intensity. Kitch Christie was determined we would by the fittest team in the competition, and he had devised a range of 20-minute power sessions, packed with push-ups, sit-ups and bench-steps. He thought he was pushing us hard. We wanted to prove he was not pushing us hard enough.

'Give me twenty push-ups,' the coach barked.

'No, we'll give you thirty!' we would shout back. And, this time, it was not just the Transvaal guys shouting; and, this time, it was not just the players in the Test team who were shouting. It was everyone. The sheer enormity of the challenge had shattered any remnants of provincialism.

'Give me thirty sit-ups!'

'No, we'll give you fifty!'

One of these high-octane sessions was abbreviated by the arrival of a military helicopter at the training field. We had been informed that President Mandela wanted to visit the team before the opening match, and the players pulled on their tracksuits, but Morne had suggested that he and I change into formal No.1 dress (blazer, tie and slacks) to greet our head of state.

The President smiled from the moment he arrived until the moment he left, and I led him down the line of players. He wished good luck to each one, and seemed delighted to be presented with a green Springbok cap by Hennie le Roux. His visit proved a source of huge encouragement to a squad starting to sense an unprecedented, united surge of national support.

It is hard to overestimate the significance of President Mandela's clear decision to support the Springboks, not simply because it persuaded millions of black South Africans to stand behind a team which, for so many years, had represented something entirely foreign to their lives, but also because it gave us, the players, an enormous emotional boost. The fear, the uncertainty and the divisions between black and white melted in his embrace, and we started to realise we could help bring our nation together.

There has never been a match in the history of South African rugby so rigorously and repeatedly analysed and previewed as our opening match of the tournament, against the world champion Wallabies. Kitch Christie had even taken ten videos of Bob Dwyer's team to Hermanus over the Christmas holiday, and he had been watching them ever since.

Gysie Pienaar, our assistant coach, and David Waterstone and Hennie Bekker, the technical assistants, analysed every Australian player in terms of his strengths and weaknesses, and all this information was then processed to produce our game plan for this most crucial of opening matches.

We knew precisely what was at stake: victory would keep us on track to win the group and follow a high road to the final against teams such as the Pumas, Western Samoa, France and Ireland, while defeat against Australia and second place in the group would set us on the low road, in all probability having to face England and New Zealand on our way to the final.

'And, personally, I want to take the high road,' Kitch smiled during one of many team meetings in advance of the match.

His strategy to defeat Australia at Newlands centred on applying real pressure on two Wallabies: scrum-half George Gregan and David Campese, the legendary winger; and on winning all the restarts.

Gregan had become a crucial link for the Australian team, and we developed patterns whereby Joost van der Westhuizen, Ruben Kruger and I would make his life as uncomfortable as possible around the scrums, and James Dalton would harass him from the front of the lineout.

We decided to focus on Campese because he was exactly the sort of inspired player who could win a match on his own. If he performed at or near his potential, it would be difficult for us to win. We needed to unsettle him. A major part of his threat was his ability to kick the ball from the hand. Playing for New South Wales against Transvaal, he had dominated the match with a series of long, spiralling kicks down either touchline. We needed to ensure he would not receive a supply to deliver a repeat performance.

It was also agreed that we would kick the ball into open field behind him, challenging his famed vanity to run from deep inside in his own half and, we hoped, tempting him to take risks and make mistakes.

The third element of our game plan was to concentrate our efforts on winning the restarts after scores by either side. We worked endlessly on the patterns of support to the main jumpers, planning our response to every kind of kick and ensuring every man understood his role. In any game, Kitch had estimated there would be between 10 and 15 restarts. If we could dominate this source of possession, we would dominate the game.

Thursday, 25 May 1995 dawned clear and bright over Cape Town. As I opened the windows of my hotel room overlooking the harbour, I briefly closed my eyes and prayed that the day would unfold as perfectly as it had begun. I went down to breakfast, and found the guys clearly focused but relaxed and joking with each other. There was no grim tension. I had not even buttered my toast, but I could sense the mood was exactly right.

We loosened up with a jog through the streets of Woodstock and, just before we left the hotel, Kitch delivered a memorable team talk, scribbled on a piece of paper but delivered with the passion of a man who sincerely believed in his team's ability to win the match. There can be no stronger message for a player on the brink of a major game than an expression of confidence that he has the capacity to win. Kitch conveyed that belief.

James Dalton, Joost van der Westhuizen and the other confident guys took their usual seats in the back row of the team bus, and I seized the place where I would be most comfortable, roughly in the middle. As captain, I wanted to be in a position where I could see everyone and judge the mood.

We travelled to the ground in silence, as usual, but the players' eyes were not grim and staring. They were alive with excitement, soaking up the cheers of the crowds milling around Newlands on this beautiful day. It was a special occasion, you could see it in every face, in every smile. Arriving at the ground, we dropped our kit bags in the changing room and rushed out to see and feel the atmosphere of Newlands on this historic day.

As we emerged from the tunnel in our blazers, we were drowned in noise, in patriotic bedlam, in unbridled enthusiasm. It was hard to believe this was the selfsame stadium where we had been so roundly booed during the match against Western Province just four weeks before.

This day, we were heroes. I looked at the faces in the crowd, studied the expressions of the people cheering, and I saw this match and this whole tournament meant as much to every one of them as it did to every one of us. South Africa was laying itself on the line, nothing less. There was nowhere to hide, no excuses to be made. We were confronted by the world champions, and we were being willed to play the game of our lives.

I felt a lump in my throat, and so did the coach when the Newlands crowd started to chant his name. As a team, we were amazed by the sense of occasion. That seemed to be the greatest danger: would we be overwhelmed by the moment? As we changed, I became concerned. Os du Randt, our prop forward and a mechanic from Bloemfontein, was almost white with nerves and tension, and I could see lock forward Mark Andrews, focused, slowly tapping his thigh as he stared straight ahead, breathing deeply.

They looked too tense, too rapt in thought, almost frozen with nerves. I impulsively walked across to where Mark was sitting.

'Mark, are you OK?'

He didn't move. His stare was fixed, his manner aggressive.

'Are you OK?'

Still no movement.

I hit him, with an open hand on the shoulder. Some of the players later said I had punched him, but that was not the case. He jolted, and looked at me. I repeated the question, and he said he was fine. Mark was a player at the top of his game, motivated almost beyond words and playing excellent rugby. Some life returned to his eyes. We needed to be right.

'Come on, guys,' I implored everyone. 'Relax, concentrate on what we have planned, be accurate and precise in all your movements and enjoy yourselves. This is going to be one of the great days.'

We could hear the strains of music from the Opening Ceremony being played out in the stadium, from time to time picking up the national anthems of the teams. There would be time to watch the video later, to swell with pride at the quality of ceremony devised by South Africans, but our challenge was to separate ourselves from the pomp and focus on the rugby.

As we ran on the field, it felt as if the roar emanated not just from the stands but from the every corner of the country. It is hard to explain the depth of emotion throughout a population, isolated for so long, as it approached this first global sporting event to be hosted on South African soil.

I sang both parts of our national anthem, 'Die Stem' and 'Nkosi sikelel' iAfrica', at the very top of my voice. In fact, I almost shouted the words. Prop Os du Randt was standing next to me, too emotional to sing, so I tugged him closer to me, assuring him we were all in it together.

At last, we were ready for kick-off. All the analysis and prediction, all the build-up and aspirations came down to a simple game.

The match was played at a tremendous pace and the Australians had the better of the first 30 minutes. Michael Lynagh scored a try, and it seemed to some observers that they would prove too clinical for the enthusiastic Springbok team. That was not my perception on the field. In my eyes, this was never a match we could lose.

A few minutes before half-time, we executed a counter-attack that calmed the nation and vindicated my own sense of the way the game was going. James Small retrieved possession on halfway and set off on a run upfield, passing to James Dalton who fed Mark Andrews. I hit the resulting ruck at speed and the ball was popped neatly out to the backline. Then it was James Small who turned up on the opposite side of the field and fed Pieter Hendriks. He dipped in, and used his wonderful acceleration to beat Campese on the outside. The try was scored in the corner, and our World Cup had begun.

155

We were playing with intensity but also with control, and there was not much for me to say or change as we gathered for half-time, leading 14–13. Our aggressive defence was working well and would become a feature of the tournament. We would kick deep, move up in a line and apply pressure so effectively that we would force an error or a turnover.

Early in the second half, we gave our coach an ultimate compliment by scoring a second try from a carefully planned and practised move. 'Steker' was implemented from the back of an attacking scrum: the No. 8 picked up the ball, passed to the scrum-half fanning wide; the No.9 then flipped back to No.10 bursting through on the inside; the fly-half would utterly wrong-foot the defence and have a clear run to the line.

The execution was perfect, Joel Stransky scored the try and we were able to defend for the rest of the match. Phil Kearns did score for Australia late in the game, but the 27–18 victory was no more than we deserved. At the final whistle, I raised my right hand in the air and ran off the field. I don't think I was even smiling. I wanted to convey sincere gratitude to the crowd for their fantastic support on the day, but also to make clear we had not won anything yet and this win was only the first step in a long campaign.

Our changing room was perfectly poised afterwards. There were no wild whoops of delight, no crazy celebrations. We knew we had been tested, and we knew we had passed the test. Some pundits did try to minimalize our success, subsequently complaining the Wallabies had been past their best at Newlands, but that was nonsense. Lynagh's side had not lost a Test match in 12 months and they were the World Cup favourites on merit. Humbly, I would suggest they were beaten by the luckier side on the day.

If we, the Springbok squad, managed to keep victory over Australia in calm perspective, there was absolutely no need for the rest of the country to maintain such decorum. The triumph prompted a nationwide party, notably at the Victoria and Alfred Waterfront in Cape Town.

Most of the players arrived at Bertie's Landing, a landmark pub on the waterfront, and were literally carried into the bar on hundreds of hands. I had never known such a vibe. After a couple of beers, I called Nerine Winter, my fiancée, on her cellphone and discovered she was patiently waiting for me at a fish restaurant somewhere else on the Waterfront. I hurried across to meet her, and was carried shoulder-high into that restaurant as well. I had never seen such happiness so intently shared by so many people.

After dinner, we joined most of the players at the Gecko club in Loop Street, finally getting back to the hotel at four o'clock in the morning. 'Doc's run' was scheduled for nine o'clock in the morning – Kitch was being kind on this occasion, but this exercise turned into something of a victory lap as the players ran through the City bowl out towards Sea Point, all the while being cheered by passers-by recognizing the national heroes.

These were rare days.

The following day, again at Morne du Plessis' suggestion, the squad was joined by their wives or girlfriends on a tour of Robben Island, including a visit to the prison where President Mandela had been held. It was another exceptionally sensitive piece of management. Morne was aware that keeping the players' wives and girlfriends feeling involved and happy can represent at least 50% of ensuring that the player is content.

Our visit to the island proved a humbling experience. We peered into the small cell where Nelson Mandela had spent so many years, and were left to wonder how he could have emerged to govern South Africa in such a spirit of forgiveness and reconciliation with so little bitterness in his heart. It is hard for ordinary men, like me, to conceive of such feats.

The island was still being used as a jail and we were invited to spend some time with the prisoners in the main hall. I addressed this audience about the 'One Team, One Country' theme of our challenge for the World Cup and expressed the hope that our efforts would unite the nation.

While I was waiting to speak, I had noticed James Small

standing to one side, in a corner, and I saw a tear roll down his cheek as he watched the prisoners. I have no idea what was going through his mind, but I saw again that he is a person who cares about others; and he was strong enough not to mind showing that he cared. I admired that in his character.

Victory over Australia had set us on the high road to the final and Kitch had determined that what he called the 'Green' team would be chosen for the remaining group matches against Romania and Canada. His primary aim was to ensure his leading players reached the knock-out phase of the tournament as physically strong and injury-free as possible, but he was also eager that all 26 members of the squad should play a part of the campaign.

When people questioned the coach's refusal to choose his strongest side, he replied bluntly: 'If you are asking me whether I believe what could be called the Springbok second team is strong enough to beat Romania and Canada, then I tell you I do. I have every confidence in them.'

Adriaan Richter led the team against Romania and scored two tries in a steadfast 21–8 victory. Having watched from the grandstands, I attended a post-match cocktail party in the President's room at Newlands and happened to be standing near the door when the Romanians arrived, carrying their kit in plastic bags from a local supermarket. I was dumbfounded.

It seemed astonishing that a team could compete in the World Cup, and not have enough financial backing to provide their players with kit bags. I quickly contacted some representatives from Adidas, and was grateful when they agreed to provide the Romanians with basic kit.

Kitch Christie reacted typically to the Romanians' plight, declaring he would find them a sponsor. I was surprised to see the coach in such animated spirits after what I thought had been a relatively low-key performance. In fact, he seemed happier than he had been after the match against Australia; when I asked him why, he explained how the subdued display had ideally slowed the pace of our campaign after a flying start, not only reducing the overstated public expectations but also calming down the players.

Throughout the tournament, the coach would remain keenly aware of the 'pace' of our campaign. He recognized the nature of the task, and had mapped out in his mind not only how he would reach the final but also how he would ensure his team would peak at the right time, reaching that final in the correct mental and physical condition to win the trophy.

This was not just a clockwork coach 'taking every game as it comes'. His preparation and thought processes were constantly more advanced and more original than those of any coach I have known.

We headed to Port Elizabeth for our concluding group match against the Canadians, a match which had been given added significance by other results in the group. The calculations were such that, technically, we could still lose to Canada and be eliminated from the tournament. Effectively, we had entered the knock-out phase one match early.

Under these increasingly tense circumstances, I wondered whether the coach might drop his avowed intention of playing the 'Green' team and name his strongest possible side for the Boet Erasmus stadium ... but Kitch Christie was not so easily swayed, not so easily panicked.

He remained attached to his pre-tournament plan, with one exception: he decided I should captain the team to provide what he believed a firm hand on the rudder in case matters started to get out of hand. I was flattered to hear he considered my presence on the field to be of such value.

Our game plan against the overtly physical Canadians could not have been more simple. We would play safety-first, zero-risk 'kick and klap' rugby, punting the ball deep, playing in their half and seizing our chances. Our aim was to win the match while conserving as much energy as possible, to avoid injuries and absolutely to withstand any provocation.

The road to disaster is always paved with good intentions. Ever since the Test against Argentina the previous September, there had been a running joke within the squad that 'something always goes wrong in Port Elizabeth'. We had repeated the mantra, and laughed, on the flight from Cape Town but when the stadium floodlights failed twice during our training on the eve of the match, the joke was becoming reality and it wasn't funny.

We discussed what would be the effect on the situation if the floodlights failed the following night, forcing the game to be abandoned. No-one seemed to know, but we didn't worry. That sort of thing would not happen in a Rugby World Cup, not in South Africa, surely not.

The team talks successfully hyped up the guys, and I was confident of a successful evening when we lined up for the national anthems.

'*Uit die blou...*'

The floodlights failed.

The packed stadium was plunged into darkness. As one of our players made the knee-jerk remark about things going wrong in Port Elizabeth, I told the team to return to the changing room and keep calm.

Candles were set on the physio's table, and I asked the players to lie on the benches and relax, before imploring them to keep their minds on the game, not to worry about the floodlights, to concentrate on what they would have to do to make the game plan work. For 45 minutes, we sat in this surreal situation, not knowing whether we would play or whether we would simply go home. We had been primed for an enormous effort, but the delay left us cold.

Mercifully, the engineers were successful and we were informed the match would start soon after nine o'clock. The first exchanges with the highly physical Canadians confirmed we would have a battle on our hands, but we stuck to the basic game plan, and scrum-half Johan Roux kicked for position all night long, provoking the crowd's irritation but our admiration. The crowd wanted to see champagne rugby, we wanted to qualify.

As a brutally competitive match ran its course, we made no fewer than 147 tackles, the most by any team during any match of the tournament. As a result, the Canadians found themselves pinned in their half and we were able to score two pushover tries from scrums near their line.

With 70 minutes played, we had established a solid 20–0 lead and seemed for all the world to have capably survived a potentially catastrophic evening. I felt proud of our discipline and professionalism.

Then, in a matter of only 30 seconds, the match, and our campaign to win the World Cup, literally exploded. Pieter Hendriks was manhandled into the billboards by the Canadian full-back Scott Stewart, and James Dalton rushed in to keep the two players apart. The conflict spread through 20 of the 30 players on the field, as punches flew in all directions.

By the time Irish referee David McHugh had regained control, Hannes Strydom had left the field with a badly cut eye and, most significantly, James Dalton had been sent off on the grounds that he was the 'third man in' to the brawl. The International Rugby Board guideline stipulated the referee should identify and dismiss the third player to join the fracas, rather than either of the first two brawlers, on the basis that he had provoked the mass fight.

I appealed vehemently and emotionally to McHugh.

'He was trying to stop the fight,' I said. 'He didn't even throw a punch. Come on, referee, we came to play rugby and they came to a fight. Let's keep things in perspective. He'll be banned from the tournament!'

But a referee's mind is seldom changed, and James walked slowly off the field, his hands resting sadly on his head and his dreams in tatters. The match finished quietly and two Canadians, Rod Snow and Gareth Rees, were also dismissed. There were no celebrations in our changing room. James sat silently in his sagging kit, utterly miserable and broken.

A disciplinary hearing was held at midnight, during which our hooker received a mandatory 30-day suspension for being sent off. His World Cup had been brought to a sudden conclusion. I tried to console him, but there was nothing to say. I wondered whether there was anything I, as the captain, could have done differently, but there was not.

Rugby remains a physical sport in which tempers are liable to explode at any moment. One needs to maintain discipline for 80 minutes, but a situation had developed and James was the unfortunate man to be singled out and punished. As he sat in silence, five or six players must have realized they might easily have been in his place.

We should have been celebrating our progress to the quarter-finals, but dark clouds scudded in over the squad's outlook. There was no laughter, no buzz, and the mood deteriorated further when we learned the following day that Pieter Hendriks and Hennie le Roux would be cited for their roles in the brawl against Canada. Video evidence seemed to show Pieter kicking at an opponent, and Hennie delivering an extravagant right hook.

Faced by the prospect of losing not one player, but three, our sense of sadness turned to seething anger; although we did calm down with the news later in the day that Hennie would, in fact, not be cited.

Perhaps we overreacted. Maybe these events were simply a spark to ignite the pent-up pressures and tensions of the tournament, which, until this period, we had impressively controlled. Whatever the reason, the emotional impact on the squad was devastating. We felt let down by the management (although it is hard to say what they could have done), and we felt victimized by the citing officers. For a Springbok squad contemplating a World Cup quarter-final, we were ridiculously grumpy and sullen. Our wheels may not have come off, but they were certainly wobbling.

The entire squad spent the Sunday after the Canada match at the Fish River Sun resort, an hour east of Port Elizabeth, where the staff did their best to improve our mood by laying on a day of crayfish, golf and bowls. Our bus was due to return home at 6 p.m., but I asked Morne du Plessis if I could stay behind to have dinner with the resort manager, Melville Vogel, a friend of mine, and to return in a separate minibus. Two of my team-mates, Andre Joubert and Gavin Johnson, were soon at my shoulder, also asking to return later.

Morne appeared uncomfortable with the idea, but agreed on condition that Douw Mans, one of the security policemen travelling with the team and, strangely, the cousin of my former girlfriend, would stay with us and drive us back to the hotel in Port Elizabeth after dinner.

Inevitably, we lost track of time. Dinner dragged on and we headed for the casino where the cards started to fall kindly. We were on a roll, and I was grateful for an opportunity to unwind from the pressures of the tournament. It was not until after 12 midnight that we left the Fish River Sun, but, while Andre and Gavin slept in the back, I took care to sit in the front with Douw, talking to him to make certain he stayed awake.

We arrived back at our hotel in Port Elizabeth at three in the morning. Morne, looking pale and drawn, was pacing up and down in the reception. He was furious, saying he had tried to telephone me but that the receptionist had told him I was not available to take his call. That was ridiculous. I told him I would always take his call. He seemed unconvinced.

'We'll discuss this in the morning,' he said angrily.

I felt shattered, confused and disappointed, and, at eight o'clock the next morning, I told Morne and Kitch that I resented being treated like a child. They explained what would have been the consequences of a road accident, and I could understand their point of view, but I was becoming irrational and angry. In my mind, everything was twisted and blurred.

We returned to Johannesburg where James Dalton lost his appeal on the Monday and, after holding a tearful, dignified press conference, the hard man packed his suitcase and left. Hendriks was handed a harsh 60-day suspension by his

Disciplinary Committee, and also checked out of the team hotel with tears in his eyes soon afterwards.

I had become sullen and silent, making no contribution to the team in any way at all. During training at Megawatt Park, north of Johannesburg, we were asked to undertake a five kilometre run. When we got back to the start, some of the guys manfully tried to inject some spirit by saying we should tell Kitch Christie that we wanted to run another five kilometres.

They looked at me. I shrugged at them and set off on another run without saying a word. I was flat, fed-up and disinterested.

It was not until the Tuesday evening that Kitch called me to his room at the Sandton Holiday Inn. He had also been less than enthusiastic around the training ground and the team room. We were in a rut.

'Cappie,' he said, 'are we going to win this thing or not? We are three days away from a World Cup quarter-final, and only three matches away from winning the World Cup. But we're letting it slip. If this Springbok team is going to get back on the road, it is you and I who must do it. What do you think? And what are we going to do?'

I would like to be able to record at this stage that I leapt to my feet and told the coach we would move forward and win the World Cup, but that was not what happened. I told him that I didn't know what we should do; I told him I felt depressed by what had happened to Pieter and James, annoyed that I had stayed out late at the Fish River Sun, disappointed that Morne had thought I would not take his telephone call – that I was generally out of sorts.

'OK, coach,' I concluded. 'We'll wait and see what happens.' And I left his room, still confused.

A team meeting had been scheduled for 9.30 a.m. the following morning, and I attended with no clear strategy or intentions. After a brief opening talk, Morne took me by surprise by asking me to address the squad. I stood from my seat in the front row of chairs and turned to face the players.

I was angry, and whenever I get angry, tears are never far away.

I told the squad why I thought things had gone wrong and I apologized for being grumpy over the previous couple of days. I said sorry to Morne for betraying his trust in Port Elizabeth and, with a cracking voice, I pledged myself to the squad and to winning the World Cup. It was then agreed that Gavin, Andre and I would each be fined R500 (£55) for being late, and the saga was banished to history, never to be raised again.

The players strode purposefully out of that team room, straight to the team bus and on to one of our most effective training sessions of the World Cup. We had turned the corner. Our resolve and the will was back and, with only 84 hours remaining before kick-off, we belatedly turned our minds to the challenge of a quarter-final against Western Samoa at Ellis Park.

In accordance with generous World Cup regulations, Chester Williams and Naka Drotske had joined the squad as replacements for the suspended players, and I was profoundly encouraged when Chester took the trouble to tell me how proud he had felt of the team's achievements in the group phase. He had seen the impact of the tournament on people, and he seemed thrilled to have been granted this second chance of taking part.

Kitch Christie had studied the Western Samoan team carefully and the essence of his game plan was to put points on the board in the first quarter, to kill the game as a contest and then cruise to the semi-finals while conserving energy and minimizing the chance of injury. The 60–8 victory at Ellis Park in April provided the sure knowledge of our superiority.

In the event, on a bright sunny day before a 68,000 capacity crowd, we did score early in the game and we did kill the contest but no game plan could offer us protection from the Samoans' physical approach to the game. Andre Joubert was flattened twice inside 15 minutes, and the full-back left the field with what proved to be a broken hand. By the end of our

42–14 win, at least seven players were nursing significant injuries: Kobus Wiese was icing his knee; Ruben Kruger could not lift his arm above his shoulder; Mark Andrews was suffering from chest pains; Joost van der Westhuizen had been struck in the throat; James Small had missed the match with a sore hamstring; and Joel Stransky's eye was only now starting to open after being closed during the match against Canada.

Andre Joubert's broken hand, however, was causing the most concern, although he seemed the least worried of all. Kitch had gazed at the famously relaxed full-back, aghast, as he managed to knot his own tie with his swollen hand. It seemed as if Andre was feeling virtually no pain. Richly talented and easy-going beyond description, the full-back was all class.

He underwent an operation that same Saturday evening to stabilise his hand with metal pins and, contrary to medical opinion, never seemed likely to miss the semi-final against France in Durban. He spent two highly publicised sessions in a decompression chamber to reduce the swelling, and a special protective glove was flown out from Ireland for him to wear, but Andre always indicated he would be fine. 'No problem,' he would smile.

The tournament had, meanwhile, produced its first big surprise when Australia were defeated by fly-half Rob Andrew's late drop goal at Newlands, taking England through to a semi-final against New Zealand. The All Blacks had been impressive in overpowering Ireland, Wales, Japan and Scotland, and were being touted as odds-on favourites to win the World Cup, but we were not overly focused on the form of our main rivals.

The coach was nothing if not unpredictable – we had changed our gameplan to suit the needs of each game – and his decision that Mark Andrews, regarded as one of the finest lock forwards in the world, would play No. 8 against France swiftly dispelled any hopes that we would enjoy a quiet, straight-forward build-up to the semi-final in Durban.

Kitch had asked me what I thought, and I told him Mark did have the athletic ability and the skills to adapt to a new role, but it was asking a great deal of a player to move to a new position before such an important match. I can't imagine how the French reacted when they saw our team. With Rudolf Straeuli and Adriaan Richter as two No. 8s in the squad, the coach had taken an option that nobody else would even have considered.

Was that genius or foolish? Judgement would depend on the result, but nobody could say the coach was scared by the occasion. With hindsight, I believe the move was primarily motivated by Kitch's resolve to find a place in the side for Kobus Wiese – the big Transvaal lock had played in France and would scrum hard and put fire into our drives – but he could not bring himself to leave either Mark or Hannes Strydom out of the side. The compromise was to move Mark to the back of the scrum. It was certainly brave.

We travelled to Durban on the Friday, the day before the match, and arrived in the worst weather I had ever seen on the Natal coast. The players watched the deluge with interest and I was pleased by their mood. We were not afraid of losing, and were excited about winning. From a captain's point of view, I could not have been happier with the vibe.

When Kitch saw the weather, he performed his usual routine of telling the players that he was going to telephone the Disneyland resort in America, where he would be given the world's most advanced and accurate weather forecast. At least, that was what he always told us.

'Who are we talking to today?' Balie Swart would ask.

'Mickey Mouse or Donald Duck?' Kobus Wiese would tease.

And the coach would smile, never troubling to tell the players that he would in fact contact Etienne de Villiers, president of Disney International and the son of Marquard de Villiers, an old friend from Pretoria, and that it would be Etienne who then secured the accurate weather forecast.

Kitch was happy to let the players enjoy the joke, even at his expense.

The Disney weather centre predicted heavy rain for Durban on the afternoon of 17 June 1995, clearing towards evening. It was not optimistic and, on the morning of the match, we sat down to adapt our game plan to suit the wet conditions. Shelving our intention to run the ball at the French, it was clear we would have to concentrate on retaining possession. The team that could best control the wet ball would win the match.

Still the rain came down.

My fiancée, Nerine, was flying to Durban on the morning of the match as a guest of South African Breweries, and the windscreen of the light aircraft in which she was travelling was actually cracked by the downpour. On any normal day, I doubt whether aircraft would have landed in Durban under such appalling conditions. But this was not any normal day.

We only started to wonder whether the match could go ahead as our bus started to wind its way through flooded streets. There appeared to be no break in the clouds, and still the rain came down. Upon arrival at King's Park, I borrowed an umbrella and walked out to inspect the field. An area beneath the posts at the City end had been transformed into a genuine lake, and the surface water was clearly visible everywhere else.

I was not at all surprised when Derek Bevan, the Welsh referee, came to our dressing room and said kick-off would be delayed by an hour. Some of our players seemed unsettled, but most of us shrugged our shoulders at just the latest bizarre development of our World Cup campaign. We had reached a point where we started to expect the unexpected: after the floodlight failure in Port Elizabeth, now we faced the floods of Durban.

Morne du Plessis and Kitch Christie wandered around the room, giving advice, urging the guys to stay focused. One of the Natal officials arranged for a television and video to be installed in the changing room, and we tried to relax by watching tapes of the French in action.

'What happens if the rain doesn't stop?' someone asked.

'We would go out,' Morne replied. 'The game would be decided by the number of players dismissed during the tournament and the French have had none while we have had James sent off in Port Elizabeth.' I was shocked.

No-one said anything, but nobody failed to understand that we needed to get on to that sodden field and play this game. The French team, waiting in their changing room down the corridor, understood the situation as well. With the benefit of hindsight, it seems to me that their mindset would have been different: they didn't want to play the game in the wet, and would surely have been quite happy to reach the final on a technicality.

When Bevan arrived to say the rain had stopped for long enough and the match would start at 4.30 p.m., perhaps we had secured a decisive advantage. We were hungry for the contest while they were hoping there would be no contest.

I won the toss and, following Kitch's advice, opted to play the first half with the wind and the rain at our backs. The latest forecast from Disney had been for the wind to die down after 5 p.m., putting us at no disadvantage in the second half, and it proved absolutely correct. It is not widely known that Donald Duck was entitled to some glory in our victory.

We started the match exceptionally well and Ruben Kruger powered over for a try during the first half, but Joel Stransky and Thierry Lacroix both kicked magnificently in the conditions, and this bizarre contest, played out in spectacular sprays of surface water, came down to the wire.

We were leading 19–15 with three minutes left to play when Joel failed to kick a restart 10 metres, and the French were given a scrum on halfway. It was an uncharacteristic error and placed us under pressure. France won the ball and fly-half Christophe Deylaud launched an up-and-under. I was running back, and I saw James Small steady himself under the ball.

Perfect, I thought. James will claim the mark. But he didn't. He knocked on.

Two unforced errors had awarded France with an attacking scrum, and I could hardly contain my anger. Gathering the entire team around me, the air turned blue as I urged the guys to concentrate.

'We've come so xxxxxxx far,' I shouted, drenched with sweat, rain and mud. 'Let's not xxxxxxx give it away. Please, xxxxxxx concentrate.'

Deylaud launched another chip kick from base of the scrum, and the ball fell into the arms of Abdelatif Benazzi, who surged forward to score what would have been the winning try. I was running behind him, and thought he had wrestled over the line to score the try, but Hennie le Roux and James Small had courageously thrown themselves in his path and the referee signalled for a five-metre scrum. As the bodies untangled, it became clear that Derek Bevan had made a magnificent decision.

There was no doubt.

Benazzi had grounded the ball six inches short of the line, but France were not beaten yet. As we prepared to defend yet another five-metre scrum, the forwards bound arms in a tight huddle and Kobus Wiese famously took hold of his old friend, Balie Swart, and said: 'Listen, Balie, in this scrum, you are not coming back. You can go forward, you can go up, you can go down or you can go under … but you're not coming back.'

Kobus was shouting. I had never seen such resolve, passion and guts. We were drenched and exhausted, but this felt like a defining moment in our lives. Would we hold firm? Would we hold our position?

History records that we did hold firm, and we won the ball, and Joel Stransky cleared to touch, and the final whistle sounded, and we had reached the 1995 World Cup Final. In those desperate closing scrums, Kitch Christie's decision to select the scrumming power of Kobus Wiese, even at the expense of playing Mark Andrews out of position, paid off handsomely.

I threw my arms in the air. We had peered over the edge of failure, and somehow hauled ourselves back to celebrate another immense triumph. The front row left the field together, still arm-in-arm, three big men in tears. Os du Randt, Chris Rossouw and Balie Swart had proven themselves.

Of Andre Joubert, it can only be said his performance was so solid and secure that everyone forgot he was playing with a broken hand. I saw heroes in each direction. The five non-playing squad members came to the changing room, dressed in blazers but looking as exhausted as us, and began shaking the hands of every player. We were a family, a winning family.

The following day, returned to Johannesburg, the squad sat together and watched on television as New Zealand mightily overwhelmed England in the second semi-final, at Newlands. Jonah Lomu had literally run through the tackles and I told our guys that our defence would have to be on form. It was correct that the All Blacks should have carried the tag of over-whelming favourites into the final. Lomu had been the star of the tournament.

Lomu's performances had been tremendous during the week leading up to the World Cup Final and I suspect the Jonah-mania might have rattled our coach. We had arranged to spend the Monday and Tuesday away from the madding crowd at Sun City, and it was there that Kitch suggested that, man for man, we could outwit the All Blacks. He wanted us to play the 'Brains Game' in the final, a brand of rugby where everything is executed at double speed, tap penalties, short lineouts, quick scrums.

Such a strategy appeared too risky for such an important match, although I was never going to argue with Kitch and we implemented these tactics at our training. But the guys were nervous, and a series of bad passes and dropped balls persuaded the coach to adopt a more conventional pattern: we would move the ball, but we would also confront the All Black pack.

Lomu hardly featured in our team talks thereafter. Kitch would simply say 'James will look after him' and move on to something else. James Small approached his task with care and had spoken to his friend, Inga Tuigamala, a powerhouse All Black wing from another era.

Tuigamala's advice was to stay on Lomu's outside, always forcing him inside where he would be taken by the cover defence. That became our plan for Lomu, and we moved on to discussing how we would play.

By Wednesday, the spirit within our team had reached new levels. At one point, the backline players were sweating through some bench-steps, inevitably with their shirts off, and they started counting their steps out loud. We, the forwards, were doing sit-ups nearby, and began counting aloud as well, working to outpace the backs. Louder and louder, faster and faster: I have never known such an intoxicating atmosphere.

On Thursday, we were joined by golfer Ernie Els, soccer star Marks Maponyane and cricketer Fanie de Villiers at a press conference attended by almost 200 journalists and 15 camera crews. Ernie had withdrawn from a golf tournament especially so he could attend the World Cup Final and he came up for a couple of beers in my room after the press conference. He could not have been more encouraging or constructive.

Our last training session of the tournament progressed quietly at some Rand Afrikaans University playing fields in Melville, and I was in the process of taking my boots off when my cellphone started ringing in my kit bag.

'Hello,' I answered.

'Hello, François, how are you?'

President Mandela's voice was unmistakable. He had called me before the opening game, again before the semi-final and now before the final just to wish me luck and to ask how the players were feeling; and he had even dialled the number himself. These were not the conscious acts of a politician, rather the impulsive acts of a man who genuinely supported the Boks.

'And, good luck for the game. I'll see you tomorrow.'

'Thank you, sir.'

Saturday, 24 June 1995 dawned bright and clear in Johannesburg, as if any other weather was conceivable for the World Cup Final; the players woke as usual and found their own way down to breakfast sometime between nine and ten in the morning. Armed with cereal and fruit juice, I found Kobus Wiese and Japie Mulder together and sat beside them. Conversation turned swiftly to the match, the All Blacks and how to beat them.

'We must mimic their gamesmanship,' I told the guys. 'We must do to them today exactly what they did to us in New Zealand last year. If you're standing up from a ruck or a maul, take care to push one of the All Blacks in the back or, even better, hold him down on the ground. If you're walking past them, take care to shove them in the shoulder.

'And never get involved in any kind of retaliation, never get angry or upset and complain. Always stay calm, do the deed and walk away. Focus on the ball and get on with the game. We must take command on the field. We want to be the epitome of controlled aggression on the field.'

I had repeated the message several times through the week, believing it to be crucial that we stand man-to-man against the New Zealanders. I have always thought they win 50% of their matches before they even step onto the field because they transmit this aura of superiority. We had to challenge and threaten that status. We needed to be in their face.

Around eleven o'clock, the players gathered outside the Sandton Sun hotel and we set off on a jog through the streets of the suburb. Again passing motorists hooted their horns as they recognized familiar faces and passers-by stopped to cheer their support. Some of the guys selling newspapers at main junctions even stopped selling and ran beside us.

I was eager to keep the guys focused, but it was impossible to ignore a sense that, on this particular day, this one country would be standing together and standing behind one team of 15 players and reserves. It sounds too sugar-sweet to be true, but wherever we ran, wherever we looked, people smiled and gave us a thumbs-up. It was strange. It was a special day to be a South African in South Africa, and it was a wonderful day to be a Springbok.

Returning to the hotel, I wanted to spend some time alone in my room, running through plans, getting my head in order. I took a long cold bath to get the blood pumping around my body and the sheer enormity of the occasion persuaded me to dispense with some familiar habits.

Many years before, my brother Kobus had said to me that every time I had my hair cut before a game we lost the match. The remark had stuck, and I never cut my hair before a game, but I did cut my hair before the World Cup Final. Similarly, I had never shaved before matches because I knew my skin would be more resistant to cuts if it was rough. But, before the World Cup Final, I did shave. Why? To this day, I don't know.

Gumguard, boots, studs and Speedo: all the essentials were safely in my kit bag. I was ready. There were still fifteen minutes before we were due to get together in the team room, so I lay down on my bed. We had arranged for three final team talks before we left for the ground, one each from Morne, Kitch and myself, and I had calculated that, once Morne and Kitch had given their rousing orations, there would not be much more to say. So I resolved to be very brief – 'Enjoy it, concentrate, good luck' ... that sort of thing.

As I stood to turn off the television in my room, by coincidence, the commercial being broadcast was the one featuring Morne du Plessis in which he recalled how he did not have the opportunity to play in a Rugby World Cup when he was a player but that he is pleased to be involved as the Springbok manager. The commercial finished with a voiceover stating: 'For South Africa, the waiting is over.'

I left my room. The waiting was over.

The team room was very quiet. Guys were staring ahead. There was no idle chatter, no jokes as Morne stood to address the squad. He thanked the team for their co-operation throughout the tournament, said how he had enjoyed working with them and quoted a moving passage about giving your best. He also congratulated the players on what they had achieved for the country. Then he sat down.

I was surprised. I had expected Morne to beat the drum. By this stage, I was relying on Kitch to deliver the blood-curdling words. The coach moved to the front of the room and started: 'Guys, we've come a long way. There is not much to say other than you know what we have to do. Get out there, play your hearts out and, when we win, we can celebrate. I want you all to know I am very proud of you.'

That was it! I was starting to panic.

We were moments from a World Cup Final and the players were looking at me, who had prepared nothing. There was no escape.

'One thing certain about today,' I began, 'is that we are all going to make mistakes. The challenge will be to keep our heads, not worry about any mistakes and get on with the game. We know what we must do.

'If we play our guts out this afternoon, we will win this match. There is no doubt about that. I am certain. We must just back each other and play the game of our lives. That's what this is: the game of our lives. If we all come off the field having given everything we have, then I am convinced we will be world champions.'

We filed out of the team room in the Sandton Sun conference centre, through the corridors, passing more cheers and cries of 'Good luck!', on to the team bus parked outside the main entrance. I was looking at the faces around me. We're too quiet, I thought. We're far too tense.

I have always believed music can be a most effective means of shaping emotions, and I had made a point of carrying a cassette of the song 'If' by Roger Whittaker. Many of the players had been concerned about what would happen *if* they knocked on, or *if* they dropped a pass. I wanted to get the message across that they should forget about the 'ifs' and just play their natural game, without fear of failure and without inhibitions.

It had long been a Springbok custom to drive to a Test in total silence, but I unilaterally decided we needed something different before a World Cup Final, and so I strode to the front of the bus and pushed the cassette into the tape machine. Suddenly, the bus was filled with music.

*No, I don't believe in 'If' any more.*
*'If' is for children*
*'If' is an illusion...*

As we approached Ellis Park stadium, the sirens of the police escort became deafening as they blasted a path through the massed crowds. There was noise, colour and excitement on each corner. Living through this day had begun to feel like surfing on an enormous wave: the trick was to stay balanced and to ride the occasion, the danger was to fall and be submerged.

Some players walked to the edge of the field when we arrived, but Ellis Park held no surprises for me and I decided to stay with Dr Frans Verster, the team doctor, and have my ankles strapped. I then moved across to the room of Evan Speechly, the physiotherapist, for a final rub to stay loose and relaxed.

Ten minutes later, I returned to the changing room, and was stopped in my tracks. President Mandela was standing beside my place, wearing a No.6 Springbok jersey. He beamed and stretched out his hand to greet me. It was an incredible gesture on his part. Suddenly there was a lump in my throat. He wished me luck. I thanked him.

He then walked around the room, wishing each player luck and, within a few minutes, he was gone. I swallowed hard, refocused.

Within a moment or so, it seemed as if the entire stadium was shaken by some kind of explosion. A South African Airways jumbo jet had executed an audacious flypast, passing less than 200 metres above the stadium. The stunt had been the centrepiece of a closing ceremony every bit as effective as the opening ceremony at Newlands. Watching later on video, I felt so proud that South Africa had produced two such stirring spectacles.

Each minute the occasion soared to a new peak, threatening to take over our senses and overwhelm us. Each minute we would have to refocus our attention on the match, and concentrate on the game plan.

In essence, we had decided to concentrate on basic strategies such as to speed up the game, move their forwards around the field and to play as much of the game as possible in their half of the field. We had also resolved to test the defensive abilities of their back three. Jeff Wilson, Glen Osborne and Lomu were devastating players in attack, but we devised a kicking plan to put the ball behind them and smother them with pressure.

Kitch agreed we should not be too expansive. Every final I had played had been won by the team making the fewest mistakes on the day. We would not take risks and we would, at all costs, maintain discipline.

Ed Morrison, the English referee, had been appointed ahead of Derek Bevan to handle the Final, a decision which might have rattled us because he had been the referee who sent off James Small in Australia, but we remained calm. Kitch pointed out that no referee had ever changed his mind on account of players complaining, and said we should leave him alone to do his job. We were resolved to accept his decisions, without any fuss.

Just before ten to three, I led the Springbok team onto the field for the World Cup Final, and a stadium full of people thanking their lucky stars that they were present erupted. I felt emotional, but focused. I felt on the brink of tears because I was so consumed with national pride. I felt strong. I felt as if I could take on anyone. I felt proud of being a South African.

The introduction of President Mandela to the two teams was a blur and I decided not to sing our national anthem when it was played because I was frightened I would burst into tears. I searched for Nerine, my fiancée, in the crowd and clenched my jaw, determined to stay in control.

I had wondered during the week how we should respond when the All Blacks performed the *haka*, but still we had made no plans. I respected the tradition and, in no way, sought to offer any disruption. We lined up around ten metres from the New Zealanders, but Hannes Strydom decided he would edge closer as the chanting grew louder. Others followed.

Immediately Lomu started moving towards James Small but, famously, Kobus Wiese stepped across between James and Lomu, as if to say if you're thinking of going for him, you'll have to deal with me first. It was a magnificent gesture of solidarity and spirit on Kobus' part and it contributed substantially to a sense that we had somehow survived the *haka* intact.

At last, the match began ...

*The All Blacks try a short kick-off, but get it wrong. Joel and Joost miss touch-kicks. It is a nervous start by both sides. New Zealand mount their first attack on the blindside, trying to exploit Mark Andrews' inexperience in the still unaccustomed position of No. 8. Osborne slips through a gap, but Japie Mulder wraps up Frank Bunce and we stand firm.*

*Andrew Mehrtens and Joel exchange penalties, and the All Blacks try another strange kick-off but mess it up again. They must have studied our match with the Wallabies and seen how we had controlled the restarts. It is obvious they are worried about us. I am encouraged.*

*After 12 minutes, the All Blacks bring Lomu into the game, setting him up to loop round the centre and charge up the middle. I desperately want to be the first Springbok to tackle him, but I overrun the challenge and it is left to Joost to go low and bring the huge wing crashing down. But we give away the penalty and Mehrtens is successful to move 6–3 ahead.*

*I am happy with the way we are playing, moving forward and holding possession for long periods. Any thought that the All Blacks would overwhelm us as they overwhelmed England have been swiftly banished. Mark Andrews takes the ball forward, Joost darts forward, Ruben takes over and bursts for the line. We score! We score! No try. Ed Morrison says no try.*

*We did score. Beneath the pile of bodies, we did score. You can often tell what happened by the expression of the defenders – the resigned look on Olo Brown's face gave it away – and you can also tell by the look on the face of the man who claims the try – Ruben looks almost distraught. Morrison has made a mistake but, true to our pre-match pledges, we don't complain and simply get on with the game. The All Blacks pull down the next scrum, Joel collects three more points. 6–6.*

*Joel then kicks a drop goal, putting us 9–6 ahead and Joost is alive, alert and threatening, always liable to produce the unexpected and extraordinary. He chips off his left foot and scampers forward. A kind bounce and he'll score, but the ball falls for the All Blacks and they still knock on. We have a scrum, and I see Balie and Os, our props, want us to go for the pushover.*

*We start to edge forward, but the scrum is to be reset and our efforts are interrupted by the half-time whistle. I am frustrated because we have let slip two excellent scoring opportunities. We lead by three points when, with a little luck, we should have secured a 10-point advantage.*

*During the interval, we gather in a tight, arm-linked huddle as I tell the guys we are on the right track. Our scrumming is superb. We must just make no stupid mistakes and we will win the World Cup.*

*I glance across at the All Blacks and see them standing loose, apart as Sean addresses them. That is the typical New Zealand way, but the thought struck me that we were the more intense, hungry side on the day.*

*Into the second period, it becomes clear they are trying to* bring Lomu into the game more often. Osborne joins the line and feeds the wing who then accelerates around Andre Joubert. The crowd gasps. He is approaching full speed and heading for the try line. Japie Mulder tracks across, measures his pace perfectly and executes one of the great tackles of all time.

As he stands up, our centre pushes Lomu's face into the ground and epitomizes the spirit and resolve within the squad. Lomu is clearly irritated and he shakes his head as he jogs back to his mark.

The second half wears on, and the All Blacks grow stronger. Mehrtens levels at 9–9, and Hennie le Roux and Japie Mulder make a series of crucial tackles, holding our midfield defensive pattern together. Time starts to drift away, and it is still 9–9. Keep your discipline, boys.

Our scrum remains powerful, again vindicating Kitch Christie's bold selection of Kobus Wiese at lock with Mark Andrews as No. 8. And yet we still derive the benefit of calling Mark to the front of the lineout when we urgently needed to win our own ball. With four minutes left, we face such a lineout near our own line. Mark takes the catch, Joel clears.

Two minutes remaining, the All Blacks are pressing and Mehrtens has an opportunity to drop the winning goal, but he misses. I sigh with relief. It is a wasted chance. Everyone knows that. Maybe this will be our day.

Full time. Level at 9–9. Both teams are exhausted at the end of a long and hard tournament, but the trophy has yet to be won. I tell the players to look around them, to watch the flags waving and to look at all the people who are relying on us to pull this game through for them. I finish by saying we should play for them and become the new world champions.

The All Blacks go back to playing basic rugby, and Mehrtens kicks a long range penalty to put them 12–9 ahead. But we are still daring to attack, daring to win the game. Five minutes into extra time, Chester Williams takes the ball deep inside our half *and counter-attacks. Joost takes the ball on the blindside and feeds to Joel. He's clear. He's going to score!*

*Forward pass. Ed Morrison signals for an All Black scrum, and he is correct to do so. It had been forward, fractionally forward.*

*Moments later, the referee excels again. Joel kicks an up-and-under and the All Blacks are offside. Fitzpatrick sees his team will concede another penalty and hurls himself backwards as though he has been hit, but nobody has touched him! The referee spots the charade, and declines the invitation to reverse the penalty. Joel kicks the penalty, level again, 12–12.*

*Into the second half of extra time, I suddenly realize I have strained a calf muscle in my left leg. It is sore and running is difficult, but I don't stop for treatment for fear they will take me off the field. We kick on their back three again, Osborne is snared in our defensive blanket and we earn the scrum in an attacking position. I call a blindside move, from where we will be able to lay a solid forward platform. The scrum wheels and is reset. Joel cancels my call from fly-half. He says he wants the ball immediately.*

*Joost passes, Joel collects and strikes the most perfect drop goal. It soars higher than the uprights, but passes between them. We lead by 15–12. I start shouting to the guys: 'Now we stay in their half. Whenever we get the ball, we kick it down there, and we stay down there.'*

*The stadium is alive. No mistakes. No mistakes. The minutes start to tick away. With two minutes left, we win another penalty but Joel pushes his kick to the right of the posts. Stay tight. A maul forms from the drop-out. We win the scrum, and stand solid yet again.*

*I watch referee Morrison put his whistle to his mouth. He blows the final whistle, and our lives change forever. We are world champions.*

What happened next was completely spontaneous and unplanned. We had won and, in a surge of emotion, I sunk to my knees. The players gathered in a tight circle and, with bedlam breaking out around the stadium and around the country, we quietly gave thanks to God for our victory. I am Christian, and I wanted to give thanks for this wonderful moment in my life.

The bear-hugs and tears that followed remain a blur, but I remember giving Hennie le Roux, one of my closest friends in the side, the biggest hug of all. The atmosphere, the pride, the knowledge that the entire nation was in a state of celebration combined to create an unforgettable mood. I have since been surprised to read how many people, from other countries, recall the day as the fondest memory in their rugby lives. Somehow, the emotion within the stadium and throughout the country went far beyond sport. It represented the unification, however brief, of a country once so cruelly divided.

Amid the smiles and congratulations, the players were being herded to a podium in front of the West stand and, before the presentation of the World Cup had even taken place, I found myself guided towards the SABC's David van der Sandt to conduct a live interview to a worldwide television audience of 500 million. Drained and exhausted, I steadied myself.

'François, fantastic support from 63,000 South Africans here today?'

'David,' I replied, 'we didn't have the support of 63,000 South Africans today. We had the support of 42 million South Africans.'

The crowd cheered, and the words became legend. People said I must have planned the response, but I was too tired for that. I said what I felt. As players, unlike any Springbok side before us, we had been able to feel the committed support of the entire country. It made a huge difference.

When the interview had finished, I felt more anonymous pairs of hands guiding me towards the podium where President Mandela, still wearing the same No.6 jersey, stood with various blazered officials. I stepped through the throng of players and photographers, and onto the podium.

Can any rugby player ever have known a prouder moment? Can any Springbok ever have been so fortunate to be on that podium on that day?

The President passed me the Webb Ellis Trophy, the cup which I had stared at so intently before the opening lunch, and said: 'François, I want to thank you most sincerely for what you have done to our country.'

'Mr President, I want to thank you for what you have done,' I replied, before taking the trophy and raising it above my head. I was the first forward to raise the World Cup, the first South African to raise the World Cup. I kept telling myself to remember this moment – and I do.

We posed for a squad photograph and then started on a second lap of honour, this time with the World Cup. The crowd had become less noisy now, creating a wonderfully serene atmosphere of waving flags and people trying to take in every ounce of the occasion. There was an air of huge satisfaction, of sheer pleasure at the fulfilment of a national dream.

FW de Klerk was one of the first people to arrive in our dressing room which seemed fitting since it was his courage in ending apartheid which had started the process of enabling us to host the World Cup at all. Every player posed with the Cup as the celebration of all celebrations began.

More than an hour after the match, I finally showered and it was past seven when we eventually arrived back at the Sandton Towers. A crowd of 3,000 had gathered in the forecourt and the foyer, cheering the guys as they walked to their rooms. We had never felt so happy.

The squad then gathered for a last team meeting which could not have been postponed, all of which meant that it was almost nine o'clock by the time we arrived at Gallagher Estate for the official World Cup dinner.

I walked into the room, still smiling, and immediately sensed the mood was entirely wrong. Dr Luyt was furious that we were so late, and I could see the other squads present – the All Blacks, France and England – were already growing restless.

The vibe was that nobody really wanted to be there, and it seemed ironic that, on this night when perhaps the greatest parties of all time were being held all over the country, we were stuck in this terrible, sour atmosphere where nobody was smiling.

Dr Luyt delivered a speech in which his intended humour utterly failed to impress the audience. He said our victory proved we would have won the World Cup in 1987 and 1991, presented a gold watch to Derek Bevan rather than Ed Morrison who had refereed the final and lavished unctuous praise on his son-in-law and tournament director, Rian Oberholzer.

The English players began to mock him openly, All Black Mike Brewer was brazenly heckling and I was ashamed to see Springbok players feeling uncomfortable when they should have been enjoying the proudest evening of their career. After the match, I had specifically asked the players to remember we had won a close match which the All Blacks might easily have won, and I urged them to be humble in victory.

It was my fate to speak after Dr Luyt, and I could sense people were not interested in what I had to say. I noticed Will Carling looked bored and concluded my thanks as swiftly as possible. The All Blacks and the English left the dinner before the main course had been served.

The New Zealanders, of course, were bitterly disappointed although their reaction to defeat did them no credit. The allegations of deliberate food poisoning before the final rumbled on for several years, but without ever producing any shred of evidence to substantiate the claims. Some of their players might have been suffering from an upset stomach of sorts, but we had players on the field with physically broken hands and cracked ribs.

If I recall their intensity during the *haka* and their domination deep into the second half, it is difficult to accept this was a team in any way debilitated by illness. To my mind, they were defeated by a better side on the day, and it was a pity they failed to concede that reality.

We arrived back at the team hotel around eleven o'clock and decided to rescue the evening from the ruins of the official dinner. But we were stuck at the hotel without any transport, so Hennie le Roux, Joel Stransky, me and some other players flagged down a couple of cars in the street and asked for a lift to a bar in Rivonia called Rattlesnakes. The drivers were surprised, to say the least, but all appeared more than happy to oblige.

Rattlesnakes was packed, the sheer number of people crowded in on us, and I suddenly felt an urge to celebrate this evening with people who were most important to me, most of all my fiancée, Nerine. We decided to go back to the hotel and spend some time alone. The evening had been somewhat of a disaster, but my mind was buzzing and I could not sleep.

At four o'clock in the morning, still wide awake, I sat down in the middle of the room, reflected on the day and slowly and quietly drank an entire bottle of champagne. That was my celebration.

I did manage to sleep for a couple of hours, and staggered down to breakfast with some of the guys at around nine o'clock. There was a great mood around the tables. We knew we had been through a lot together and it seemed to me we had become more than team-mates. It seemed to me that the 1995 World Cup Springboks had become friends who would always share a genuine bond. That was what Kitch Christie had wanted.

Time will tell whether the bond will hold.

There are plans to launch an annual reunion of the 36 members of that World Cup squad, players and management, and I, for one, will always make a point of being there, of renewing friendships and recalling happy days.

Strangely, I had not sat down to watch the video tape of the World Cup Final until forced to do so during the preparations for this book. I had almost been frightened to challenge the precious recollections in my mind.

But they are safe, unsullied by subsequent events.

During the aftermath of the final, someone came to me and suggested it was depressing to think that most of us involved in the World Cup were less than 30 years old but that we could live to be a hundred and never see a day which could remotely compare with 24 June 1995.

'It's all downhill from here,' he smiled ruefully.

# CHAPTER SEVEN

# *Money Games*

*Someone is sitting in the shade today*
*because someone planted a tree a long time ago*
Warren Buffet

In an ideal world, the Springboks would have basked in World Cup glory for several months after the tournament – and we were hailed memorably by 200,000 people on the streets of Johannesburg during a ticker-tape parade – but the rugby world was far from ideal in June 1995 and, within eight days of the Final, we were embroiled in financial and contractual wrangling that would run for a month.

Through hundreds of cellphone calls, through ultimatums and bitter recriminations, through meetings and threats, the World Cup Springboks took a dangerous and stressful path through the wreckage of amateur rugby and on towards professionalism; on 4 August, the 28 players were offered what were then the richest rugby contracts in the world.

As captain of the squad, I was thrust to the forefront of these complex negotiations. Even though it would leave me vulnerable to ongoing accusations of being selfish and greedy, as captain it was my duty to lead.

In essence, the squad simply transferred the bond and trust which we had developed during the World Cup to a different environment. From our first meeting to discuss contracts, we had resolved we would consider all the options and reach a decision together. One for all, and all for one had worked for the Three Musketeers. It would work for us, too.

Money brings evil. I understood that. Money would bring greed, money would bring temptation, money would bring jealousy. Ever since childhood, I had understood the value of money and I realized my central involvement in this awkward process would bring criticism and enemies. This was inevitable and beyond my control. It needed to be enough for me and my conscience to know I had been absolutely honest at all times, that I had been direct and that I had always acted in the interests of the Springboks.

This epic saga started during the week before our World Cup quarter-final against Western Samoa. I received a telephone call at the Sandton Holiday Inn from Ian MacDonald, my Transvaal team-mate, who told me there was an exciting project in the pipeline and asked if I would meet the organisers. I said I would talk and we fixed a time.

Rumours that rugby union would finally turn professional, in some or other way, were common during the tournament and I was aware that media giants such as Rupert Murdoch and Kerry Packer were prepared to invest many millions of dollars in the game. Against this uncertain background, I would have been foolish to ignore any proposal.

I was pleased, however, that the Springboks had not discussed money or professionalism at any time during the tournament. Our focus was purely on winning the Webb Ellis trophy, and I resolved to protect that status at all costs. So I agreed to attend a meeting with Ian MacDonald, and neither invited anyone else along nor told anyone I was going.

'Mac' picked me up in his car and, while we were driving, informed me we were going to meet Harry Viljoen, the former Transvaal coach. We arrived at Harry's home in Sandton, and he outlined detailed plans for the launch of a professional rugby championship, staged outside the official structures of the game and apparently bankrolled by Kerry Packer. Every major national team would take part and, according to Harry, it would be my personal task to sign up the entire Springbok squad for this venture.

I immediately responded that I would do nothing until after the World Cup, and Harry accepted that, concluding that I should meet Ross Turnbull, the main organiser of the project, as soon as possible.

My initial reaction to the concept was that it had been tried before and never got off the ground, but I recognized that the chances of something like this taking flight were increasing with every day that the rugby union establishment stubbornly clung to their amateur code. It was not a question of anyone wanting the game to turn professional. In terms of rising revenue and demands on players, the game was already professional. The IRB's task was simply to recognize that fact and legitimize an open game.

I did not meet Turnbull until a week later, before our semi-final against France, and the former Australian rugby union official impressed me with the quality of his research and preparations. Sitting in his room at the Sandton Sun, I told him I was personally committed and on board, but would not be able to speak for the squad until we had met after the World Cup.

As the closing stages of the tournament unfolded, I did take a decision to tell Joost van der Westhuizen and Hennie le Roux that something exciting was emerging, because I was aware they were receiving lucrative offers from rugby league and I did not want them to commit themselves before they had considered all the worthwhile options available to them.

I did, however, take the opportunity to read through one of the TWRC (The World Rugby Championship) contracts, and I was enthused by the basic principles of playing in a global conference system, playing fewer matches of higher quality and of taking the game to the new markets such as the United States and Japan. Basic salaries for the Springbok players would range from R400,000 (£45,000) to R1.5m (£160,000) per year. Those numbers looked almost unbelievable set alongside the fact that, during 1995, most of the guys were taking home basic earnings from the game of approximately R70,000 (£8,000) per year.

Harry Viljoen had also presented me with a list in which he had divided the Springbok squad into three categories. He did not ask my opinion, and I would not have given one if he had. His instructions were direct: to make the offer to the players based on these three categories. I asked Harry who would coach the side, and, to my relief, he said it would be Kitch Christie, but I did not approach Kitch at this stage because I felt there was a risk his loyalty to Louis Luyt would prompt him to leak information.

But this was all hypothesis. The secret remained a secret.

I was, therefore, caught by surprise when Edward Griffiths, the SARFU chief executive, addressed the players during the team meeting straight after the World Cup Final. He outlined his vision for the future of Springbok rugby and indicated that the US\$550m television rights deal signed by SARFU, the New Zealand Rugby Union and the Australian Rugby Union with Rupert Murdoch's News Corporation would result in massively increased salaries.

Out of the blue he concluded by warning the guys not to sign contracts for any kind of unofficial rugby circus without first seeing what SARFU could offer. 'This is a time of opportunity,' he said. 'We know that.'

His information was impeccable, and I felt obliged to move quickly. When he finished, I asked him and the rest of the management team to leave the room, saying I wanted to address the players alone. It was uncomfortable, especially in our moment of triumph, but I needed to tell the entire squad that there was an option on the table which we should consider and that it would be presented to them within the next week. Edward had forced my hand, but it seemed as if the situation remained under control.

During the week that followed, Sean Fitzpatrick, Phil Kearns and Will Carling, the captains of New Zealand, Australia and England respectively, all telephoned me to find out whether the Springboks were considering TWRC. The venture seemed to be assuming global proportions. I was excited.

My strategy at this stage was simple: sign the guys up for TWRC as soon as possible and wait to see what happened. I didn't know if it would happen but it was worth a try. Nothing ventured, nothing gained.

As luck would have it, seven days after the final, the Springboks, with their wives and children, had been invited by SARFU and Sun International to spend the weekend at The Palace at the Lost City. We were treated like royalty by Tobin Prior and the staff, and, on the Saturday evening, I moved to present the TWRC contracts to all 28 World Cup players.

Since the squad had been divided into three categories, I decided it was necessary to hold three meetings and these were held, one after the other, in the privacy of my hotel room. Nerine Winter, my fiancée, made the fatal error of wanting to take a bath after the first group. The second group arrived early and, since she didn't want to disturb the meeting, she found herself trapped in the bathroom for two hours.

My approach was the same to all three groups: I would outline the core concepts of TWRC, disclose their salaries, suggest the players sign their contracts and I addressed any uncertainty by giving a clear undertaking that I would retain each signed document in my own possession – I would hand nothing back to TWRC, thereby sealing any agreement – until the players, as a squad, decided that was the option they wished to pursue. I gave a further assurance that any individual player could withdraw at any stage; their TWRC contract would be destroyed upon request.

There was no form of coercion or peer pressure during the meetings. Chester Williams did ask if he could take a contract to show his lawyer, but I said we could not afford to jeopardize the secrecy of the venture by showing the document to anyone outside the squad, and I reminded him of his option to have the contract destroyed any time he wanted.

When Brendan Venter said he wanted to read the entire text before signing, I said that was fine, and, by the end of the evening, 27 of the 28 World Cup Springboks had signed with TWRC. Most of the guys were more interested in the figures than the words, but I was excited by what had happened. In the past, players had talked and talked but we had actually put pen to paper, and placed ourselves in a strong position.

Edward Griffiths arrived at The Palace later that evening, having scheduled a meeting with five senior players early on Sunday morning. He took that opportunity to outline SARFU's plans without mentioning any figures and then asked me directly about rumours of other options.

'They're only rumours,' I replied.

Again the meeting was uncomfortable, but I had little option. The clear instructions from Turnbull were to maintain secrecy and I recognized that the viability of the project now relied heavily upon his ability to secure signatures from the Wallabies, All Blacks and England players.

I was pleased to have completed my task, and I called Harry Viljoen to say the Springboks had signed TWRC contracts. After lunch on Sunday, I put two boxes of the precious documents in my car boot, drove home and eventually locked them away in the safe at my house in Midrand.

The TWRC project now launched a second phase in which appointed agents around the country would emerge and sign 140 leading South African players. With Ian MacDonald recruiting other players in the Transvaal, I was not involved in this stage and was able to sit tight with the Bok contracts and allow events to unfold. The momentum was being sustained.

The players showed admirable calm, discretion and patience through the days and weeks that followed, with the exception of Chester Williams who was persuaded by his lawyer and agent, Frikkie Erasmus, to have his TWRC contract destroyed. Upon their request, I ripped up the document and threw it away, but Erasmus called back several days later and said he insisted upon coming from Cape Town to Johannesburg and actually seeing the destroyed pieces of contract. Fortunately, my dustbin had not been emptied during the intervening time, so I hunted among the rubbish and was able to deliver the morsels of document to him.

I understood Chester's position, but it did have the unfortunate effect of somehow separating him from the squad, and this scarcely endeared him to the other players. From the outset, we wanted to act as one united group, but Chester had gone his own way. I don't believe his career benefited from being cast as an isolated individual within a team game.

While the TWRC process may have been safely on course, simmering tensions over pay and playing conditions within South African rugby boiled over when an unrelated crisis exploded on the Monday after the World Cup Springboks returned from their weekend at Sun City.

Perhaps the signing of TWRC contracts did embolden the players to stand a little taller, but there was no thought of confrontation in the minds of the Transvaal Springboks when they arrived at the Wanderers to resume training with the provincial squad. It was just before four o'clock.

Uli Schmidt had been appointed to the union committee with a special responsibility for players' affairs, and I arrived at the training venue to find Uli in discussion with several players. We had put forward proposals to the union before the World Cup, requesting discussion on various issues ranging from the ratio between retainers and match fees to medical aid, and it was soon clear that Uli had come to tell us Louis Luyt had declined our proposals but was prepared to increase our match fees by R500 (£55) per game.

My first reaction was 'so what?'

We had signed contracts worth many hundreds of thousands with TWRC, so these discussions seemed irrelevant, but most of the other players evidently disagreed. Pieter Hendriks, Hennie le Roux, Ian MacDonald, Rudolf Straeuli and others soon became embroiled in a heated debate with Uli and the Transvaal coach, Ray Mordt.

Quarter past four, half past four, quarter to five. I hardly participated in the discussion at all and, eventually, the players proposed Uli should take our formal response back to the union, and that a proper meeting be arranged to take the process forward. But the guys kept talking, asking what was going to happen if they broke their leg on Saturday etc.

At five o'clock, Ray Mordt declared it was too late to start the session and said the guys should come back the next day to begin preparations for the Currie Cup match against Eastern Province on Saturday. The arguments petered away, but I sensed there would be trouble.

Hennie le Roux called me at seven o'clock the next morning to say he had received a telephone call from the Transvaal Rugby Union informing him he had been fired and asking him to bring his sponsored car back to Ellis Park. Johan Roux called soon afterwards with the same news, except he had responded by telling the union to come and collect the car themselves. It transpired that Charles Rossouw and Rudolf Straeuli had also been dismissed. Luyt had fired four of the guys who had spoken most vehemently to Uli, although I was surprised to discover that perhaps the most vocal guys, MacDonald and Hendriks, had escaped any action. Perhaps their status as an employee of the TRU and an employee of Ray Mordt, respectively, left them unable to be seen in opposition to their employers, although the other players found it difficult to take such a charitable view when four of their team-mates had been fired.

The TRU's action was ridiculous, and I recognized that, against my instincts, I would have to become involved and lead the players' response. The players looked towards me and it would have been morally impossible to turn away. A morning full of cellphone calls resulted in a decision that all the players would gather to discuss their options in my home at 3 p.m., one hour before the time when we were supposed to train.

Japie Mulder and James Dalton, both young players wary of Luyt, were initially hesitant to attend the meeting but both appeared at my house and, by four o'clock, the driveway was full of cars. The only players who did not gather, as arranged, were MacDonald and Hendriks, both still remaining loyal to the people who signed their salary cheques.

Gavin Johnson arrived in good faith, despite being specifically urged by the union to attend training. I learned that, to my amazement, the union's CEO, Johan Prinsloo, and Ian MacDonald had visited Gavin at his house and tried to persuade him not to stand behind the four fired players.

It was a sign of the times. The world was going mad. MacDonald, the man who introduced me to TWRC and seemed to be completely on board in that venture, was now unclear. He may have felt compromised by working for the union, but his general conduct seemed bewildering. I wondered who could be trusted on such days. The sad answer, I knew well, was to trust nobody.

It was then resolved that Rudolf Straeuli and I would drive through to where training should have started at the Wanderers and inform the union of our formal position. I arrived to find Luyt there, and I affirmed to him that we wanted to play for the union and that we wanted to resolve the matter. He asked us to draw up the issues for discussion, and a meeting was arranged for nine o'clock the next morning at his Ellis Park office.

Once again, the players gathered at my house that evening and discussed the next step. At one point, Johan Roux suggested we should ask for salaries of R20,000 (£2400) per month. Japie Mulder replied that we were mad. We should ask for only R10,000 (£1200) per month. He thought that was reasonable. As they spoke, I began to realize these guys did not really believe the TWRC option was likely to materialize. If they had, they would not have been getting so agitated about these comparatively small figures.

Hennie le Roux, as ever, stood at the centre of every meeting. At stages when I would start to think we were wasting our time, it would always be Hennie who dragged us back to the principles and shored up our belief that these were principles worth defending. Gary Janks, the wise and measured lawyer who had become so supportive of the players, also performed an invaluable role on numerous occasions. If anyone needed advocate's advice or legal advice, or assistance of any kind, it would always be Hennie and Gary who stood up, took out their cellphones and made the arrangements.

Two years later, they would both play leading roles in the formation of the South African Rugby Players Association (SARPA), and I am sure their often unappreciated efforts to defend the position of rugby players in South Africa will be properly recognized for many years to come.

With Gary's assistance, we compiled a 'wish-list' to be delivered to the union. This was subsequently characterized by the TRU as 'the players' demands' and wildly costed at R15m. The union was desperately seeking to manipulate the media into casting us, the players, as being greedy and selfish.

We had arranged for the players to gather an hour before our meeting with Luyt, and I took that opportunity to warn them that, in all probability, the Transvaal president would try to divide and conquer. He would say one player had said this about that player, and another had said that about this player. I told them how Luyt was a skilled negotiator and that this would be child's play for him.

Our response to such tactics needed to be disciplined and I urged the guys to agree I would be the only one to speak. Whatever Luyt revealed, no matter how serious it seemed, we agreed to deal with it afterwards. We then went to our cars and drove, with some trepidation, to Ellis Park.

Chris Dirks and Ian MacDonald were evidently 'assisting' Luyt before the meeting, and I was sad to see the way in which some players abruptly pushed past MacDonald as they entered the room. The spectre of money was already casting shadows over once solid friendships.

It soon became evident to us that the union was planning to record the meeting, probably with the intention of seeming rational and then handing the tape to the media to portray us as the bad guys. My instinctive response to this situation was to ask one of the players to deactivate the union's tape machine positioned in the corner of the boardroom to make recordings of meetings from which to write the minutes. This was done.

We were then amused to watch Dirks struggle to switch the machine on and we barely suppressed laughter as he conceded defeat. Luyt entered the room soon afterwards and adopted a hostile and aggressive approach, apparently safe in the knowledge that the meeting was not being taped. Or so he thought ... we had arranged for two of the players to conceal pocket tape recorders in their jackets, and record the proceedings.

I punctuated his attacks by repeating we wanted to concentrate on the future, not to dwell on the past, and it was clear that Luyt was becoming very frustrated by his inability to rattle us. He suddenly rose to his feet, thanked us all for what we had done for Transvaal rugby and left. We were left hanging, and returned to discuss tactics at the Sunnyside Park hotel.

The guys believed they had now been sacked, and some started to panic. Players were asking what would happen to their sponsored cars, and who would pay their mortgages. These were legitimate concerns and I knew it was important that, in dealing with this crisis, we first removed the immediate problems so we could focus on the broader issues. I first contacted Sarel Liebenberg, at Nissan, who said he would be able to loan vehicles to players in need, and then Tobin Prior, at Sun International, who said he would look for opportunities to use the players in marketing and would assist in paying their salaries for a limited period. The saga had created daily headlines.

We were trying to keep the guys under control, calm and disciplined in their approach, and I began to wonder again why we had allowed ourselves to be embroiled in this row over comparatively small sums of money. It seemed so unnecessary, but now there was no easy way out. Luyt had been enraged and I knew he would not tolerate any kind of defeat.

It was agreed the players would outline their position at a formal press conference held at the Sunnyside Park hotel, scene of so many happier times during the World Cup (and it struck me how our moment of glory now seemed to have taken place such a long, long time ago). Milling around the hotel car park before the journalists arrived, we gathered round a car radio and were hugely emboldened to hear fellow Springboks, Joost van der Westhuizen and Andre Joubert, give interviews in which they supported our stand.

For many years, South African rugby players had been easily divided and ruled by the administrators. For the first time in my experience, it seemed as if the Springboks, at least, were finally standing together.

We read out a carefully prepared statement at the press conference but refused to answer any questions because we were so scared of saying something Luyt would be able to use against us, perhaps even in court. We should have answered questions but we were generally terrified of the union president. He had been on our side in the past, and not one of us relished him as an enemy.

Kitch Christie wanted the matter to be settled, and he advised me to find a way where we could give Luyt a way out by which he could reverse the dismissals and not lose face. With this in mind, I appeared on television and affirmed that our actions were in no way intended to insult Louis Luyt or his family, and I apologized if any offence had been taken.

My life had assumed a frantic pace.

That Wednesday afternoon, with the crisis at its peak, I was obliged to honour a long-standing appointment to give a speech at a major Liberty Life function in Nelspruit. I set aside my prepared text and spoke frankly about what was happening with Transvaal, since that was the issue which had been dominating every news bulletin and front page for three days.

It appeared as if my address had been well received, and the man who had addressed the audience after me was saying how much he had enjoyed my speech when he suffered a serious heart attack. I knew the procedures, and started with mouth-to-mouth resuscitation. I then pulled out his tongue and tried massaging his heart, but it was to no avail. The man, around 50 years old, died soon afterwards.

Such events sustained my sense of perspective, but I was growing tired and frustrated by the ongoing saga. On Thursday evening, Edward Griffiths met the players at my house where we agreed upon a scaled-down list of proposals, which he took to Luyt the following morning. The union president accepted the compromise and agreed to reinstate the four victims on condition that we, as players, apologize for their actions.

Our response was that we could not apologize because I felt we had done nothing wrong, but we finally agreed a text where the players indicated their 'contrition' for events. The dispute was over.

A virtual Transvaal 2nd XV, selected in our place, lost against Eastern Province on the Saturday and, by Monday, the province had returned to what would become a sadly familiar typical atmosphere of bad feeling, mistrust, harassment and plain hostility. The Transvaal 'family' of 1993 and 1994 had been divorced. Players began to hate the administrators and suspect each other, and, inevitably, our results suffered.

Meanwhile 27 TWRC contracts, bearing Springbok signatures, were still locked away in the safe at my house, but the pressure was starting to take a toll on this process as well.

At one stage, Harry Viljoen asked me to hand over the contracts but I reiterated I could not do this without the players' permission. He asked me if I would sign a formal statement to that effect, to provide some reassurance to the organisers. I agreed and a lawyer acting for TWRC, Jennis Scholtz, drew up a brief document which stipulated not only that I had acted as an agent to sign the Springbok World Cup squad but also that, if Kerry Packer was indeed involved in the project, I would receive an additional sum of US$300,000 for doing so.

The fact is I had not negotiated any kind of fee at any stage. Harry Viljoen had negotiated the fee with TWRC organisers. It was undoubtedly generous, but it was not solicited by me.

I signed this document which, several years later, was released to the newspapers to create an impression that I had wilfully abused my position as Springbok captain to enrich myself. That was not true. I had neither sought nor talked about a fee at any stage. It was not part of my plans; by the same token, I do not believe I can reasonably be blamed for failing to turn down this fee. It was being offered in good faith, and affecting no-one else.

Details of the TWRC plans were starting to leak into the public domain and Louis Luyt's initial reaction was to downplay the project and demean the people involved. I did not think this was either a decent or constructive tactic and, on reflection, his brutish approach made me even more resolved to support the TWRC proposals.

I am aware people have considered my behaviour during this period was tantamount to selling out South African rugby, but that was not my perspective at all. In my view, the players' choice was not between playing for South Africa and playing for Packer; it was between playing for Luyt or for Packer. Wherever we played, we would have represented our country with the same pride we had shown during the World Cup. It was our intention to still play as Springboks.

The facts at this stage were that Packer, through TWRC, had put an attractive deal on the table while Luyt, for his part, had shown no intention of offering the players anything but abuse and harassment. His behaviour had been characteristically erratic: one moment, he was sniping at me, the next moment he was greeting me in the warmest possible terms outside his office and suggesting that he would actually pay me a commission to sign up the Springboks for SARFU, but nothing came of that.

Luyt may have sought to appear unconcerned by TWRC, but News Corporation, who had just committed US$550m to televising rugby in South Africa, Australia and New Zealand, were becoming anxious that the leading players in those three countries were being poached to perform beneath the banner of NewsCorp's bitter great media rival, Kerry Packer.

Late one evening, I was contacted at home by Sam Chisholm, head of NewsCorp in London. He seemed genial and reasonable.

'So what's happening in South Africa?' he asked, and I told him that we were seriously considering the approach from TWRC.

'And how much are you being paid now?' he asked.

'Three thousand rand a month plus bonuses,' I replied.

'How much?'

'Three thousand rand a month,' I repeated.

'And how much are you being offered by Packer?'

I told him the amounts involved, and I got the clear impression that he fully understood our position and our conduct.

'Would you be interested if we made a similar offer?' he asked.

'We're prepared to listen, Mr Chisholm,' I replied, 'but it will be the players who make the final decision, and nobody else.'

He accepted that reality and called me back soon afterwards, asking again if we would consider a similar offer. I repeated we would. He then told me that he wanted to see if I was a man of my word, if I could be trusted and if I was serious in what I was telling him. He wanted to test me.

Chisholm had learned TWRC were planning a satellite link-up between Australia and South Africa the following day to confirm progress and maintain momentum, and he asked me not to play any part in the broadcast. 'If you do that,' he said, 'then I'll know I can trust you.' I gave him my word.

Was I being disloyal to TWRC by talking to Chisholm? I don't think so. Perhaps Luyt's bold statements that TWRC only had an idea but no financial backing began to play on my mind. Was TWRC all hot air? Was Ross Turnbull flying kites? Perhaps, amid these growing doubts, I was willing to listen to another option from a major international organization like NewsCorp, who, in stark contrast, had already put plenty of their money where their mouth was, with respect to rugby union.

These were testing days. I was walking along a tightrope, needing to be alert and suspicious at all times, ever keeping in mind the goal of securing the best deal for the entire Springbok squad.

These were exhausting nights as well. Players, TV executives and rugby administrators from within South Africa and around the world kept my telephone ringing incessantly 24 hours a day. I wondered how so many of them had access to my home number. There was no time to relax and think out loud. Every person – every single person – had to be assessed and reassessed, every word measured. Traps lay everywhere.

Perhaps the purest approach was made by Johan Rupert, the wealthy businessman from Cape Town and head of the Rembrandt empire. He called me and said he would pay the players if we needed to buy some time before making a final decision. I may have been naïve, but it seemed to me this offer was made with no strings attached. There appeared no possible advantage to him, and I appreciated his empathy with this group of sportsmen paddling in deep waters clearly populated by many outstanding, sharp businessmen. He repeated several times we must not make a decision under pressure and said he wanted to help. As the saga unfolded, however, events assumed their own pace and we did not need to take up Rupert's offer.

The day of the proposed TWRC satellite link-up between

South Africa and Australia now shaped as a particularly awkward time for me. I had given my word to Sam Chisholm that I would not take part but it was impossible for me to offer that explanation to the TWRC people. I told them I could not be involved that afternoon because of another commitment.

I sensed the stakes were being raised.

That morning, after I had spoken to Chisholm, I was informed that Jamie Packer, the son of Kerry Packer, had travelled to South Africa to show his organization's commitment to TWRC, and I was asked if I would meet him at Harry Viljoen's house a couple of hours before the satellite connection was due to be made. The mere presence of Jamie Packer among us appeared to provide evidence of substantial financial muscle and intent which the TWRC venture had been lacking until that point.

With hindsight, I wish he had arrived 24 hours earlier.

If I had been aware of Packer's serious intent only the night before, I don't know if I would have been so accommodating and receptive to Chisholm on the telephone, but I had not known and I had given my word. My tightrope was swaying in these powerful cross breezes: Rupert Murdoch was gusting from the east, Kerry Packer was blowing from the west.

I duly arrived at Harry Viljoen's house and it was not long before Jamie Packer asked if he could speak to me alone.

'What will it take for you to co-operate with us?' he said. 'What will it take for you to hand over the contracts your players have signed?'

'It's not my decision,' I replied. 'The players must decide.'

'No, you don't understand. What will it take?'

I sensed he was asking me to name my price, but I had given my word to the players and I was mindful how Kitch Christie had always told me a man is born with his word and if he gives it away, he has nothing.

'I'm sorry,' I said. 'It's not my decision.'

Packer said nothing, turned and left the room. He was evidently a man experienced in concluding major deals, and he knew when to walk away. I was impressed by both his manner and his demeanour.

James Small and Hennie le Roux eventually took part in the satellite crossing with the Australians, while I stood around in the background. I could sense various TWRC people feeling I had let them down, and I am aware these sentiments were shared by many leading players in Australia and New Zealand, who were embracing TWRC with enthusiasm.

These people failed to recognize my first, and only, responsibility was to the World Cup Springboks, of whom I was one. The players had trusted me to guide them towards the best possible contracts, and that was my only aim; not to fight for Packer, or Murdoch, or Luyt, but to secure the best deal.

We had started our campaign on an 'all for one, one for all' basis and, Chester apart, that had not changed. Combined with our status as the world champions, this united approach gave us decisive leverage in negotiations with TWRC, with Luyt and with NewsCorp. We would not be split.

If Sam Chisholm's aim was to break TWRC, why did he call me rather than Sean Fitzpatrick or Phil Kearns? Why did he identify the Springboks as the link in the TWRC chain which he could address? Maybe it was because he knew TWRC could not thrive without the World Cup winners, maybe it was also because he knew that we would stand together. When he dealt with the Springboks, he dealt with the entire squad. There was no split. One for all, all for one: united we stood, divided we would have fallen.

Several days after the satellite link had taken place, Sam Chisholm contacted me again to inform me that Louis Luyt would be instructed by News Corporation to match whatever we had been offered by TWRC. SARFU would effectively act as NewsCorp's agents in the matter.

My initial reaction to these dramatic developments was the Springboks would jump at a NewsCorp offer whereby they would earn the massive sums of money promised by Turnbull but without any disruption to their lives; they would remain in South Africa, playing within familiar structures.

NewsCorp were effectively offering the best of both worlds, yet there was a further dimension: TWRC had promised to pay us 20% more than any other offer we received at any stage of negotiations. Once again, I was reminded how carefully and cleverly the architects of TWRC had planned their venture. The choice remained complex and far from cut and dried.

The Springboks obviously needed to meet, and this opportunity was provided when we were invited to a meeting at Luyt's home in Saxonwold, Johannesburg, at ten o'clock one Sunday morning. As the players arrived and walked through the garden towards the entertainment area where we would gather, I found myself standing in the study with Edward Griffiths, Kitch Christie, Rian Oberholzer and Luyt himself.

'I'll match Packer,' Luyt said boldly, pretending he had made this huge decision himself, unaware that Chisholm had contacted me with the news several days before. In essence, he was the messenger.

'Thank you, Doc,' I replied.

'That's it,' he said. 'We will contract all the World Cup players on the same terms as they have been promised by Packer.'

'Thank you, Doc,' I said again.

We walked up to join the players and the discussions ran their course. When Luyt had finished, I reminded the players of the TWRC commitment to better any other offer by 20%, but I started to sense the mood among the 11 Springboks present was that they wanted to sign with SARFU. Some of them were young men on the brink of becoming very rich and, when considering the content of any contractual agreement, were clearly still more interested in the numbers than the words. You could spend the numbers.

We agreed to make arrangements for a meeting of the entire

Springbok squad at the Midrand Protea hotel later that week, at which we would make our final decision.

Through the intervening days, I saw Luyt several times at Ellis Park and he was variously hostile and charming. Only 24 hours after making 'his' offer, he was taunting us that we would have to sign on the same terms as the TWRC contract and that we would be 'signing our lives away'. He liked to create an impression of always understanding a contract better than anyone else, although I saw nothing especially punitive in the terms. Yet, on other occasions, he would be genial and amusing, evidently pleased to be winning a 'war' against what he regarded as an external force.

The SARFU contract was derived from the TWRC contract, with some amendments to cater for South African conditions, most notably Luyt's insistence that we would be paid in Rands and not in US dollars. Johan Roux, a stockbroker by trade, tried manfully to argue for dollars on the basis that SARFU was receiving its television rights income from NewsCorp in the US currency but Luyt was adamant and, perhaps foolishly, we lacked the energy to argue with him.

With hindsight we should have backed Johan's position, even to the point of threatening not to sign, but we yielded. The contracts were signed in Rands converted from dollars at a rate of R3.62 : US$1. By the end of August 1998, when the three-year deals ended, the South African exchange rate had plummeted to approximately R5.4 : US$1. Luyt's uncompromising stance was saving SARFU more than 30% of the total contract cost. Once again, it was impossible not to admire his business acumen.

I was determined our final meeting at the Midrand Protea hotel would be properly structured and represent a fair debate between the TWRC option and the NewsCorp option represented by SARFU. As the players arrived and greeted each other, I sensed the camaraderie and spirit from the World Cup had remained intact. In many ways, we were still a family.

The meeting began with a brief overview of the situation, followed by an update on the TWRC project. We showed a video recording of the satellite discussion with Australia and noted that James Packer had confirmed the full commitment of his father's organization to the venture. We then outlined the SARFU/NewsCorp proposal, offering the same money but for playing in the familiar Currie Cup, provincial and Springbok structure.

Edward Griffiths arrived soon afterwards and, together, we answered questions for almost an hour. Some of the players were becoming frustrated by the delay because they wanted to sign with SARFU and move on. Others evidently didn't trust Luyt, and sought more reassurances.

As the discussion advanced, it became evident that a clear majority would vote to accept the contracts being prepared by SARFU. Personally, I was feeling disappointed. Even at this stage, my preference was to support TWRC. If it had been my decision alone, I would have handed the contracts to Ross Turnbull and moved ahead with the new venture.

Why?

First, I could see the three-year contracts with Louis Luyt's SARFU would swiftly translate into three years of harassment and strife. The deal had been forced upon him by NewsCorp, and he would never be reconciled with the fact that we had purely identified our market value. It seemed clear to me that he would bitterly resent some World Cup Springboks. Effectively working for such a disenchanted man was not going to be much fun.

Second, I sincerely believed TWRC could catapult rugby union into a fresh, honest and professional era where the game would be marketed on a level far, and to an audience, far beyond it's traditional frontiers.

The votes were duly cast by a show of hands. I was determined the process would be handled in a fair and transparent manner.

'Who votes for TWRC?' I asked.

Hennie le Roux raised his hand, James Small raised his hand, and I raised my hand. That was all. Three votes.

'And for SARFU?'

The rest. With the exception of three abstentions – I am not certain what those players thought they would achieve by abstaining, but the majority was clear and the conclusion was reached that the entire squad, with the solitary exception of Chester Williams, would sign with SARFU.

Players immediately began filing through to an adjacent room where Corlia Oberholzer, a lawyer by trade and Luyt's daughter by coincidence, was sitting with a pile of SARFU contracts to be signed. The appropriate numbers were filled in each contract, and the signatures were applied.

There was a delay when Johan Roux and Rudolf Straeuli noticed an extra punitive clause had been inserted to the original TWRC text. Edward Griffiths immediately called Luyt, who authorized the removal of the clause. Even at this time, we had to be careful.

The campaign was over, and I was perhaps predictably overwhelmed by a sense of anti-climax. Most of the players were delighted because they had increased their salaries by ten times with minimal change in their working conditions, and a few of them even thanked me for my efforts on their behalf, but I felt strangely flat and concerned that we might have made the wrong decision.

Later in the afternoon, I drove through to Ellis Park to discuss several outstanding issues with Luyt. The first was the matter of two players who had asked to be raised from the 'C' category to the 'B' category. I put their case to Luyt and he consented with a wave of his hand.

The second issue was the more awkward matter of the US$300,000 promised to me first by TWRC, and then by Sam Chisholm. Luyt's response had been for me to contact Chisholm directly, but I wanted to raise the issue again and I did so, with Edward Griffiths and Kitch Christie present.

Luyt replied that he had said he would 'match' Packer, and

he would honour that commitment. Whatever we had been promised by TWRC, either as a salary or commission, we would be paid by SARFU. That had been the deal, and I felt completely entitled to clarify the agreement. It is important to note that I only raised this matter after the Springboks had signed with SARFU. I did not in any way hold him to ransom over my personal issue.

But that was the deal. If Luyt had stipulated he would only match the salary, I would have accepted that, but that was not the case. I heard no more until December when, after some gentle reminders, I was paid a cheque of R1m (less than the correct conversion of US$300,000) made out in the name of the Transvaal Rugby Union. My understanding is that Luyt paid me a sum that had been directly forwarded to him by Chisholm.

The Springboks' decision to sign with SARFU dealt a fatal blow to the TWRC venture, even if Turnbull did proceed with an ultimately unsuccessful legal challenge against SARFU in the high court. He had signed most of the leading international players, and more than 100 provincial players in South Africa, but these contracts were worth nothing without the Boks.

An unpleasant situation developed where the World Cup Springboks were accused of looking after themselves at the expense of leading players around the world and their teammates at provincial level. We were perceived as having scooped the cream, and left everyone else stranded.

I could understand this reaction very well, but it was probably too much to expect of any young man to sacrifice his own position to give other people a chance of securing better terms. The Springboks did look after themselves, but nobody else was going to look after them and it is hard to believe anyone else, at home or abroad, would have acted differently in their position.

Money did bring jealously and envy. Money did fracture long-standing relationships. Money did change the mood of the game.

As I feared, the contracts between the Springboks and SARFU swiftly became a battleground.

The hostile mood, however, hardly affected the players based outside Johannesburg. They were able to settle and enjoy the benefits of what was a tremendous deal for the players. It was the Transvaal Springboks who had to bear the brunt of regular threats and harassment as the exact wording of the contract became a bitter and enduring matter of conflict.

Meetings were held to reach agreement, but they invariably ended in more antipathy. Edward Griffiths did make sincere efforts, in his words, 'to make the contracts work for everyone', but he was abruptly and inexplicably replaced as the SARFU chief executive in February 1996 and his conciliatory approach towards the World Cup players went with him.

Rian Oberholzer eventually took over as the new CEO and, although he and I had become friends while he worked at Ellis Park, he predictably adopted a similar approach as Luyt, his father-in-law. During one exchange, Rian told a group of players they should co-operate with SARFU 'or we'll send you to coach in the townships for five days every week'.

If these administrators struggled to accept what, after the IRB decision in August 1995, had become an openly professional environment, then it also needs to be said that we, the players, cannot be absolved from all responsibility for the wretched atmosphere which settled like a thick mist.

Perhaps with reason, the players became so scared of their contracts being cancelled that they sought external businesses on which they could fall back in a worst-case scenario. Yet, as they launched coffee shops, chemical products, restaurants, furniture dealers and antique dealerships, they allowed themselves to be distracted from their job of playing rugby.

The Transvaal squad began to dissolve as a family and, confronted by the union's hostility, players became more interested in their businesses than on who we were playing on

Saturday. Towards the end of the 1995 season, I was featured in a profile for an Ellis Park match programme, and I listed my job as being a 'professional rugby player'. Some of the guys laughed at me, but that is what I was and that is what they were too.

On one occasion, I warned Japie Mulder that he should not spend so much time on his business and ought to devote more to his rugby. He said that was easy for me to say because I was earning twice as much as him. He was working really hard, but I was astonished by his response. This was somebody who had said barely two months before that he would happily play for R10,000 (£1200). Japie remains a close friend, but this type of angry exchange was symptomatic of a period when money started to infect established relationships.

Perhaps the relationship between Louis Luyt and me suffered as much as any. Kitch Christie used to tell me that every time the SARFU president signed a cheque to a World Cup player, he saw my face on it, and I accept this was probably the reason for the bitterness which developed.

Luyt was the man who I had respected for so many years, a man who I had admired for his business skills and plain guts, a man with whom we had scaled the highest peaks of the game at provincial level and with whom we had become the world champions. This was the man who used to call me 'my son' in lighter, happier moments.

Through the aftermath of the 1995 World Cup, we had clashed over a matter which he seemed to believe was personal. He was wrong. It was my responsibility to secure the best deal for the Springboks, and I believe I was successful in that respect. But he preferred to see everything in a personal dimension and I think he grew to feel such antipathy towards me because it irritated him that, in his mind, we had somehow won the battle.

At the end of the 1995 season, the Transvaal squad gathered for the annual squad photograph. The officials and players were milling around, waiting for the photograph to be taken.

Louis Luyt turned to me and uttered the following words: 'There is thin line between love and hate, and I hate you.'

I didn't reply. That was the epitaph of the money games of 1995. The photograph was taken. There was nothing else to say.

# CHAPTER EIGHT

# *Meltdown*

*You can buy a man's time.*
*You can buy his physical presence at a given place.*
*You can even buy a measure of his*
*skilled muscular motions per hour.*
*But you cannot buy enthusiasm.*
*You cannot buy loyalty. You cannot buy the devotion*
*of hearts, minds or souls. You must earn these*
Clarence Francis

South African rugby could hardly have bounded towards the end of 1995 with greater enthusiasm and promise. The triumphant Rugby World Cup had promoted such universal excitement in every suburb and town that the game once regarded as the symbol of apartheid had essentially been born again as a dynamic vehicle of national unity and reconciliation.

Rugby's public image had never been better: the Springboks were well paid, safely contracted and winning; the development programme was finally discovering real momentum; and SARFU appeared every bit as dynamic and visionary as the model United Cricket Board. We were bringing the country together, we were making a difference. It was fun to be involved.

Yet, through the following year, the key figures in this transformation were removed from the game, and rugby lurched into a dismal cycle of conflict and crisis where all recent gains were lost. History may well regard the meltdown of the 1995 Springbok World Cup squad as one of the most foolish and miserable acts in South African rugby history.

In September 1995, Morne du Plessis, Kitch Christie, Edward Griffiths, and myself were all enthused by the future.

Barely 12 months later, we had all been consigned to rugby's past.

Why?

I suspect – and this is only my personal impression of what happened – that the paramount factor was jealousy. We were too successful to survive in a world ruled by amateur administrators who were irked that, in contrast, they were repeatedly lampooned. There was truth in the contention that, for example, Louis Luyt's contribution was not properly recognized, but his wounds were often self-inflicted, most pitiably when he was bitterly and universally criticized for his speech after the Rugby World Cup Final: he had only had to say 'Thanks for coming' to receive warm congratulations from even his most determined critics.

Second, we were moving the game forward far too quickly for the men wielding power on the Executive Committee. Whether it was my activities with regard to professionalism, or Kitch's desire to develop a new National Rugby Centre, or Morne's views on waving the old national flag at Tests or Edward's bold initiatives to fire the development programme, we were all too resolved and, humbly, too effective to survive in an environment where the people who survived were those who maintained the status quo.

South African rugby was ripe for progress and, in our different ways, we wanted to change it ... quickly. The Executive Committee of 1995 and 1996 differed and, in my view, squandered a unique opportunity to secure for the game a meaningful role in the new South Africa.

The 1995 World Cup presented rugby with this golden chance. I hope and pray the historians of the next century do not look back and consider the invitation of 1995, so rudely declined, was not the last chance.

In September 1995, we were filled with hope and optimism. The money games had left scars, and animosity did linger within Transvaal, but there was harmony and excitement within the Springbok squad. We had won the World Cup and, in our hearts, we believed we had scarcely hinted at the potential of an essentially young squad. In our minds, the 1995 World Cup was the end of nothing, rather the beginning of everything.

When President Mandela invited the entire squad to receive medals at a special banquet in Pretoria, we were proud and touched but still focused on improving our performance in the next match, a one-off Test against Wales at Ellis Park in the first week of September. Our defence may have been fine but we believed our talented backs had barely stretched during the World Cup, and we knew the pack's ball retention could be more clinical.

'Cappie,' Kitch Christie said to me during this period, 'do you realize how strong this side can become? I think we can be awesome.'

This was not arrogance for the media, this was a private observation. Despite the magnificent support of a flag-waving crowd in Johannesburg, we somehow failed to click on the day against Wales and yet still finished with a 40–11 victory, and some fine tries for the memory bank.

The post-match headlines were dominated by the 30-day suspension imposed on Kobus Wiese for punching the Welsh lock, Derwyn Jones, early in the match. In the new professional era, this sentence translated as 30 days without pay, equivalent to a fine of around R50,000.

Kobus accepted the harsh reality like the big man he is, and I was pleased to see a fundamental understanding of professionalism spread through the squad: it is not just about the arrival of huge sums in your bank account, it is also about self-discipline, good conduct and responsibility. On and off the field, we were growing as a squad.

We approached the brief end-of-season tour to Europe, comprising Tests against Italy and England, with the stated goal of being 'champions away', of proving that our World Cup success reflected genuine domination rather than mere home advantage, but we nearly came dramatically unstuck at the Olympic stadium in Rome. After trailing the brave Italians with 15 minutes to play, we were flattered by an eventual 40–21 win.

As wake-up calls go, this proved extremely effective, and we arrived in London on the back of 13 successive Test victories, grimly resolved to extend our run at the newly redeveloped Twickenham, home of the most consistent and powerful team in the northern hemisphere.

The squad checked in to the Westbury Hotel, off Regent Street in the West End, shortly after four in the afternoon and swiftly changed into T-shirts and shorts. We had been asked to run off the effects of the flight from Rome, and, shoulder to shoulder, we headed out towards Hyde Park.

It was intended as a gentle jog, but our spirit and shared resolve soon transformed the simple exercise into a ferocious race. Mark Andrews and Kobus Wiese usually trundle along at the back, but we were amazed to see them push themselves to the front, setting the pace.

The challenge was laid down, and the quick guys, James Small, Andre Joubert and Jacques Olivier, picked it up, sprinting to the front again. At one point, I stopped to tie up my shoelaces and was passed by the entire squad. I had never experienced such intensity, such raw spirit before. On and on, we ran, racing each other, challenging each other, responding eagerly. Up the park, down the park, passers-by stared at us in wonder.

When we finally stopped, every player was drenched in sweat and shared pleasure. Each of us realized something special had happened, and I beckoned the guys together in a tight huddle. I spoke quietly, staring hard into the players' eyes as I looked around the circle.

'All right, I only want to say one thing,' I almost whispered. 'There is no way we're going to lose to those guys on Saturday.'

That was all. The squad returned to the hotel and, in my mind, there in a public park scarcely two hours after arriving at the airport, we had started to defeat England and justify our status as world champions.

Our preparations had also been assisted by Mike Catt, the former South African now playing for England, who had described me in the media as 'an average player'. Asked to respond during our opening press conference, I merely said I thought he was a good player.

Kitch relished such sagas and, through the week, he would chuckle at me: 'Ho, ho, ho, average player!' I was surprised to find several Boks were genuinely upset by Catt's remarks and it soon became clear that his tongue had earned himself a notably awkward afternoon on Saturday.

Toks van der Linde, the Western Province prop playing in his first major international, was hyped beyond description and epitomized the fierce resolve shared by the entire team as he crashed into the first three mauls of the Test match, sprinting at top speed and shouting out loud 'Yes! Yes! Yes!' as he thudded into English jerseys.

Jim Fleming, the Scottish referee, called me over and asked me, as captain, to calm Toks down. I walked over to our super-motivated prop and, while wagging my finger and pretending to admonish him, actually told him he was playing tremendously well and he should carry on.

England presented a powerful challenge, never more so than when Tim Rodber performed probably the most bone-crunching tackle I have ever suffered in my career, but I sensed we were always in control. Fleming ruled out a perfectly good try by Chester Williams in the first half, and we secured a decisive advantage when Joost van der Westhuizen scored a fine individual try immediately after the interval, chasing his own kick.

We won far more convincingly than the final score of 24–14 suggests, and had achieved our goal of confirming world champion status. The Boks had played 10 Tests, and won 10 Tests, during 1995. We had earned our ranking as the strongest team in the world, and looked forward to developing our level of performance to new heights during 1996.

Relaxed together, happy together and winning together, the

team had started to consider the twin challenges of 1996 – the inaugural Tri-Nations series and the first full All Black tour of South Africa for 20 years – with great excitement. Far from resting on any laurels, we were eagerly contemplating the opportunities and the new glories which lay ahead.

I spent the Christmas and New Year holidays happily in Cape Town, bidding farewell to 1995 as a genuine vintage year and welcoming 1996 with excitement. It would be even better, I felt certain. On 20 January, after all, I was to be married to my fiancée, Nerine Winter.

We had met while students at RAU and started a relationship in what were considered at the time to be awkward circumstances because Nerine's previous boyfriend, Wayne Willemse, was also a close friend of mine. A sniff of scandal proved irresistible to gossips, and a whispering campaign at RAU and around rugby accused me of luring my friend's girl but this was far from the truth and, early in 1994, we started going out with each other for the purest of reasons. We simply followed our hearts.

I had asked Nerine to marry me just before the World Cup, and she accepted the invitation. We told our families, but decided to delay a public announcement until after the World Cup because we sought the minimum of media attention.

Nerine and I were, however, happily caught by surprise during the official banquet for the Springboks, hosted in August by President Mandela at the Presidential guest house in Pretoria. I had been speaking to him, telling him of my engagement, and had asked if I could introduce him to Nerine. He said 'of course', and was standing in deep conversation with other people as the two of us walked towards him. With typical charm, he saw us coming and immediately broke away from the group.

'Nerine,' the President began, remembering her name, 'would you be very offended if I came to your wedding in January?' Those were his opening words to her. We were amazed, and to say we were honoured would be an understatement.

The President's attendance raised the profile of the event and it soon became clear that, if we were to retain any measure of privacy, we would have to award photographic rights to the wedding to one media group, and keep the rest away. The alternative would have been an uncontrollable scrum. The Sunday newspaper, *Rapport*, was duly contracted although its rival, the *Sunday Times*, apparently sent in two reporters masquerading as wedding guests, to take stolen photographs with a small camera.

Happily removed from such issues, we planned our wedding to be the best day of our lives. It was as simple as that. I bought my suit and tie from a shop in London, George Boys designed beautiful invitations and cards, and Marianne Fassler agreed to make Nerine's dress.

My brother, Kobus, would drive Nerine from her home to the chapel in Midrand, and I had arranged for him to pour her and her bridesmaid, her sister-in-law Karien Winter, a glass of champagne as he welcomed them to the car. I had also left her a watch, as my wedding day present, in the glove pocket, and planned for her to hear all her favourite songs during the course of the journey.

Nerine looked fantastic on the day and, after the ceremony, we moved to the reception at Gallagher Estate before, at half-past four in the morning, leaving to spend the night in a suite at the Sandton Towers, organized by the manager, John de Canio. When breakfast was served in our hotel room at noon, we reflected upon a truly wonderful event. Nerine's parents, John and Miemie Winter, had truly given us the best day of our lives.

We spent our honeymoon in the Far East, being treated like film stars. In Bangkok, we were whisked to waiting transport without appearing to pass through passport control. The hotels and locations were magnificent, and the highlight was perhaps a candlelit dinner for two on the beach, arranged three metres from the sea with our own waiter and musician.

The year could hardly have started in more uplifting

fashion. Nerine and I had trained during our honeymoon, and I arrived back in South Africa in the second week of February raring to start the new season. It would, I felt so certain, be even better than 1995. Everything was perfect.

Within an hour of arrival at Johannesburg airport, it very soon became clear that everything was not perfect. It had long been an ambition of mine to play in the Dimension Data pro-am golf tournament at Sun City, where amateurs like me could have the opportunity to play alongside professionals, like Nick Price, and I had earlier secured permission from the coach, Kitch Christie, to accept this invitation immediately upon my return from honeymoon. As we headed for Sun City, I was telephoned by Johan Prinsloo, the TRU chief executive officer, and instructed to be at training that afternoon. I said I had been given permission. He said my contract would be cancelled if I did not attend training that afternoon.

So I called the organisers of the golf, offered my apologies, turned my car around, returned home, packed my kit and headed for training. This type of incident was typical of the conditions in which the Transvaal players were expected to perform. Some would call it harassment.

Kitch Christie had been persuaded to return and coach the Transvaal team through at least the first half of the season, when the Springboks were effectively not in action. I advised him not to accept the dual role, but I think Kitch was afraid of having too much time on his hands. He had been fighting lymphatic cancer for more than 16 years, and it seemed to me he needed the day-to-day involvement in rugby to stay fit and focused.

The coach could not abide inactivity, and Luyt duly regained the services of the man who had guided the provincial team to glory in 1993 and 1994. He would coach Transvaal and the Springboks at the same time, and we set our sights on our first goal, the inaugural Super-12.

In sport, however, it is almost always true that you can never go back. Transvaal team had played and won as a family under

Kitch's leadership in 1993 and 1994 but, only two years later, that spirit had evaporated amid the tension and mistrust between the players and the union. Kitch tried manfully to bridge the gap and regain the old camaraderie, but there was nothing to be done while the TRU was making life difficult for some of its players.

In the golden era, we had played for each other. In 1996, the players' paramount aim was to protect their contract, and ensure the money arrived safely at the end of each month.

Our Super-12 challenge was over almost before it began. The draw had not been kind to us, forcing us to play our first four matches on tour to Australia and New Zealand within the span of 13 days. Increasingly ravaged by injuries and reduced to flying out stand-in youngsters, we lost all four games. It was the worst run of defeats in my career. To exacerbate a bad situation, the coach had been confined to his hotel room for most of the tour and played a minimal role as he struggled to recover from a bout of influenza.

Rumours were starting to destroy the team.

Kobus Wiese had been injured during our opening defeat against New South Wales in Sydney and was told to return home, coincidentally just in time for him to attend the opening of one of his chain of coffee shops. People began to speculate Kobus had faked his injury because his business was more important to him than his rugby. I know that was not the fact, but it was typical of the petty nonsense which began to undermine solid friendships and systematically to eat away at our once strong morale.

Other rumours blew through the squad. Perhaps, as captain, I should have called a meeting and confronted the issues head-on, but the rumours frequently related to personal matters and were better left alone.

We did regain some pride by defeating Auckland, the eventual Super-12 champions, at Ellis Park, but finished out of the semi-final places at the top of the table. Transvaal had used a total of 36 players in their 11 matches, and only three players had taken part in all 11 games: Pieter Hendriks, Japie Mulder and me ... and yet the rumours still spread that I was not interested in the game, not truly committed to rugby, more interested in making money, and so on. A paranoid person might have believed there was a deliberate campaign to discredit certain individuals.

There was no end to the bad news.

Kitch's state of health had failed to recover and, in April, he stepped down, first as Transvaal coach and then as Springbok coach. Anyone could see he was not well, but it seemed as if he was placed under inappropriate pressure to resign in a hurry from both positions.

What was the hurry?

When the coach had fallen sick in 1993, the union had stood by him, he had recovered and we went on to win a clean sweep of trophies during that season. Three years later, he was no more seriously ill and seemed certain to recover, but, as Kitch suggested in his biography, he felt Louis Luyt was eager for him to make a final decision. I was bewildered by the rush. The Springboks were not scheduled to play their next Test until 2 July, and I was sure Kitch would have been back to full fitness by then.

Luyt, the ultimate decision maker, appeared less certain. 'I don't want to have Kitch's death on my hands,' the SARFU and Transvaal president told me at the time, perhaps explaining his actions.

Thus, the decisions were made: Ray Mordt was named as Transvaal coach and Andre Markgraaff installed as the Springbok coach. The speed of their appointments suggested a measure of planning. Suddenly, in a matter of days, Kitch had been completely removed from the scene.

The players had known for some time that Markgraaff would ultimately become Springbok coach, although some did question his credentials. His claim to fame was to have coached Griqualand West, then considered to be a minor province which had been strengthened by buying players from nearby Free State, to a series of 'friendly' victories over several of the big provinces, and there is no doubt that he had proved an effective coach at that level.

I discounted the widespread notion that Markgraaff was benefiting from a strategic alliance with Luyt, established in 1994, whereby Luyt would give money for Griquas to buy players and guarantee Markgraaff the Springbok coaching job at some stage; in return, Markgraaff would marshal support among the small unions for Luyt's election as SARFU president.

This seemed too far-fetched to be true, and I was encouraged when Markgraaff and I exchanged a few words after a friendly between Griquas and Transvaal in Kimberley. He asked me how I was feeling, and I told him the first priority was to sort out the enduring contract disputes between the players and Luyt. If these were left to fester, I warned him, they would start to affect the Springbok performance in exactly the same way they had undermined Transvaal's Super-12 challenge.

'I agree,' he replied. 'Don't worry. We'll sort it out. We can't allow that sort of thing to affect our preparations.'

I was pleased by his reaction, and excited when he asked if we could meet at the Sunnyside Park hotel to discuss the season ahead. There was no doubt in my mind that we could work together. Indeed, I had started to feel as if Markgraaff might be the answer to all our problems. If anybody could talk to Luyt effectively on our behalf, it would surely be him.

Markgraaff opened the private meeting by telling me I should not think of my three-year contract with SARFU as the be-all and end-all of my earning potential in the game. He told me how professional rugby union was going to boom and assured me there would be additional opportunities.

I agreed with everything he said, but each time I thought he was going to start talking about rugby, he kept talking about money. Perhaps he was determined to allay my fears about the wrangling over the contracts, but I wanted to discuss how we were going to win the next three matches and set a new record for the longest winning streak in history. He didn't.

As I drove home, I felt confused and uncertain of what to make of the meeting. He had assured me that I was part of his plans, and I had affirmed to him he was the captain of the ship and I would follow his instructions. I had told him wherever he wanted us to go, we would follow, but I was keen to talk about the actual rugby sooner rather than later. Kitch had always managed to keep the two issues apart, and we needed to do the same.

Markgraaff and I met again in Cape Town soon afterwards and, with Christiaan Scholtz, spent a day looking at properties, getting to know each other better. I liked him. He seemed honest and sincere.

When the squad gathered before a Tri-Nations series warm-up Test against Tonga, however, there was one matter which I needed to be resolved between Markgraaff, Ray Mordt, who had been appointed as assistant coach to the Springboks, and myself; and I wasted no time.

Ray had been the only person to decline an invitation to my wedding, explaining he had prior family commitments. This seemed a poor excuse, particularly since the invitations had been sent out three months in advance. Ray raised the matter with me during Transvaal's Super-12 tour, and told me the genuine reason for his decision to stay away.

It transpired that Markgraaff had told Luyt that I had been speaking to a group of bankers and declared I had no respect for Ray, either as a coach or as a person; and Luyt had then told Ray Mordt.

I was amazed. The story was a complete lie, and I asked Ray why he had not picked up a telephone to ask me about the incident. He said he had been too disappointed. I said we should confront Markgraaff face to face and get to the bottom of the unfortunate saga as soon as possible.

The first opportunity to do this was on the day the Springbok squad gathered at the Pretoria Holiday Inn to

*Below:* The jubilation sinks in as Joel Stransky joins Ruben Kruger and I moments after the final whistle of the 1995 Rugby World Cup final at Ellis Park.

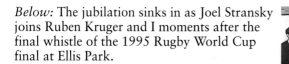

*Above:* One happy Springbok squad, and one Webb Ellis trophy – we were a family, that was the key.

The lap of honour was conducted amid a serene air of calm – you could almost hear 67,000 people thanking their lucky stars that they were present. Hennie le Roux, great player and great friend, was on hand to give me an even better view of the celebrations.

*Above:* I would have enjoyed leading South Africa against Martin Johnson's Lions in 1997, but circumstances with which Louis Luyt, right, was familiar meant I was otherwise occupied on the other side of the world.

*Above:* Wearing her colours, and wearing a smile shared by every South African after we were crowned rugby World Champions.

*Above:* Unable to sustain the family of 1995 – it struck me that Morne du Plessis was never comfortable with Andre Markgraaff during 1996, and Morne did not hesitate to step down at the end of the All Black tour.

*Right:* Sean Fitzpatrick was the most astute captain I have ever played against on a rugby field, and a genuine legend of the game all around the world.

*Left:* Phil Kearns, scoring against Argentina, led Australia with distinction, while, from left, John Eales and David Campese were always respected opponents.

*Right:* It is one of my greatest regrets that I left my Springbok rugby on a stretcher – carried off towards the end of the 1996 Tri-Nations Test against New Zealand at Newlands, and never to return.

*Above:* Transvaal endured an unhappy Super-12 campaign in 1996, although I was pleased to have been the only forward to play in every match – retaining the ball under challenge from Cabous van der Westhuizen, James Small and Wayne Fyvie against Natal.

*Above:* The World
Champions tour was held
four months after the final,
but many thousands braved
the rain and filled the
streets of Cape Town, and
we were happy to sign
autographs all day long.

*Above:* Nerine and I were
privileged to have President
Mandela attend our marriage
ceremony. It was a very special day
for us all.

*Left:* As part of the World
Champions tour, we conducted
coaching clinics around the country
– here, at the famous Orlando
stadium in Soweto.

*Left:* Three weeks after being left out of the Springbok side, I was desperate to lead Transvaal to victory in the Currie Cup final, but Natal were too strong on the day at Ellis Park. Here, I'm tangling with Jeremy Thomson, who was destined to join me at Saracens.

*Above:* Less than 12 hours after agreeing to join Saracens, I attended a formal press conference at the Trocadero Building in Piccadilly Circus – Michael Lynagh and Phillippe Sella welcome me to the club.

*Left:* It's a fact that I have never had a contract to play for Saracens – ever since the first day we met, the word of club owner, Nigel Wray, has been good enough.

*Above:* Getting the guys together – Saracens have the potential to become the leading club in Europe, our task is to realise that potential.

*Left:* Saracens' ground share arrangement with Watford Football Club, recently promoted to the Premiership, has given the club use of a comfortable and modern 21,000-seat stadium just north of London.

*Right:* At Saracens, we have tried to create a club organised specifically for the players, and the players have responded to the challenge of professionalism. Here, Richard Hill, left, and George Chuter sweat in the gym.

*Above:* It was a privilege to play beside Michael Lynagh for Saracens in 1998 – it's hard to think of a more skilful flyhalf and more decent man in the game.

*Right:* Sometimes the game boils up inside you, and it just comes out – I think that's what's happening here.

*Left:* Leading the way at Saracens.

*Below:* My first match for Saracens was played in the mud of the Recreation Ground in Bath, but our narrow defeat that day would be avenged the following season.

*Left:* Every opportunity to give something back to South African rugby is welcome, and I enjoyed conducting a series of clinics with Guinness during 1998, this one at the University of Pretoria.

*Below:* A crowning moment for Michael Lynagh in the last major match of his career – Wasps have been beaten, and we have won the Tetley's Bitter Cup final at Twickenham, May 1998.

*Below:* The ears have just about survived intact, and I enjoy working for television – here, I'm preparing with the ITV team at the 1999 Calcutta Cup match at Twickenham.

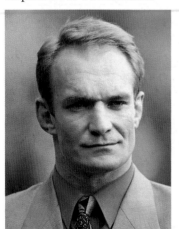

*Above:* One of our aims at Saracens has been to nurture Test players, and lock Danny Grewcock, scoring here in the 1999 Tetley's Bitter Cup final, is one of several Sarries who have advanced to play for England.

prepare for the Test against Tonga on 2 July. I had not even unpacked my suitcases when I found Ray Mordt and asked him to come and meet Markgraaff in his suite.

I started by explaining what had happened and concluded this matter would have to be amicably resolved before we could trust each other and work together as the coach and captain of the Springbok team.

Markgraaff seemed taken aback. He said he had had a conversation with Luyt but denied he had mentioned any names. He said he had spoken about the team in general, and suggested the entire situation had arisen from a foolish misunderstanding. Ray didn't say much, but I accepted what the coach said and asked him if we could please be open with each other on all issues. I then assured him he could rely upon my support at all times.

We duly defeated Tonga 43–18, but the arrival of a new coach with new tactics immediately and inevitably created a different atmosphere from that which we had nurtured in 1995. Henry Honiball's selection at fly-half ahead of Joel Stransky also delivered a clear message that World Cup form and reputations were but a distant memory.

Continuity seemed lost. Far from building on the solid achievements of 1995, the squad was being asked to start all over again.

The Springboks' first two matches in the Tri-Nations series were to be played against the Wallabies in Sydney and the All Blacks in Christchurch, and we needed two wins to secure the world record for the most successive Test wins by any international team ever. We glimpsed a place in history and we should have been heading west with confidence and excitement; instead, a bewildered Springbok squad was muddled and uncertain.

'We will play rugby the world has never seen before,' Markgraaff had extravagantly told the media before our departure and the wild expectations that we would demolish Australia in Sydney increased when they conceded 40 points to the New Zealanders the previous week. These events combined to place an already nervous team under huge pressure.

My foreboding of pride before a fall deepened when the coach handed me a piece of paper on which he had written the game plan he wanted us to implement against the Wallabies. I saw he wanted us to take quick tapped penalties, to throw quick lineouts, to punt the ball deep into their half rather than into touch and, if we won a penalty in their half, to kick for a lineout in the corner rather than to kick for the posts.

I did not feel comfortable with the idea of introducing a new strategy before such an important match, but I had promised the coach my support and I was not going to break that pledge.

We lost the match 21–16, and blew our chance of setting a new world record. Our performance lacked pace and discipline but, even then, we had come close to beating an indifferent Wallaby team which seemed far weaker than the side we had defeated at the World Cup. I was as disappointed as at any moment in my career, but said nothing to anyone.

The team had patently not been ready for a strategic upheaval and the manner in which we wasted no fewer than eight attacking penalties was clear evidence of the confusion in our side. I think those penalties were tapped by eight different people, and the possession was wasted.

Morne du Plessis had remained with the squad, and I confided in our much respected team manager my concern that Markgraaff's game plan was unsound. I understood what kind of rugby he wanted us to play, but there had to be more gradual process of transition. Morne agreed with my concerns, but felt in no position to exert any influence. The dynamics of the management team had also changed since the World Cup. Kitch had relied upon Morne, but I received the impression that Markgraaff appeared reluctant to take advice from anyone. Later in the year, indeed, he would seek and be given the responsibilities of both manager and coach.

We advanced from Sydney to Christchurch and found New Zealand rugby whipped into a fever over the prospect of revenge for the World Cup final the previous year. Amid the bitterness and allegations of food poisoning, this was to be the day when the All Blacks proved once and for all who was the strongest team in the world. The country was buzzing.

Unfortunately our preparations were hampered by the inexperience of our new coach. Guiding Griquas into a pre-season friendly was one thing, but guiding the Boks in New Zealand was another. Markgraaff's inexperience was manifested in his obsession with the opposition. Through Monday and Tuesday, he spoke incessantly about Jonah Lomu, and how on earth we would stop him, and about Zinzan Brooke, and Kronveld, and...

He was on the wrong track. International rugby is played by imposing your game on the opposition, not by worrying about what they can do. I knew that and the players knew that, but Markgraaff did not know. I was becoming increasingly frustrated and, this particular week, took refuge by playing pool in the team room with Johan Ackermann, the young lock who had come into the side. Pool provided a distraction from our problems, and took me away from the television and radio in my hotel room.

And yet, despite everything, I knew we remained a world-class side capable of defeating New Zealand. We only needed to get the tactics and the mental preparation right and we would win.

By Wednesday, I had decided to take action and, in tandem with Morne du Plessis, who also recognized the difficulty, staged a situation during a squad meeting where I asked the management team to leave the room. Left alone with the players, I set about trying to put things right. Even before the door had closed behind Markgraaff, some of the exasperated players wanted to make their views known first. I had not said a word.

'What the * * * * is going on?' asked one.

'Does anyone understand the game plan?' asked another.

'Does the coach think we can't beat these guys?' asked a third.

I tried to calm the players and explain how we certainly did have the talent to win the Test. Look at the history, I told them. We lost here in 1994 when we should at least have drawn the series and we completely deserved to beat them in the World Cup Final. I pointed out how they had made only two changes from the final, with John Hart replacing Laurie Mains as coach and Christian Cullen emerging as an exciting full-back, but that Sean Fitzpatrick's team would present essentially the same intensely physical challenge. 'Of course, it will be close,' I concluded. 'It's always close against this lot, but we can win here. The All Blacks know that too.'

I left some facts unsaid. While the All Blacks had stayed calm after the World Cup final defeat, and sustained the develop-ment of their side, we had adopted a new coach, a new game plan and new players in key positions. It appeared to me as if we had tossed away whatever advantage we may have won at the World Cup and found ourselves underdogs again. I was frustrated but I tried to channel my fury at the opposition.

Almost unbelievably, Markgraaff delayed selection of the scrum-half to play at Lancaster Park until the morning of the match before finally settling for Johan Roux and a kicking game, ahead of Joost van der Westhuizen, in what seemed likely to be wet and heavy conditions. Everyone knew such indecision plays havoc with a team's confidence and stability.

Despite these circumstances, and maybe because of them, the team arrived at Lancaster Park in a ferociously determined mood. We were angry, we were frustrated and, perhaps above all, we wanted to prove ourselves as genuine world champions all over again.

Following tradition, the squad watched a film on the Friday night before the match, on this occasion *The Rock*; and, standing in the changing room before the game at Lancaster Park, I recalled the story of the captain who took his troops to

Alcatraz and held them ransom for money owed to veterans of the Vietnam war. In one of the most dramatic moments of the film, the captain asks his men: 'Are you ready?'

And they shout back, in unison: 'Yes!'

So, with the guys changed, I asked the team if they were ready.

'Yes!' they shouted.

I sensed we were. John Allan had been recalled as hooker, and was as up for the contest as anyone could be. He had shot past me like a bullet when we ran on the field and he suddenly started shouting abuse at the All Blacks while they performed the *haka*. His approach was fine, although it did cost us three points when he conceded a penalty by head-butting Fitzpatrick at the first scrum. Battle was mightily joined.

Moments later, we appeared to have won a kickable penalty not far from the All Black line, but the decision was reversed after a late challenge by Pieter Hendriks on Cullen. We were a physical side, and that was fine. We had also been physical in 1995. The difference was that in 1995 we had also been controlled. We lacked that quality a year later.

Nonetheless, when Mark Andrews set up an excellent try for Andre Joubert, I became convinced we would win the match. Referee Ray Megson, however, had a crucial impact on the game, awarding the All Blacks a penalty on their own line when they had collapsed a scrum which we were moving forward. His basic error cost us seven points, and the Test. We had played all the constructive rugby, we had looked the more cohesive side throughout the 80 minutes, but we had lost 15–11.

Sean Fitzpatrick, the All Black captain, approached me as we were leaving the field after the final whistle, shook me by the hand and said: 'Sorry about the ref.' I appreciated the gesture, but I was seething again, and my emotions boiled over when I slammed my clenched fist into a door when I reached the changing room. I was beyond despair.

'It's his fault,' I shouted to Morne du Plessis. 'You know that.

This is all the coach's fault. We should be winning these matches. This is bullshit.'

Morne put his arm around me and ushered me to a corner. Markgraaff had not heard my outburst. The team was desolate.

Soon after arriving back in South Africa, my relationship with the coach suffered a further blow when I was told how Markgraaff had stood in the hotel bar after the Test match in Christchurch and regaled two journalists with his view that we had lost because I had made two bad decisions when we had a scrum near the All Black line during the second half.

My policy in such situations is to be direct, so I walked straight to the coach and asked him to explain what he had said. Once again, he denied he had mentioned my name but did concede he had said we may have made an incorrect decision at the scrum close to the All Black line.

I continued: 'And do you recall the moment in the teamtalk when you clearly stated that you wanted Gary Teichmann [the eighthman] to be able to call moves from the back of the scrum. Well, that is exactly what he did in that situation. Now I have no problem with that. He made his decision, and that is fine, but I will not accept you holding me responsible.'

Once again he protested his innocence, but I no longer believed him.

The squad settled in Bloemfontein for our first home Test of the series, against the Wallabies at the Free State stadium, but we had become divided against ourselves. I remained loyal to Markgraaff in public, but the situation was becoming almost unbearable in private.

No sooner than we had arrived at the hotel, the coach called Gary Teichmann, Ruben Kruger and myself to his room. When we sat down, he asked us why we were not combining as a unit. It was the sort of question which any decent coach should have answered himself. That was his job. After all, he had selected us as the loose forward trio.

I didn't want to do too much of the talking because Gary and Ruben are naturally quiet guys, but the meeting eventually became a taut dialogue between captain and coach. Markgraaff asked me if I should play on the blindside or the open side, or maybe switch between the two.

'Coach, I will play wherever you want me to play,' I replied.

'I am not saying we should do that,' he said, becoming agitated. 'I am only saying we should consider it as an option.'

'Fine.'

The meeting was going nowhere and I could sense Gary and Ruben becoming increasingly uncomfortable. I was quickly reaching the conclusion that Markgraaff was not exactly sure of what he wanted. I could see he was a clever man and his understanding of the game was beyond question, but his manner did not inspire confidence.

In these circumstances, I took a decision to take a much stronger hand as captain on the field. Joel Stransky had been recalled to the team to face Australia and, contrary to Markgraaff's game plan, I asked the fly-half to kick the ball to touch rather than into space. We needed to establish field position, and the tactic paid dividends as we led 16–3 at half-time.

The Wallabies did fight back in the second half, but we held on to win 25–19. It might be imagined that the coach would have been delighted to get back on the winning road after two defeats, but Markgraaff was evidently not too excited when we returned to the changing room.

My frustration at Markgraaff's impact on our playing performance was matched by Morne du Plessis' reaction to events off the field. Management had worked as a team during 1995, from Edward Griffiths as the SARFU chief executive officer to Morne and Kitch, to me as captain and on to the players. The media was handled expertly, situations were handled sensitively and, week after week, the team was happy to be free from controversy and crisis.

In 1996, Morne appeared deeply suspicious of SARFU after

Edward's departure and was unable to communicate freely with Markgraaff. His instinct was to follow the same kind of pro-active, visionary course of 1995 but, all of a sudden, he found himself out on his own.

He had been distressed by the number of old South African flags being waved from the grandstands during the Test in Bloemfontein and, off his own back while waiting at the airport the following morning, he issued a powerful media statement condemning the situation, saying the Springboks did not want to be supported by anyone waving the old flag.

I understood what he wanted to say, but nobody had told me exactly what he had said. Communications were breaking down and I suddenly found myself being asked to comment on the manager's remarks. There was no real control, and we were being needlessly driven into corners.

'We want to unite the entire country, whichever flag anyone is waving at the stadium,' I said, trying to pacify those players who had come to me to say their families had been upset by Morne's statement. I had tried to steer a tight middle line, but my comments were then received as implicit criticism of Morne and, amazingly, I found myself being cast in a public dispute with the outstanding team manager in my experience.

When SARFU announced the team manager had been speaking in his personal capacity, it seemed to me that Morne was being hung out to dry. His sense of honour and duty would keep him bravely at his post until the end of the All Black tour, but it became clear to me that he was staying under sufferance.

The meltdown of the squad was under way. Edward Griffiths had been dismissed by fax in February, and denied any sort of hearing or opportunity to answer any charges set against him. Luyt mentioned the CEO had become 'too important' but I sensed he had become too successful. Luyt's style was to act as an executive president, and he did not relish the idea of a CEO with his own strategies, especially when he was successful.

Kitch Christie had been moved aside in April and, now, Morne du Plessis was being made to feel uncomfortable as manager. Even then, in July, I began to sense the direction the wind was blowing.

My response was to keep battering away. The most effective defence of any player who senses he may be unpopular with the coach or officials is to keep winning on the field. Winners become untouchable. I remained loyal to Markgraaff in public, but I had passed the stage of implementing his game plans without question. I wasn't going to stand inactive while matches were lost.

The All Blacks had already secured the inaugural Tri-Nations title by the time they arrived in Cape Town for the last match of the competition; that was to be followed by three more Tests against the Springboks, to be played on successive weekends as a separate series.

In contemplating our strategy, I noted Christian Cullen, the bold, young full-back, had emerged as the star of the season. He appeared a magnificent runner of the ball from deep positions, but I was also aware this kind of player could be less comfortable when kicking the ball clear.

So I suggested to Joel Stransky that he should play a kicking game, constantly driving the ball into open spaces behind the young star. I then sat with the backs to develop a blanket of pressure which they would throw over Cullen and, within a few moments, we had developed a key tactic which we, the players, could help us win the game.

For the first 30 minutes against New Zealand at Newlands, we played perhaps our most impressive rugby of the series. Japie Mulder scored a great try and we were driving powerfully up the channels. Cullen had been caught twice while retrieving the ball and he seemed generally unsettled. I sensed the All Blacks were wilting as we established an 18–6 lead.

Then, shortly after half-time, I was sprinting back in cover defence to tackle Sean Fitzpatrick when I managed to get my head on the wrong side of his legs and his knee crashed into the side of my head. I was gone, lights out, but the doctor revived me and I decided to play on.

I had felt a similar sense of numbness in my arm and dizziness around my head when striking a tackle bag awkwardly while on tour in New Zealand with Transvaal earlier in the season, and I was starting to believe something might be wrong, but I badly wanted to remain on the field. At such times, the passion of the moment overwhelms all logic. It shouldn't. But it does.

And I did play on. It was only when my vision began to blur deep inside the second half that I realized it would be impossible for me to remain on the field. It had long since been irresponsible, but now I was being bloody-minded. I had heard people questioning my commitment before the Test, and I wanted to show everyone how much I wanted to play and win. I was still shouting to Joel to "kick the ******* ball", as I had done all afternoon, when I finally yielded to the medical reality and collapsed to the Newlands turf.

I was strapped to a stretcher and carried off the field amid applause from the stands. It was, in fact, the second time I had been stretchered off the field in Cape Town. Eight seasons before, I had suffered a fit while playing for Transvaal Rooibokke against Western Province B and swallowed my tongue. My life may have indeed been saved by one of my team-mates, Wittes Buitendag, who pulled my tongue out of my throat.

So history repeated itself, and I found myself once again lying on the treatment table in the medical room near the changing rooms. Morne du Plessis came down from the stand to check whether I was all right, and he returned some 15 minutes later to tell me we had lost 29–18.

'What?' I exclaimed. I could not believe his words. I lay there, alone, wondering what on earth had gone wrong in the last quarter.

Thabo Mbeki, the deputy president, put his head around the door and wished me well, as did Jim Bolger, then Prime

Minister of New Zealand; and the third man to visit me was John Hart, the All Black coach.

Markgraaff stayed away. Luyt stayed away. As I lay still and sore, the message seemed to be becoming clear: I was neither needed nor wanted by the Springbok coach, but I resolved to stand tall and hold my head high. This was the fourth serious concussion of my career, and I felt distinctly groggy as I took off my playing kit and walked to the showers.

I returned to the main changing room to find Luyt sitting with a beer in one hand and his other arm wrapped around the neck of Gary Teichmann, who had taken over the captaincy when I left the field. On this occasion at Newlands, my place was directly next to Gary and I had no option but to sit down immediately beside Luyt.

Silence. I sat alone.

The SARFU president didn't greet me, didn't ask me how I was feeling and didn't acknowledge me at all. Markgraaff appeared equally indifferent, failing to enquire about my state of health at any stage. I was amazed by their conduct, and there is no point in denying that it hurt. Other players could see what was happening, and the atmosphere was terrible. I had captained the Springboks for more than three years, and given everything to the cause. I kept asking myself if I had deserved to be treated like that.

Os du Randt had also left the field near the end of the match and, together, we were taken by ambulance for observation at the Groote Schuur hospital. I stopped the driver on the way to vomit by the side of Main Road, but I started to feel better later and the scans were duly taken.

'François, you have suffered serious concussion,' the doctor told me on the Monday. He was holding the X-rays of my brain in his hand.

'I know, but I need to play against the All Blacks on Saturday.'

'I think that is out of the question.'

'Can I sign an indemnity form?'

235

'What do you mean?'

'I will indemnify you from any responsibility for what might happen to me if I play in the Test match on Saturday. Will that be OK?'

'Look, at the end of the day, you can do what you want,' the doctor told me, 'but you have your whole life ahead of you. It would be stupid to take any risks. In my view, you need five weeks' rest. Have you seen Muhammad Ali recently? He thought he could ignore medical opinion as well.'

His advice was offered in such a way that it could not be rejected, but it remained desperately hard to accept the reality. I called Markgraaff with the doctor's verdict and explained I would be ruled out for the rest of the series. The telephone call lasted around a minute, and the Springbok squad moved into a three-Test series against New Zealand without me.

The experience of watching on television at home as the Boks sung the anthem before the Test at King's Park was painful. I missed the challenge terribly, and was bitterly disappointed when the guys lost the Test narrowly and were shaded out a week later in Pretoria. I had sent faxes to wish them well before the games, but that was all. It was Gary's show.

On the Monday the Springboks arrived at the Sunnyside Park hotel ahead of the third and final Test at Ellis Park, a new bombshell was dropped. Theo van Rensburg, the former Bok full-back, phoned me to say he had heard from within the Springbok camp that Markgraaff was claiming I faked my injury at Newlands and was not seriously hurt at all.

I had been furious several times during the course of 1996, but rarely more furious than when I put the telephone down to Theo. I walked directly to my car and drove from Midrand to the Sunnyside Park hotel. I arrived to find most of the players milling around after the team photograph had been taken in the hotel garden. I greeted players and wished them well, but I was looking for Markgraaff. Upon finding him, I managed to keep control.

'Hello.'

'Hello.'

'I understand you think I faked my injury at Newlands.'

'What?'

'I understand you think I faked my injury at Newlands. You were saying my injury was not as serious as I had made it look. Is that true?'

'No, that's not true,' he said. 'I never said anything like that. Of course I wanted you to play. I needed you in the team.'

I looked him in the eye. I sensed he was lying through his teeth. I could see it in his face. I walked away, wished Gary Teichmann the very best of luck, posed for a photograph with the new Springbok captain and drove home. That would be the last time I ever spoke to Andre Markgraaff.

The Springboks won the third Test at Ellis Park, salvaging some pride after four successive defeats against New Zealand, and the players returned to play out the conclusion of the Currie Cup season. Rumours had already reached me that I should not consider myself an automatic selection for the Springbok squad to tour France and England at the end of the year, and my response was to treat Transvaal's remaining matches as trials.

Markgraaff's dislike for me was evident, but I also knew I was playing well enough to secure my place in the squad. I had been very happy with my form for South Africa during 1996, and I was completely prepared to prove myself again at provincial level. I had no complaints about the process. That is sport. You get injured and you fight your way back. I had no control of the coach's intentions, but I knew I could control my own form.

We were playing Western Province at Ellis Park on the Saturday the Springbok squad was to be announced. Ray Mordt, Transvaal coach as well as a national selector, had warned me that Markgraaff didn't like either me or the way I had captained the team earlier in the season. He didn't say I would not be selected, but maybe he was trying to prepare me.

Not lacking in motivation, I played my full part in a comprehensive Transvaal victory and, fearing the worst, allowed events to unfold after the game. It was during the standard post-match captain's press conference that I heard official confirmation that my name was not among the 30 announced for the Springbok squad to tour France and England.

I took the news on the chin, but I was hurt. I felt so bad, so miserable. Scarcely 15 months after winning the World Cup, I had effectively been dropped from the Springbok squad. Adding insult to the injury, the coach had not even telephoned me with the news. He subsequently claimed he had tried to contact me several times during the week. Whatever the truth of that assertion, no message was left either at my office or my home or on my cellphone.

The press conference continued. There was not much to say, other than to express my disappointment and to wish Gary Teichmann, my successor as captain, and the rest of the side the best of luck in Europe. I returned to the Transvaal changing room and, out of the blue, was approached by Louis Luyt.

'I can change it,' he said. 'I can change it.'

'No, Doc,' I replied. 'Leave the coach to select his own side. There is no need to interfere. It must be his decision.'

Maybe I should have been touched by Luyt's gesture in offering a late reprieve (and no-one doubted he had the power to reverse any decision) but I believed it had been the SARFU president who created the enviroment where Markgraaff could exact his wrath on me.

I drove home quietly, sadly and, the following day, flew to Cape Town to play golf with Howard Jones, CEO of Grinaker Construction. The facts sunk in when I read Markgraaff's statement on the front page of the Sunday newspapers. 'François Pienaar is not a part of my vision for the future,' said the Springbok coach, who had been formally appointed until the 1999 World Cup.

So that was it? Not part of his vision, not part of the Boks: it appeared as if I had played my last Test match for South Africa. Was that my fate, to be carried off on a stretcher directly into history? At the age of 29, in my prime as a player and a captain – it was incredibly hard to accept.

The public response during the week that followed, manifested in radio phone-in programmes and newspaper polls, demonstrated enormous support for my reinstatement but I had accepted that the higher structures of South African rugby were hardly in mourning at my omission. Markgraaff's will would prevail against the outrage. I may have been the Springbok captain, I may have been at the peak of my game and I may have had widespread popular support, but I remained as essentially vulnerable as any other player. If the coach doesn't pick you in the side, he doesn't pick you. There's no reprieve.

Transvaal played Northern Transvaal at Loftus Versfeld the following weekend, with a place in the Currie Cup Final at stake, and I was moved when my team-mates pledged they would win the match for me. On the Friday night our Midrand home had been ransacked while Nerine was alone in the house (I was at the hotel with the team) and, having coped with that scare, I pulled myself together to produce one of the most compelling performances of my entire career, leading the team to an emphatic victory.

With around five minutes remaining, I had looked towards the Loftus scoreboard and seen my name flashed up as Man of the Match. The Pretoria crowd that had sometimes booed me in the past suddenly cheered. I sensed tears were starting to well in my eyes, and I could not hold them back when my team-mates carried me off the field at the final whistle.

The ideal reaction to my Springbok omission would have been to lead Transvaal to victory in the Currie Cup Final against Natal at Ellis Park the following week, and we were leading into the second half, but Andre Joubert scored a superb try to secure the Durban team a well-deserved victory. It was my first defeat as a captain in any final, at any level.

As the Currie Cup ran its course, I had grown more disappointed that I had not secured even a place in the Springbok squad. Markgraaff had picked Theo Oosthuizen, a house friend of his in Kimberley and a decent provincial flanker who was approaching the end of his career. I kept asking myself if I had really been a less attractive candidate than Oosthuizen.

The coach countered such questions by declaring he could never have selected me as an ordinary player. Why not? Even if he had wanted Gary to captain the Test team, I would have instantly accepted an opportunity to lead the midweek side and force my way back into contention. I deeply craved any opportunity to prove myself again, to regain lost ground.

As the days passed, the pain increased.

Why had this happened?

It took Louis Luyt four years to admit why I was dropped when, after much huffing and bluffing, he finally told a television interviewer that I had been 'too strong' for the coach. Markgraaff, he suggested, had declared he could not work with me because I was simply too strong.

This seemed nonsensical. John Hart had taken over as the All Black coach and had not dropped Sean Fitzpatrick, even to the extent of taking him on tour to Britain, when he was injured, simply to have the benefit of his experience from the bench. Jack Rowell had been appointed as England coach and had not dismissed Will Carling. If I did threaten Markgraaff's sense of security, then the fault surely rested with him.

The facts were that I had supported him in public and among the players at all times. I had wanted to help him settle as an international coach, but he appeared unwilling to listen to my views or opinions. Was he too proud or too insecure to learn from an experienced captain? Why could he not have arrived and been happy to build on the foundations of 1995?

The answers to these questions must hang in the air, but I frequently wonder what might have happened if this inexperienced, but obviously clever coach had approached his task differently in 1996. If we could have trusted each other, if he had been prepared to sustain our success of 1995 rather than to establish a new dynasty, the results might have been so different, not only for me as captain but also, ultimately, for him as coach.

I derived no pleasure from Markgraaff's dramatic resignation only five months later when a secret tape recording of a private conversation in which he had made racist remarks was released to the public, and I sincerely hope he will enjoy success as a top coach in the future.

There is no doubt in my mind that his decision to drop me was his own decision. He was not acting under orders, but there is equally no doubt in my mind that Louis Luyt was not at all distressed by my demise.

He had made no secret of resenting me since the World Cup players had signed their SARFU contracts, and probably felt I had received my just rewards for, in his eyes, daring to take on the establishment. He would also have noted that my fall from grace effectively completed the meltdown of the leading figures within the Springbok World Cup squad.

Edward Griffiths and Kitch Christie had gone before Easter, Morne du Plessis had resigned as manager after the All Black tour, and I had not been selected for the Springbok tour. Yesterday's heroes were washed up and unwanted, seeking new horizons.

Was I bitter then? Maybe. Am I bitter now? No. There is no time or point in wasting valuable time on such negative emotions. I would become angry with acquaintances who suggested I would somehow be perversely pleased when the Springboks were defeated by the British Lions in 1997. Nothing will ever dampen my support for my country, and the team which will always hold such a special place in my heart. The Springboks remain special.

I was distressed to watch from afar as South African rugby was dragged through crisis upon crisis, and eventually the courts, through 1997 and 1998, but I felt in no way vindicated by Louis Luyt's ultimate resignation when his own executive committee turned on him.

On the contrary, I felt sad that this man who had contributed so much to the game over two decades, from his dynamic leadership of Transvaal to his legendary business acumen, should have suffered such a humiliating and undignified exit. I felt sad, but it must be conceded that he was largely the architect of his own downfall. He had created everything with great skill, and yet then appeared to preside over its destruction. He created a truly great Transvaal team, and appeared to preside over its destruction; he had created the world champion Springboks and then appeared to preside over their destruction.

'Yet each man must kill the thing he loves.' The words of Oscar Wilde might have been written exclusively for Louis Luyt.

I had started to realize his charming, genial nature was balanced by a relentless and ruthless streak. This was the peculiar paradox of Louis Luyt. We had enjoyed many happy and wonderful days together, but our links were broken during 1995, and a kind of love became a kind of hatred.

We parted ways at the end of 1996, and it is unfortunate that sporadic skirmishes still erupt in the media. During 1998, he misread a meeting which the National Sports Council asked me to attend and lambasted me publicly as a 'Judas' who had tried to sell the Springboks after the World Cup. Three years on, it was clear the pain of signing the World Cup players' contracts has remained with him. I genuinely hope his resentment eases with time, and that the talented and driven Louis Luyt that I know finds peace and fulfilment again. He says he hates me. That is his decision.

For my part, I would be lying if I claimed no longer to feel any pain at the events of 1996, and the end of my Springbok career. I feel the pain each time I watch South Africa play, either at the stadium or on television because part of me still yearns to be involved, in green and gold.

And I will always bitterly regret that I was unable to leave

Springbok rugby on my own terms, on my own feet. With all due modesty, I believe I did deserve better than to depart the stage on a stretcher.

But that was what happened. As the Springboks departed for France in October 1996, my task was to find a brand new challenge.

Within weeks, the telephone was ringing...

# CHAPTER NINE

# *New Horizons*

*Man cannot discover new oceans until he has the
courage to lose sight of the shore*
Anon

The voice was evidently English, and the manner was gentle. The man on the other end of the line had introduced himself and was now asking whether I might be interested in playing rugby for a club in London. I was at home and it was late in the evening, so I listened to what he had to say.

'Thank you very much for calling,' I eventually responded. 'I am extremely flattered by your suggestion, but my intention is to remain in South Africa and win back my place in the Springbok team.'

He said he completely understood and that appeared to be that. The idea of playing in England had hardly crossed my mind. Some officials from Richmond had sounded me out during the 1995 Springbok tour but I had told them my goals all lay in South Africa, at home.

Now this gentleman had called me out of the blue. He said his name was Nigel Wray, and he had spoken about the Saracens club. My instinct had been to decline his enquiry as well, although I did wonder during the following day how he had found my telephone number.

'Cappie?'

It was Kitch Christie calling.

'Did Nigel Wray call you?'

I said he had, and the coach proceeded to tell me how Ian Robertson, BBC radio rugby correspondent, had suggested to the Saracens owner that I could be a possible recruit. Nigel Wray had first contacted Kitch who, in turn, had given him my telephone number.

'So what did you tell him?' the coach asked.

'I told him, no thanks, because my body needs a rest after playing four tough seasons with hardly a break, and I want to come back stronger than ever for Transvaal in the Super-12 next year. I'll play my way back into the Springbok team, coach. You just watch.'

The coach was silent on the other end of the line.

'Cappie, I think you should seriously consider that option.'

'What do you mean?'

'Well, you have achieved everything you can in South African rugby. You've won all the domestic trophies and you've won the World Cup but now it seems as if you're not welcome here any more. People are trying to pull you down. Don't give them that pleasure, cappie. Look at the way you have been treated. You've got nothing more to prove to anyone here. Maybe you need a new challenge.'

No-one's words weighed more heavily on my mind than those of Kitch Christie. He went on to say life would not be easy overseas, he said it would be tough, but he also believed I could be successful over there. I considered his advice. Playing in England? Was that what I wanted to do? It was not as if my entire career in South Africa had collapsed. I was still firmly established as the Transvaal captain, and we were as strong as any team in the country. That night, I raised the option of a move with Nerine, my wife.

She was completely objective, and seemed excited by the idea from the outset. I am cautious by temperament, but Nerine loves to strike out on a new adventure. She said she would support me in whatever I wanted to do, but she then set out the issues with cool perspective.

'It has reached a stage where people in South Africa are setting you up to fall,' she said plainly. 'If Transvaal win, people say that was expected. If Transvaal lose, they say you are not committed to rugby and it's your fault. If you do get back into the Springbok side, and you win, they will say that was expected as well. And if you lose, well, they will take great delight in blaming you. We're almost in a no-win situation here.

'I think we should seriously consider putting the drama behind us, and making a fresh start. Maybe you do need a new challenge.'

I understood her view. Markgraaff could not have been more adamant. I was 'not part of his vision for the future'. On the other hand, the fact was I still had two and a half years to run on my hard-earned contract with SARFU, and that would remain fully in place whether I played for the Boks or not. In fact, the act of being released from any commitment to international rugby would give me more time to concentrate on my business ventures. That was not such a bad prospect, was it?

As the days passed, both Kitch and Nerine were urging me to consider the England option seriously, but I was uncertain how to proceed. I would wait and see. Then, four weeks after his initial call, Nigel Wray was suddenly on the line again. I have always wondered who passed a message to the Saracens owner that it might be worth his while to contact me for a second time. I suspect Kitch Christie was looking out for me again.

'Mr Wray, yes, hello. I would certainly be interested.'

We spoke. He outlined his club, and what he wanted to achieve, and I could sense the enthusiasm in his voice. It soon proved contagious. He was offering me a challenge, a genuine rugby challenge.

The first step in what was always going to be a delicate process was to secure an agreement from Louis Luyt to release me from my contract with SARFU. I did not think he would have any objection to getting rid of me, but I understood his complex nature by now and I knew he could prove awkward if he felt so inclined. I needed to approach him with respect.

I arranged a meeting with the SARFU and Transvaal president in his office at Ellis Park, told him about the offer and explained how I needed a new challenge. My approach was not to ask his permission to leave, rather to ask his advice on what I should do, and he responded in a benign, almost paternal manner. He agreed it was correct for me to seek a new adventure overseas, he thanked me for what I had done and he wished me well. For a moment, he seemed almost moved by our parting. As he had said himself at the end of 1995, there is a thin line between love and hate.

As I left his office, I mentioned how much I liked the statue of two rugby players displayed on his television. It had been presented to SARFU by the Ukraine Rugby Union on the occasion of the 1995 World Cup. Luyt looked at the item and impulsively said I could take it with me. It became my leaving present, and has stood in my hall ever since.

We parted on amicable terms. Luyt could easily have been awkward (he had the power to make me stay or he might have placed a prohibitive transfer fee on my head) but he was decent and I had secured the release which enabled me to start discussions with Nigel Wray.

Some time before, I had met John Bredenkamp, a Zimbabwean who had launched a sports marketing company, Masters International, that acted for golfer Nicky Price, among others, and I contacted him in search of an objective assessment of Mr Wray as a businessman in London. The response could not have been more encouraging. Furthermore, John Bredenkamp offered to take negotiations with Saracens forward on my behalf.

'The situation is simple,' I told him. 'This is what I am currently earning in South African rugby. If I can get somewhere near that in England, based on the current exchange rate, I will be very happy. My paramount motivation is to find a new challenge, not to earn more money.'

John Bredenkamp understood and swiftly resolved the financial issues with the English club. I had secured the release from Luyt and Saracens had agreed the package: the bridge to a new life was in place. All that remained was for Nerine and I to identify the challenge, become excited and take the final decision to leave South Africa and strike out abroad.

I had planned to attend the Million Dollar golf challenge at Sun City, as I did every year, and it was proposed that, immediately upon completion of the final round on the Sunday evening, Nerine and I would fly to London with John Bredenkamp in his private Gulfstream jet.

Arriving at the small Sun City airport, I glimpsed the amazing lifestyles of the leading golfers in the world as an impressive queue of private jets lined up to fly them to the next tournaments on their schedule. There were clearly several compensations to the lonely, airport-hotel-stadium life of an individual sportsman ... even if these fabulously wealthy men would never experience, say, the camaraderie and team spirit of the scrum.

Our plane refuelled in Harare and we flew north amid fine food and champagne, in the lap of luxury. We were met by cars on the runway in London and driven directly to John Bredenkamp's house. The meeting with Wray had been scheduled for later that evening.

It would be easy to look back and reflect that we knew exactly what we were doing, and we were magnificently resolved throughout. But that was not the case. There were frequent moments when I wavered, when I felt as if we were being carried along on a tide of events. It was Nerine who maintained a positive outlook. The move to London would place greater strains on her than me (that is invariably the case when South African couples move to Europe), but her amazing strength and resilience kept us both going during this crucial period in our lives. The likelihood is that, if she had not been so enthusiastic, we would probably have opted to stay at home.

Arriving at his offices in London's Thayer Street, I knew little more about Nigel Wray than that he had become one of Britain's wealthiest men following various deals in property, and that, in his youth, he had played on the wing for Saracens.

With the means now at his disposal, he had set his heart upon transforming the unfashionable north London team into one of the most dynamic and successful rugby clubs in the world. He wanted me to join him in realizing that ambition. That was his proposition.

Would I want to work for him? This was the issue.

I walked into an office decorated with sports memorabilia from around the world, and immediately felt at ease. As Nigel Wray outlined his vision for Saracens, it became clear that the values which were important to him were the same values that were important to me. He wanted to build something of enduring value, he wanted to treat the players as assets, and he aimed to be successful by operating in an honest, open manner.

Most important of all, I instinctively liked him. There was no mention of financial matters because they had already been resolved, and Nerine and I reached a decision there and then that Nigel Wray was precisely the sort of essentially decent person I wanted to work for.

We shook hands, and the deal was done. Neither of us saw any need for a formal contract and, to this day, that remains the nature of my employment. We would work together on the basis of mutual trust.

Arrangements were confirmed for a press conference the following day at the Trocadero building in Piccadilly Circus, where the club's new signing would be announced to the world. Nigel asked if that was all right. I nodded. It sounded fine, but events had assumed their own pace.

Driving away from his office that evening, I had suffered another bout of nerves, suddenly struck by fear that I had made a mistake. Not for the first time, nor the last, it was Nerine who calmed me down, reassured me that we had made the right decision and moved us forward.

I took care to make two telephone calls that evening before the news became public. First, I telephoned Kitch Christie and sensed from his tone of voice that he was delighted for me. I made a point of thanking Kitch, again, for all his assistance.

My second call was to President Mandela because I did not want him to hear on the television that I had decided to play abroad. He told me he could understand the reasons for my decision, wished me well and said he hoped it would not be too long before I returned to South Africa. I thanked him for his support through difficult times, as well.

The Trocadero was awash with journalists and, for once, it seemed a sporting organization was able to break news which nobody had leaked. My staged arrival in an elevator provoked a ripple of such genuine surprise that the only awkward question at the press conference was when one journalist asked if I was simply cashing in at the end of my career.

My response was delivered with calm conviction. I explained I did not regard myself as being at the end of my career, but in the prime of my career and that, for various well-publicized reasons, my career was being blocked in South Africa. I said I needed a new challenge and was lucky to have received an offer to help build Saracens into a major club. I concluded by saying I was happy to be judged by my performance, week in, week out.

No, I was not cashing in. I could have earned the same money by staying in South Africa and with far less disruption to my life. People could say what they liked: we moved for the challenge, not money.

As the questions continued, I cast my eyes around the room and took special note that the entire Saracens playing staff had been asked to attend the glamorous West End launch; that would have meant a round trip of more than an hour from the north London suburbs where most of the players lived. I wondered how they would react. Would they be supportive, or would they quietly resent the acquisition of a high-profile foreigner? I searched the line of strange faces for an answer, but could find no clues.

In fact, the only faces I recognized among the players were those of the two legends signed to the cause the previous season. Phillippe Sella, the French international centre and most capped Test player of all time, and Michael Lynagh, the record-breaking Wallaby fly-half, joined me at the main table to answer questions. I greeted them both and was then introduced to Mark Evans, the club coach.

The club wanted me to start playing as soon as possible, but I had asked for a couple of weeks to tie up loose ends in South Africa. Nigel Wray agreed, so Nerine and I flew home where the public response to my decision was happily positive and understanding. Through a frantic and emotional period of packing and increasingly sad farewells, we were overwhelmed by the number of people who took the trouble to say we were doing the right thing and wished us the best of luck.

At petrol stations, in shops, in the street, in restaurants, my concerns were soothed by this sense of general support. A thousand small reactions, the look in the eye of a stranger, may seem individually irrelevant to the life of a Springbok rugby captain but, collectively, they have the power to embolden or depress, to encourage or destroy, and I was mightily cheered.

President Mandela's invitation to have lunch alone with him and Graca Machel at the Presidential guest house capped what we considered to be the perfect send-off for this new period in our lives. Our families did weep at the airport, and so did we, but a new adventure had begun. I cleared my mind of the antagonism and petty jealousies, ripped up my World Cup contract, and started to focus on the new challenge. I was excited.

John Bredenkamp had kindly provided us with an initial house to rent, west of London. Within nine hours of arriving, I was invited to attend my first training session at seven o'clock that evening.

'We need to be at the club by seven,' I told the man enlisted to drive me to training. 'So would it be all right if we left here at about half past six?'

He laughed.

'What's wrong?' I asked.

'You'll get used to the traffic,' he replied. 'If you want to be certain of making seven, we should leave at half past four.'

Two and a half hours to training! It seemed incredible. We would take some time to adapt to London living, but Nerine and I had promised each other we would remain positive and make light of such obstacles. We had arrived in mid-December, the coldest and greyest month, and it was usually pitch dark by four in the afternoon. No problem.

I turned up at Bramley Road, the Saracens training ground in Enfield, north London, prepared for the conditions to be primitive and more in keeping with rugby's amateur era, but they were far worse than I had ever imagined. I saw a group of players standing by a small, dark building in what appeared to be a public park and, apprehensively, I found my way to the dusty, unheated changing room with mud left on the cement floor from the last session.

We changed and found our way to what was called the 'third paddock', a playing field thick with ankle-deep sludge and mud and inadequately lit by floodlights which amounted to not much more than a few torches on a couple of poles. I was amazed, even bewildered but I said nothing.

In fact, not many people said too much. Michael Lynagh and Phillippe Sella, perhaps anticipating my sense of surprise, took the trouble to shake my hand and welcome me, other players mumbled some form of greeting and a few of my new team-mates preferred to say nothing at all.

There was no formal welcome at all, so I was hardly surprised when the coach said we would start with a physical contact session. This was going to be my formal welcome to Saracens RFC. As the shoulders began to thud into my chest, I realized I was being tested, challenged to be tough. That was the way I played, and I returned every contact with interest.

Of course, there were moments when I gazed across in amazement at legends of the game like Lynagh and Sella as they jogged around in the mud, and there were times when my mind drifted back to the pampered luxury that I had taken for granted at Ellis Park or Loftus Versfeld or Newlands. But these were brief. I saw a major challenge and I wanted to embrace it.

At the end of the training session, the players returned to the changing room and tried to wash off the mud in the small showers. I could not face that ordeal, packed my muddy kit into a plastic bag, said goodbye and eventually arrived home to Nerine at 11.30 p.m. My Saracens career had begun.

We spent Christmas alone together, missing our families to such an extent that I took Nerine to see the famous street lights on Regent Street. We were gradually settling in London, and Nigel Wray was sensitive to our situation, often calling to check everything was all right.

My debut neared, a Division One league match at home to Orrell on 28 December 1996. The club had arranged a pre-match lunch for sponsors and VIPs, at which commemorative paperweights were distributed to the guests, and I was moved by the number of South Africans, based in London, who arrived at the 8,000-capacity home of Enfield soccer club to witness this landmark in my career.

In the event, we were all disappointed because the referee took his car key and, when he was unable to push it into the soil, proclaimed the field was frozen. The match was duly postponed. I had seen pitch inspections like this in cricket, but never in rugby. I was learning all the time.

Our next scheduled fixture was to play Bath at the Recreation Ground, where Saracens had never won, but the English winter was closing in again and I began to wonder when we would ever start a game. The Bath officials had, however, gone to extraordinary lengths to get the match played, laying huge blankets over the field and using an industrial heater to blow warm air beneath them. I was impressed. The game was on.

Tony Daley, the prop forward who had scored the winning try in the 1991 World Cup final at Twickenham, was playing in our front row, and the genial Australian took me to one side before the game. 'Mate,' he said. 'I just want to warn you some of these guys go crazy in the changing room before a game. You've never seen anything like it. Don't be shocked.'

I told him he must be joking. He insisted he was serious.

As kick-off approached, I sensed the guys becoming quieter. That was normal but Greg Botterman, our hooker, launched into a routine in which he adopted aggressive karate poses and became animated. It worked for him but, all the while, I was aware of Daley trying to catch my eye from the other side of the changing room. He was mimicking Greg, but I resolutely looked in the opposite direction to avoid revealing any lack of concentration.

Then Phillippe Sella and Paul Wallace, the Irish prop forward, began butting heads together in the middle of the changing room, and Tony Copsey, the Welsh lock, started pacing up and down the room, saying, 'We're going to kill the bastards, come on, we're going to kill them.'

Daley was right. Northern hemisphere teams do work themselves into a kind of crazed fever which is almost unknown in South Africa, Australia or New Zealand, and I did wonder whether they were not wasting energy which would be better channelled on the field, but I had not arrived in England to sit in judgement on anyone. It was my challenge to fit in.

We should have beaten Bath that day, eventually losing by two points after a penalty try had been controversially awarded against us in the closing stages, and my first impressions of the team in action were encouraging. I had been desperately disappointed to lose but we had challenged one of the strongest clubs in the country on their own ground, and I was becoming aware how much we could raise our performance.

Placed securely in the middle of the league, we wanted to focus on the Tetley's Bitter Cup competition in the second half of the season although we received a tough quarter-final draw, away to Harlequins. I could hardly have any complaint, however, because it was me who made the draw. The match became the focal point of our season.

We had meanwhile moved to a flat in Hampstead and started to find a routine to our lives in London, but training continued to be a slog in the poor conditions at Bramley Road. I was starting to become frustrated by the lack of decent training facilities. We wanted to be a professional team, but we were being asked to prepare our game plans on indifferent pitches and my irritation finally boiled over when, four days before the Harlequins match, I stumbled in a pothole at the training ground and injured my shoulder.

In considerable pain, I wanted to finish the training and ultimately vented my frustration by swinging a punch at one of our players, Mark Burrows, who kept coming offside. He saw it coming and ducked, and we laughed about it later, but I was becoming tense.

I wanted to win with Saracens. It was never going to be enough for me to bank Nigel Wray's cheque each month and go through the motions. Some people might have thought I would behave that way, but I wanted to perform, and to win, and to take the club forward. Our entire season hung on the game against Harlequins, and I wanted to be part of the action.

Under these circumstances in South Africa, I would have made routine arrangements for the team doctor to inject cortisone into my shoulder before kick-off and I would have been able to play without difficulty, but I could see both the Saracens coach and the team doctor were uncomfortable when I put forward that suggestion on the Wednesday before the game.

The doctor arrived on the day of the match and, almost an hour before kick-off, called me to take the injection. I said that was too soon – we needed to wait until barely three minutes before running out to play. He was nervous about the entire process. This was not done in England.

So we waited, but the doctor then said he had been unable to get any cortisone and that I would have to take a local anaesthetic. I was not going to argue then, but I was furious. I knew very well the anaesthetic would have no effect because it was the joint that was sore. I needed the cortisone. Then he couldn't get the needle in and, when he did, he missed the spot.

The situation was becoming frustrating, and the result was that I ran on the field for this crucial match with an unprotected and sore shoulder. I managed to play my part for a while but, after an hour, I found a Quins forward was running directly at me. I had to make the challenge, but I wanted to protect my sore right shoulder, so I turned to tackle him with my left side. In doing so, I ripped my hamstring and Harlequins ran through to score.

I was forced to leave the field, Lynagh and Daley soon followed with injuries of their own, and the match was lost. I was angry because I had been foolish to play with an injury and, as a result, let down my team-mates.

In the aftermath of defeat, Michael Lynagh and I started to discuss the challenges faced by the club, and I was relieved to discover he was also concerned that, as experienced Test players, we were not being used to our full potential. We became close friends, and we shared the view that we were scarcely being invited to give our opinions either on the training grounds or in the way our game plans were put together.

I had arrived at Saracens, resolutely determined to fit in with the ways of Mark Evans, the coach, and Tony Diprose, the captain, but I did confide in Michael my general sense that, perhaps as foreigners, we were being kept on the outside of the decision-making process. I wanted to be respected by the players and I was prepared to work for that respect. I was eager to make friends, not enemies, but I was certainly not going to accept a situation where I was being made to feel like an intruder within my own club.

There had been occasions when I had spotted something wrong as we watched a match on video and been afraid to point out the problem for fear of causing offence. It was ridiculous. I believed there was a division in the club between the foreign players and English players, and I realized we were not even a basic unit, let alone a team, much less a family.

Some wet nights, I left Bramley Road wondering whether the sullen and suspicious atmosphere would ever come right. There were times when I considered whether I should not return home with my tail between my legs and play out the rest of my career in South Africa, but these were fleeting moments. I had never run away from anything, and I wasn't going to run from what remained distinctly solvable problems at the club.

I reached a firm decision. If I needed to be tougher in my approach to getting the club right, then I would be nothing less.

Our season began to drift aimlessly and, following a particularly poor defeat at Northampton, Nigel Wray asked me to take over responsibility for the coaching of the side.

He said he wanted me to run the show. I knew Mark Evans, Tony Diprose, Steve Ravenscroft and other established Saracens players would not be at all delighted by the decision. They had grown up together at the club, and would ideally have liked to remain together, in control, but something needed to be done. We were not winning. My first responsibility was to the club owner, and I enthusiastically accepted his invitation to coach the team.

That night, I telephoned Kitch Christie. We had remained in weekly contact since I arrived in London, and, even though he had been through a brief and unhappy return to provincial coaching with Northern Transvaal, he sounded as eager as ever to assist me in any way. For hours on the phone, we mulled over the challenge at Saracens, dissected all the strengths and weaknesses of the individual players and identified the brand of rugby we were striving towards. Kitch had never watched us play live, but I had sent him video tapes of our matches. I valued his opinions.

We had three league matches left to play when I took over as coach, against Orrell, Northampton and Bath; and, with a little luck, we won all three to finish eighth in the league.

These victories propelled new optimism through the club, and, newly encouraged, I set myself the off-season task of creating an infrastructure designed solely for the benefit of professional rugby players. It was a unique opportunity to start from scratch and get things right.

Nigel Wray agreed a reasonable budget of £30,000 to overhaul and develop the facility at Bramley Road and, using the Kitch Christie dictum that you only need a bit of paint, spit and polish, we set about creating what I envisaged as being an ultimate player's environment.

We installed new, clean, modern showers, stripped out the old changing room and built individual lockers for each player. We employed an attendant who would work at Bramley Road, wash their kit after training and supply fresh towels whenever they were required. Never again would players have to take dirty kit away with them to be washed at home.

A physiotherapist's room and doctor's room were equipped, together with a suite of offices for the coaching staff. We wanted to be professional in every respect, to aspire to the highest possible standards.

When it became clear there were not sufficient funds to erect floodlights of adequate strength, it was resolved we would train in the mornings rather than the evenings. The significant savings on electricity costs would further contribute towards the overall cost of the refurbishment.

With training scheduled to start at 10 a.m., it was agreed the players would stay at the club for lunch each day and a qualified chef was recruited to prepare excellent and nutritious meals. Nigel Wray, himself, contributed some furniture and an old juke box and, when we leased a pool table, we had created an environment where the players could relax, spend more time together, get to know one another and be a family.

Every wall was washed and painted. A Saracens mat, bearing the club logo, was positioned by the front door, and old team photographs were set in decent frames and properly displayed. It was important to create a sense of belonging to something worthwhile, a focus for pride. This process started with Nigel and permeated throughout the club.

All this was done within the budget. What amounted to a once-off 10% increase in costs on the annual bill would deliver a 120% improvement in the players' attitude. That was a bargain. I had wanted to give the players the opportunity to become the best players they could, and I hoped the refurbishment would take us towards that goal.

Nerine and I had also visited America during the off-season, enabling me to spend time with Reggie Williams, a former Cincinnati Bengals gridiron footballer who now runs the Disney sports centre in Orlando. My tour of that astounding facility opened my eyes to new opportunities, and I spent half a day noting down his latest training schedules, dietary details and even the configuration of lockers in the changing room. I was learning, looking for new ideas to bring back and adapt to Saracens' needs.

The players discovered a new club when they arrived at Bramley Road for the 1997/98 season, and I wanted to capitalize on the new start by holding a goal-setting seminar for the entire squad. My opening message to the guys was that there would be no more excuses. We had created one of the finest training facilities in England, and the players needed to recognize it was their responsibility to use the venue to improve performance.

The second message raised eyebrows. I told the players my motto would be 'Losing is not an option', and I was not surprised when a couple of the guys almost laughed out loud. This was a club which had had an all-time record winning streak of only five matches in the Premiership, but we needed to transform that perception in the minds of the players. My position was simple: if you train properly, if you get your preparations right, then the logical conclusion is that you should win the match. Losing should not be an option. There are no short cuts to success, but we needed to make winning a clinical process.

At some stages, I believed we may have been dealing with an English condition whereby losing is tolerated far too easily. Even during my first few months with Saracens, I had occasionally been frustrated by how comfortably some of the home-grown players accepted defeat. When I would be grumpy for the rest of the day, turning over in mind what had gone wrong, it appeared as if they would shrug their shoulders and rationalize what had happened as just a bad day at the office.

Perhaps I was being unfair. It might be true that English sportsmen are just as determined to win as anyone else but that they keep their emotions in check more than, say, South Africans or New Zealanders. But I wanted our players to approach every match with a serious resolve that losing is not an option available to them in our club's black jersey.

Several days later, we were working out the budgets and this meant calculating how much money should be set aside for win bonuses. I became extremely animated when I saw an estimate that we would only need to pay 20 win bonuses in the season when we would probably play 30 matches. I asked the official concerned why he was budgeting to lose.

'We have to be realistic,' he said. 'We will lose some matches.'

'Why?' I asked.

'Because it's inevitable.'

I understood what he meant, but it was the underlying lack of hunger for success which needed to be addressed.

Aside from the team goals, we also established individual goals, such as a place in the England team for Tony Diprose and flanker Richard Hill. I wanted to address the fact that we had very few international players in our squad, and I adopted the habit of ensuring I mentioned players like Tony and Richard in every interview or press conference after a game. This was not a token. I wanted them to know that I was backing them.

The concluding element of the seminars focused on the four 'D's which I felt would be crucial to our success during the forthcoming season: desire, determination, dedication and discipline.

Desire means wanting something because you genuinely need it, not just because it might be fun. It is more intense than 'want'. It engages more of the emotions. I told the players my prime desire was for Saracens to produce an unbeaten season and I wanted their desire to be the same. I also outlined my concern that they would become so well treated they would lose that desire to win. Taking into account the salary, match bonus, win bonus, international appearance bonus, car and the housing benefit, it became clear the Saracens players had become very well looked after.

The determination needed to be for the entire team to succeed, not for François Pienaar but for the entire club, together, as a family.

Dedication can be translated as an ability to push yourself harder in training, without anyone asking, maybe without anyone noticing. It is an ability that demands individual responsibility and must come from within.

And discipline was the fourth element: it meant developing structures which everyone understood, respected and supported; it meant always being on time for training or the bus or a meal; it meant wearing the right clothes, for training or for a function. In an ideal world, I told the players, this would also be quality which comes from within. The most disciplined sports teams in the world discipline themselves. That should be our aim.

For the hopefully rare occasion when firm discipline would need to be applied, we appointed Judge Copsey to preside over a disciplinary committee that would meet sporadically to keep everyone in line.

In planning the 1997/98 pre-season at Bramley Road, I had opted to take a tip from the Kitch Christie school of coaching. Amid groans, I informed the players we would not touch a ball for the first three weeks. We would run, and run. Some broke down, but the concept was the same as that which had worked so well with the Springboks: the squad would suffer training together and, as a result, bond together as a genuine group.

Ben Sturnham, our young loose forward, was one player who seemed to rise to the physical ordeal. Some of the other coaches had lost faith in him, believing he was lazy and saying we should release him. I did not agree and recognised in him tremendous potential, so I ensured he stayed at my side throughout the entire period of pre-season training. There was no escape. I ran alongside him, pushed weights with him, never gave him an inch, and his newly won physical fitness increased his efficiency on the field.

The overall strategy of bonding the guys together in sweat was starting to reap dividends. When I suggested we form a tight circle, with arms bound around each other's shoulders, for our team talks at half-time, a couple of the local players wondered what was going on. This was not the traditional way, but they soon became used to the concept and we clicked. We were getting players on board in our quest to be a family capable of producing consistent, disciplined and winning rugby. We had made a start.

Michael Lynagh and Phillippe Sella would play crucial roles within our structures, two wise heads on whom I knew I could rely. Coincidentally, both had contemplated retirement in May 1997, but I had made a particular plea to each man to give the club one more season, and both agreed. We needed them if we were going to mount a serious challenge.

We had further strengthened our squad in two positions, attracting Gavin Johnson, the skilful former Springbok full-back and wonderfully reliable goal-kicker, and Roberto Grau, the Argentine front row forward with whom I believed we could build our scrum. I had personally spent several months in pursuit of Garry Pagel, the powerful Springbok prop, and we reached verbal agreements twice before he eventually joined Northampton.

The Pagel episode soured my appetite for rugby's embryonic transfer market, although I knew we would have to be the sort of club that competed for the best players when they became available. The moral of that story was the need to get a signature on paper. It may suit Nigel Wray and myself to operate without a contract, but other people do not set so much value on their word. In such cases, the only deals are those signed on paper.

I approached the challenge of being player and coach by laying down a clear routine in which my separate respon-sibilities were plain to everyone at the club. Each day, I would arrive at Bramley Road by 8.30 before sitting down with the coaching staff at nine o'clock. I would run through the day's training session in some detail and let them know what I wanted to achieve. This would be briefly repeated to the players at 9.50.

When the training began, I reverted to being a player, undertaking the session exactly as I would normally have done. We typically trained for only one and a half hours, always preferring the session to be brief but conducted at a high intensity. Afterwards, we would have lunch together, maybe watch a video tape of the forthcoming opponents and each player would be expected to spend a couple of hours at the gym in the afternoon.

By the start of September 1997, I felt the club had made progress from the disillusioned team that limped to the end of the previous season. With our revamped training facility and our modern training methods, we had started to look and feel like winners.

Whatever happened, the process of constructing a structure

solely for the players had been a stimulating and rewarding experience. I was happy with my circumstances and excited about the imminent season. Life was starting to bubble along. I was whistling on my way to work.

Then, the telephone rang.

Kitch Christie had fallen ill again.

They said it was serious, time to stop whistling.

# CHAPTER TEN

# *Farewell to the Coach*

K itch Christie first discovered the lumps in his neck on his wedding day in 1979 and had been ceaselessly fighting lymphatic cancer ever since. Some days were easy, some days were harder. But he never felt pity, never asked why and, most important, never stopped living.

He had steadfastly refused to be daunted by his illness. Despite the regular check-ups and bouts of chemotherapy, he had built his own business from scratch and carved out a distinguished coaching career in rugby which culminated in South Africa's victory in the 1995 World Cup. He was the type of strong, disciplined, brave man that I most admired.

Since 1993, we had grown together to a point where our relationship could more easily be recognized as that between a father and son than that between a rugby coach and his captain. Time and time again, I had felt the benefit of his support and advice like the rays of the sun on my neck. I knew he supported me, I knew he cared for me. He never let me down.

This had been the character of our relationship. I would listen to his advice. I would implement his game plan. I would learn from him about how to conduct business, how to invest in property, how to be disciplined, how to be professional. He was the teacher, and I was the student.

From 1997, the balance began to change and, as his health started to falter, I sensed an opportunity for me to start supporting him in the same way that he had always supported me, for me to repay him.

Kitch had known these dips before: in 1993, he had spent two weeks in hospital during the middle of the season and recovered; in March 1996, people were writing him off again when he fell sick during the Super 12 tour to Australia – he resigned as coach both of Transvaal and the national team during that period, but again appeared to make a full recovery; and, early in 1997, he was appointed as the new Northern Transvaal coach, only to resign 12 weeks later during another brief spell in hospital.

I had gradually become accustomed to visiting him in the cancer ward at the HF Verwoerd hospital in Pretoria: seeing his name listed on the board as George Moir Christie, his actual name, to avoid any attention, seeing him smile amid the tubes and drips and plasters.

It would have been easy to leave such a cancer ward with a sense of dull depression, but I was never depressed after visiting Kitch in hospital. He was able to see the positive dimension of every situation, even talking about his cancer as though it was a companion: 'You have to admire this bugger,' he would say. 'I've been throwing drugs at it for seventeen years and it's still there. You have to admire that kind of determination, don't you?'

And he would smile, and you would have to agree.

With hindsight, I suppose his health had started to decline through 1997. His doctors would occasionally cut out problematic growths on his face and the wounds seemed to take longer to heal, and he would more frequently seem less able to shake off a cough or a cold. But his magnificently optimistic demeanour, together with the enduring spirit of his devoted wife Judy and son Clayton, were such that I hardly noticed any problems.

He always sounded eager and cheerful during our regular telephone conversations, and also when we spent time together during my visits home. He had shown great interest in my progress at Saracens, assisting me in every way possible for somebody 11,000 kilometres to the south.

Bruce Gardner, a close friend of Kitch who has become a close friend of mine, recalled how he had said a last goodbye on four separate occasions but that, each time, Kitch had recovered. Perhaps those of us who were close to him had almost started to believe he was immortal.

Then it was September 1997, and it seemed serious. Kitch had started to talk about a dramatic new cancer treatment which was available only in the United States. His friends moved into action. Marquard de Villiers, a medical specialist, was a long-standing rugby friend from the Pretoria Harlequins days, and the man who Kitch would describe as his 'mentor'. His son, Etienne de Villiers, president of the Disney International organization, had become a close friend of mine in London, and it was Etienne who made contact with Jonathan Lewis and Murray Brennan, both cancer specialists based at the world-renowned Sloane Kettering Memorial hospital in New York, and both eager followers of rugby union. Lewis was a South African, and Brennan was a New Zealander. They both knew Kitch, and would be pleased to help.

When Kitch and Judy had finalized their trip to New York, I telephoned Kitch and asked whether he was flying first class.

'No, no,' he replied typically. He had been successful in business, and was a wealthy man but I knew he would not fly first class. We always teased him about his Scottish heritage and he was careful with his money.

'You're sick, coach,' I said. 'You must fly first class. Don't take risks. It is more important this time that you are comfortable. The seats go right back, there is more room and you'll get more oxygen in the cabin.' He said he would find out how much it would be to upgrade, and called back later in the day to say it would cost R14,000. I told him that would prove to be a bargain. Finally he agreed and he flew first class. It was always his instinct to ensure nothing was ever wasted.

Days passed and he started the treatment at Sloane Kettering. I would phone him from time to time but I became concerned. His voice had started to sound flat and toneless. I sensed he was sliding and impulsively asked Nigel Wray if I could miss the Saracens match against Castres to spend a few days with the coach in New York. The Saracens owner is a thoroughly decent man, and he gave me his permission without hesitation.

We entered Kitch's room at the hospital, and I was shocked. At that moment, most people would probably have swallowed hard and greeted him with a smile, but I was unable to hide my genuine reaction; and I don't think Kitch would have wanted me to be anything other than direct.

'Coachie, you look terrible.'

He tried to laugh, but could barely manage a sound. He did look really terrible: soars on his face and as thin as I had ever seen him.

'What's going on here?'

I was concerned, but I think I sounded almost angry. It was clear the strain had also taken its toll on Judy and I suggested that she and Nerine go and find a cup of coffee. Kitch and I were left alone in the room. He told me how the past month had been tough, how he and Judy had been stuck in the room almost 24 hours every day. The doctors had had to remove his spleen, and found it was the size of a rugby ball.

'So, does Judy stay here the whole time?'

'Yes,' he said.

'Come on, coach, she's your wife, not your nurse. You must let her go out a bit. She also needs a break now and then. Why don't you get her a mobile phone and you would be able to call her at any time?'

He thought that was a great idea.

'And you, when was the last time you went out?'

'About four weeks ago. I don't go outside.'

'Coach, you always told us we need a game plan. Well, now I reckon it's you who needs the game plan. You've got to get yourself together. If you just lie there with no plan, you're going to die.'

'Yes,' he said.

'Right, the game plan is to get you physically fit again, and we're going to start right now by going outside.'

He didn't put up any resistance, knowing I would not be dissuaded. So I searched for a wheelchair, found one in the lobby and helped Kitch from his bed into the chair. He was frail, and amazingly light to hold.

I knew very well how brittle his bones had become. The coach had joined the team huddle just before the Test against England at Twickenham in 1995, and he stood between James Dalton and me. The usual end to such a Springbok huddle is for the players bound in a tight circle to squeeze each other and shout 'Bokke!' in unison. James and I squeezed the coach and, the team doctor told me later, fractured two of his ribs.

Kitch had said nothing, of course.

When he had settled as comfortably as possible in the wheelchair, I pushed him to the lift, through the lobby and outside into the street. I sensed each metre hurt him. He was a hard man, and he was not going to disappoint me by saying he wanted to go back to his room, but I heard him wince as we went over a bump on the pavement. He was in severe pain, and it took us an hour to travel the short distance from the hospital to Central Park.

Marquard de Villiers was also in New York at the time, and he felt a sense of outrage that this national hero was going through such a difficult time in his life and yet nobody in South Africa was aware of his struggle. So Marquard took a photograph on the steps of the hospital, of me pushing the coach in a wheelchair and sent it to the *Sunday Times*. It was published on the front page, and provoked a flood of public support.

After our excursion, Kitch and I decided we would take a walk every morning, stopping to eat breakfast at an American diner. We started to develop a routine: I would push the coach in the wheelchair for ten metres, then he would walk for ten metres, then I would push him for ten metres. This was the game plan. When we arrived at the restaurant, we would prop him up with pillows. He seemed to start enjoying himself again.

One evening, Marquard de Villiers took us all out to an Italian restaurant and the coach was on top form, smiling and laughing. The colour was coming back to his cheeks, he was fighting again.

Through six years, he had given me game plans which took us to the top of the rugby world. I was pleased to have given him at least one, even if I recognized it was not going to bring him complete success. Each walk, each breakfast at the diner, each laugh as we recalled the happy times we had spent together, these were all small victories of a kind.

Our stay in New York passed swiftly, and the morning when we had to return to London soon arrived. We packed our suitcases and went round to the Sloane Kettering to say goodbye to Judy and Kitch. He was sitting up in bed, and I congratulated him on the improvement in his condition.

'Thanks, cappie, I'll come down to see you off.'

'No, don't worry,' I said. 'You stay here.'

'No, I'll come down,' he insisted. 'And I'll walk down.'

Judy said she would say goodbye and stay in the room, so Kitch, Nerine and I walked down to the lobby and outside to where the taxi was waiting to take us to the airport. Once Nerine had said goodbye, I moved to shake his hand. As I did so, the coach leaned across and kissed me on the cheek. It was the first time he had ever kissed me. It was hard. There was a tear in my eye, and a lump in my throat.

'Thanks for coming,' he said.

'It's nothing. Look after yourself.'

We stepped into the taxi and, as we drove off, I turned to wave. There he stood, this remarkable man who had played such an important role in my life, the world champion Springbok rugby coach bravely standing without any support, waving farewell. He was wearing one of the white T-shirts distributed to the Springbok squad before the Rugby World Cup.

Then our New York yellow taxi turned the corner, and he was suddenly gone. I would never see the coach again.

Kitch did recover reasonable health and returned home in the middle of November, where he hosted the launch of his biography, most aptly titled *Triumph of a Decent Man*, and signed books for three hours. We started to speak by phone almost every other day, keeping him up to date with progress at Saracens, and keeping me up to date with his health.

The skill and care of his doctors, Jonathan Lewis and Murray Brennan, had earned him a bit more time, and Etienne de Villiers suggested we should present them with a couple of rugby jerseys as a token of appreciation. The signed Springbok jersey for Jonathan was easy to arrange, and I contacted Sean Fitzpatrick to secure a signed jersey from the All Blacks. Sean could not have been more obliging, and a jersey duly arrived in the post. In a difficult time, the fellowship of rugby came powerfully to the fore.

Through the early months of 1998, Bruce Gardner started to call me, bringing progressively bad news. We started to realize the end was getting closer, but Kitch kept going. Maybe he would prove us wrong again.

One Friday evening, just after Saracens had qualified to play in the Tetley Cup Final, we spoke on the phone about the correct way to prepare a team for a major final, about the tricks and the pitfalls; and, out of the blue, after we had both said goodbye, he completed the call with the words: 'And, cappie, remember … when we get to the final, we never lose.'

Two days later, one Sunday night, Bruce Gardner telephoned me. I instantly heard that he was in tears, and I knew what had happened. He told me Kitch had just died. I thanked him for calling, and he asked me if I would tell Rudolf Straeuli, who was playing for Bedford at the time. I said I would, and I did so immediately, struggling to hold back my own tears.

Then I walked through to our living room, poured myself a whiskey, put on some of my favourite music, turned out the lights and wept. I sat there for several hours, in tears as I played the Van Morrison song 'These Are The Days' over and over again on the CD. I had lost a father. When I eventually did go to bed, I found it difficult to sleep, turning over so many memories.

I woke the following morning, still preoccupied. I was saying a prayer, and I became so cross that I hit the wall beside our bed with my fist, knocking out a lump of plaster. And then I cried again. Nerine came to sit with me. It was the first time she had ever seen me cry. I bit my lip, and imagined what Kitch would have thought of me if he had been able to see me like this: he would probably have laughed out loud.

I flew back to South Africa for the funeral, and was able to spend some time with Judy, and with Bruce. On the flight, I had hoped the occasion would somehow bring the World Cup Springboks back together again, and the turnout of green-and-gold blazers at St Stithian's College for the funeral was impressive, but the day was simply too full of sadness.

I had arrived early at St Stithian's, and wandered through to the chapel to check the podium from where I would deliver one of the three eulogies, the others to be delivered by Bruce and Kitch's brother, Billy. To my surprise, the coffin was already positioned on trestles at the altar.

In silence, I stood in front of the coffin. The coffin seemed so small, so final. I remained, alone with my thoughts, for almost 30 minutes, bidding my own private farewell to the coach. When people started to arrive, I waited at the back of the chapel and took a sedative tablet. I knew I would become emotional, and I wanted to do Kitch justice in the eulogy. I knew I would burst into tears, but I was resolved to salute him with a steady voice.

*Ladies and gentleman, please bear with me if I become emotional, but Kitch meant a lot to me as he meant a lot to everyone that knew him. When I was leaving London, on my way to the airport to fly here, I saw a billboard advertising a new movie. The name of the movie is* Kundun, *and it tells the story of the Dalai Lama. It was the promotional line that caught my eye: 'A flower that blooms in adversity is the most rare and beautiful of all'. I know coachie would not have enjoyed being compared to a flower, but the more I thought about it, the more that line said about him.*

*'A flower grows towards warmth and sunshine, and leaves a fragrance that lingers with you long after you have left the room. Coachie bloomed with an openness and sincerity as every day dawned. There was the odd rainstorm that kept him closed and protected but, as the day progressed, he could not but help to open up once again and shine.*

*'Adversity has been his companion for long before the day I first met him, on the rocks at Hermanus, catching fish with his son, Clayton. From humble beginnings, he climbed into a vehicle aptly named determination and, fuelled by desire, set out to achieve in life.*

*'He was the boy who was sent to school in Scotland and, once there, made the most of his opportunity before rushing home to Pretoria. He was the stove-builder's son who secured his future by starting his own business and being prepared to work harder than anyone else. He was the husband and father who paid tribute to his family by saying that, without their love through his illness, he would have been dead long ago.*

*'To millions of his countrymen, Kitch Christie was a South African hero who shared and honoured their belief in working hard, worshipping God, loving their families, singing their anthem and saluting their flag. He was, however, a reluctant hero, never seduced by the limelight and never swayed by flattery. He simply loved the game…*

*' "A flower that blooms in adversity is the most rare and beautiful flower of all." And it was rare that a coach should be forced to leave the field of battle after guiding South Africa through 14 consecutive Test victories, unscarred, his dignity and humility intact, the medals pinned to his chest.*

*'Beautiful? Coachie was not a beautiful man, but he was handsome, and he boasted more hair than me. His beauty was in his ways, his manners, his speech, the way he made*

*people believe in themselves, the honesty that he unfailingly showed to his players. His beauty was in his telling gaze, his calmness under pressure and in the fact that I never heard him complain about his greatest adversary, the cancer within him.*

*'His beauty is also in his family, his lovely wife, Judy, and children Clayton, Catherine and Caroline. His beauty was in the middle of the team huddle before the Test at Twickenham when he suffered two broken ribs and never complained, his beauty was in his smile when we won.*

*'And today our grief is shared by millions of people all over the world. But this grief is mingled with intense pride in a great patriot who never gave up and never gave in, who never strayed from the decent straight road ahead. Coachie led an exemplary life. His was the triumph of a decent man.*

*'If I was a movie producer, I would make a movie about Coachie. It would simply be entitled "Kitch", and the promotional line would read: "The flower that blossoms in adversity is the most rare and beautiful of all." '*

The sedative had started to wear off during my speech, and my voice had cracked twice, but I managed to reach the end and the service finished soon afterwards. As Kitch's coffin was carried down the aisle, past the packed congregation, a group of pipers started playing 'Flower of Scotland'. I looked around and saw men crying on every side, and I wept too.

A wake was held at the Wanderers bar, on the first floor of the building which Kitch had conceived and built in 1994 as the Transvaal training base. I had a few drinks and recalled many happy times, but I felt too sad inside, too empty and numb to celebrate Kitch's life as I would have liked.

As we drank, we saw the Wanderers 3rd XV training on the field and, on the spur of the moment, decided to take 30 copies of Kitch's biography to hand out to these normal, uncelebrated rugby players. I made a short speech to say we were handing over these books to mark a sad occasion in the hope that something of Kitch would live on in all who read the book. I think, in fact I am certain, Kitch would have approved of the gesture.

I flew back to London the following night. Life would go on. Kitch would never be heard on the end of the telephone again but, for as long as I draw breath, I knew he would never be far away.

# CHAPTER ELEVEN

# *Forward with the Fez*

Nigel Wray's vision was that Saracens should become more than just a winning rugby team: he wanted the club to become a brand.

It was the players' responsibility to deliver results on the field, and the owner moved to attract one of the top sports marketing minds in Britain, Peter Deakin, of the Bradford Bulls rugby league club, to build the 'Sarries' brand. This inspired move brought outstanding, swift results. Within weeks, the club which had been playing home matches in a public park with a few hundred spectators was suddenly performing amid a fantastic vibe. Deakin's gift to the club was to make watching Saracens fun for all the family. That sounds like a cliché, but it properly describes the mood at our home matches.

Our supporters were encouraged to attend all our matches wearing a fez, a small flat-topped conical red hat with a black tassel that had its origins as the national headdress of Turkey, home of the original Saracens; and they would stretch out their hands, wiggling their fingers, as if bringing on a spell, whenever one of our kickers lined up a kick for goal – 'giving it the vibe' as the practice became known. They were made to feel they belonged, and they were encouraged to enjoy themselves.

From the 1997/98 season, the club would play its home matches at the modern 21,000-seater Vicarage Road stadium in Watford, as part of a ground-share scheme with Watford Football Club. The ground offers perhaps the finest playing surface in English rugby.

Upon this well-equipped base, idea upon idea was

implemented to build Saracens: catchy jingles were played at appropriate stages throughout the match; the public address announcer would say the entire crowd would stand to win a bag of chips if the team scored within the next five minutes; the Saracens Starlights cheerleaders entertained; youth programmes were set up to attract support from local schools.

On and on, the ideas flowed; innovative cashback schemes were implemented where schools could sell match tickets and retain a percentage of the revenue for their own purposes; kitback schemes were introduced where schools could procure kit; Chalk'n Talk was a unique programme where the rugby club supplemented children's education through courses involving questions such as Roberto Grau plays for Saracens and comes from Argentina, where on the map is Argentina, or Paddy Johns collects the ball on the halfway line and runs to the 22-metre line, how far has he run?

The club's marketing staff, numbering around 20, shared Nigel Wray's vision for Saracens and were backed by a generous marketing budget of £400,000 per year. The vast majority of English rugby clubs allocated a fraction of that amount to marketing, preferring to spend their money on the field in what seemed to be a short-sighted quest for success.

Wray's investment was structured to build a club and a brand that would last, and the players joined in the challenge, making a combined total of 200 individual appearances each month which ranged from reading to kids to opening small business forums in our catchment area.

The result of all this activity was a rise in the club's average home gate from near 1,000 to over 10,000 in the space of two seasons. This growth was earned by bold investment, of course, but it was also the triumph of hard work and a resolve to try anything and everything to create a vibe. As the new season gathered pace, Saracens was being hailed as a major success story in the otherwise troubled launch of professional rugby in the British Isles.

Club owners appeared at loggerheads with national rugby unions, all kinds of threats and ultimatums were issued concerning the Five Nations championship, the format of the Allied Dunbar league and the European Cup as the game appeared to embrace chaos and confusion ... and yet, quietly in north London, we were proving that the arrival of professionalism could take rugby union forward to new audiences and new success.

The key to all our ambitions, of course, was success on the field. Even the most inspired marketing in the country would not amount to much if the side did not perform, and that was my area of responsibility. The revamped training ground and facility represented a major step forward, and the players appeared raring for action as the season started.

Our first major match of the league campaign – away to Wasps, the league champions – presented an opportunity to measure our potential, and Lawrence Dallaglio, the Wasps and England captain, provided our primary motivation by writing in his book that Wasps should not lose to teams like Saracens. His remark irritated our players perfectly.

We prepared for the match with conviction and, sitting in the team hotel on the morning of the game, I found myself watching recent Super-12 matches with Brendan Daniels. This enthusiastic, young and quick winger from New Zealand audibly gasped as Ben Tune, the Queensland wing, scored a try with a spectacular swallow dive over the line.

'Wow!' he exclaimed. I looked across at him and could see his eyes were alight with excitement, alert to the chance of imitation.

The match against Wasps was barely ten minutes old when Brendan received the ball outside our 22-metre line, beat his man and sprinted clear of the defence. There was no way he would be caught and, five metres from the Wasps line, he launched himself into a 'Ben Tune dive'.

To his embarrassment, Brendan had not calculated that Tune slid in to score on a wet, muddy surface, and his own dive produced no forward momentum as he thudded into the unusually dry Loftus Road turf short of the try line. He knocked the ball forward and conceded the scrum to Wasps. The following week in training, amid much laughter, he was instructed to dive at the try line no fewer than 50 times to get it right, but it was difficult to see a funny side as the match wound its way to a nerve-wracking conclusion.

Leading by a single point with a minute remaining, we were awarded a penalty on the 10-metre line to the right of the posts. It is exactly at such key moments in important matches that genuinely great players step forward, thrive on the challenge and make the difference.

Should we kick for goal and risk conceding possession if we missed or kick into the corners and retain the ball? Captain Tony Diprose was weighing up the options when Michael Lynagh jogged nonchalantly to the fore, took the ball, signalled towards the uprights and kicked an immaculate penalty. We duly recorded Saracens' first ever victory away at Wasps. We had moved smartly off the blocks.

A group of four or five clubs quickly clustered at the top of the league as the season unfolded, and we continued to develop by posting an emphatic victory at Sale. We had been ceaselessly drumming into the players the need for us to become a team that travels away from home and expects to win, and it seemed as if we were achieving that state of mind.

Our season would be punctuated by important home matches, when crowds of 20,000 filled the stands at Vicarage Road creating the sort of atmosphere which emphasized not only to the players, but also the officials and the supporters, that Saracens was a great place to be. The noise and the mood were magnificent, boosting morale enormously.

The first of these cast Leicester as the visiting team and, within five minutes of the start, the Tigers forward Martin Corry struck one of our players on the side of the head. I retaliated and Richard Cockerill became involved. Tempers flared, but we kept cool, focused on the game plan and, with three minutes left, were leading by five points. The game was essentially won, but our inexperience was revealed on the brink of glory.

First, we conceded an unnecessary penalty and Joel Stransky, by now a crucial component in the Leicester side, efficiently reduced their deficit to only two points. As nerves began to seize our youngsters, the Tigers surged forward again, recycled the ball to Joel who struck a drop-kick which was heroically parried by Michael Lynagh's outstretched hand.

We were looking ever more frantically towards the referee, but Joel swiftly gathered the ball in another attacking position and this time made no mistake. The drop goal passed majestically between the uprights and we lost 21–22. I had seen him perform this feat somewhere before, and can testify it was certainly more fun to be with him than against him. We had not deserved to suffer such a fate, our changing room was quiet and the club's big Boxing Day party at Vicarage Road had been harshly spoiled.

The loss at home to Leicester marked the end of a 16-match unbeaten run, beating the club's previous record of five matches without defeat. We were becoming a different club with different standards.

Yet the players continued to work hard, and we bounced back when an outstanding individual performance by No. 8 Tony Diprose inspired a historic first victory away to Bath. In wet, muddy conditions, we had shown the greater resolve. We respected each other and we played for each other – I sensed we were starting to become a family, at last.

When we won a scrum deep inside the Bath half with three minutes left, I suggested to Tony Diprose we should play the ball. 'No, no,' he replied, grinning broadly. 'Let's scrum and run the clock down.'

It was a tremendous moment for him, and for me: after all the years of travelling to Bath and being crushed, 'Dippie' was determined to savour this long-awaited victory at the Rec. He wanted to grind down Bath in precisely the merciless way that

Bath had ground down successive Saracens teams in the past. I was encouraged by his attitude.

Another classic Lynagh penalty late in the game secured a narrow victory over Leicester in the last sixteen of the Tetley's Cup and, as winter turned to spring, we were able to contemplate the closing months of the season still strongly in contention for both major prizes.

The traditional powers of English rugby, Leicester and Bath, had faded from contention in the league, leaving what appeared to be a two-horse race between us and Newcastle, another revamped club, born again under the captaincy of Rob Andrew and with the support of Sir John Hall.

My first full season as a coach remained pregnant with potential, but not as pregnant as Nerine, my wife, with our first child. Ever since the date of our Tetley's Cup quarter-final at Richmond had been announced as Saturday, 28 February 1998, I had been aware of a possible clash because that was also the day scheduled for Nerine's delivery. I had been hoping she would be either late or early, anything but punctual.

The day dawned bright and sharp in London, and all seemed calm at home. I had spent the previous night at the team hotel, carefully preparing for the Richmond game. Not long after eight o'clock on the Saturday morning, Nerine telephoned me and said her waters had broken.

Like any prospective father, I had taken care to read all the books and I completely understood the implications of this news. There was never any chance that I would be prepared to miss the birth of my child, so I spent the next hour arranging a replacement for me in the team, and rehearsing the game plan to beat Richmond with the players. I was frantically trying to hold everything together, in an excited sort of way.

Then, at noon, Nerine reported her condition had stabilized and there were no contractions. She said she felt fine and suggested I play against Richmond, and join her after the match. A deep breath later, I put the replacement back on stand-by and, all over again, settled down to focus on the task of winning the quarter-final.

We powered to what seemed a commanding 36–17 lead, and I had even managed to score a try in honour of my imminent son. Most of the players were eagerly aware of Nerine's condition and they seemed to understand when, with ten minutes to play, I suggested I leave the field. We seemed to have the match won and I wanted to avoid the traffic congestion at the end of the game.

'Best of luck, Frankie,' said Richard Hill, as he shook my hand.

'All the best,' shouted Michael Lynagh from fly-half.

The atmosphere was surreal. I was leaving the field during a crucial quarter-final and guys were running up to me to shake my hand. After taking their good wishes in good heart, I made my way off the field, replaced by a substitute and turning to the next business of the day.

I was in the shower when I heard the first cheer, and I was buttoning my shirt when the home crowd raised the roof for a second time. It was clear something was going wrong on the field. Richmond had scored two converted tries, and kicked a penalty in the space of seven minutes. More than a mite concerned, I walked out to stand at the entrance to the players' tunnel and watched as we held on anxiously to secure a 36–34 victory.

A high-speed dash to Hampstead later, I arrived home to find Nerine calm, serene and ready to be driven to London's University College hospital. The day had been fraught to say the least, but we had remained on track and remembered what was in the books … and, early the next morning, on the first day of March 1998, my son Jean arrived in our lives.

The name represented the French equivalent of both his grandfather's names, the Johan of my father and the John of Nerine's father.

We were all back home by four o'clock on the Sunday afternoon, no longer a couple but now a small family. Nothing can prepare you for the birth of your child, and we lived through the usual uncertainties and triumphs of the first few weeks. Jean became the gurgling, smiling focus of our life together and, even if there were nights when I failed to secure my standard seven or eight hours sleep, neither of us remotely resented the imposition.

Etienne and Anita de Villiers, and their son Paul, visited us for Jean's first night at home – Etienne and Anita would become his godparents – and my small son spent the night sleeping on my chest and I even managed to complete the task of changing his first four nappies. I would grow used to sitting in his room, hour upon hour, watching him breathe.

If my son's delivery had been almost perfect, the same sadly could not be said for the scheduling of the English rugby season. The club programme almost ground to a halt through the Five Nations championship, and we went eight weeks without a home fixture. The arrangements appeared amateur in the worst sense of the word, and the club owners were right to complain that they were investing millions into a vacuum of planning and sense.

Saracens, at least, appeared in excellent condition. To the outside world, we were a powerful team of well-paid stars recruited from around the globe challenging for both the league and Cup … and we were a strong side, and we were challenging, but there were thorns on the rose. My ambition for the club was so strong that I wanted everything to be right and, as the season advanced, I started to realize this was not the case.

In simple terms, we were still not a family because there remained a discernible division between the English players and the overseas players. I don't know if this arose from a perception that the foreigners were earning more money or simply on account of the fact that they were new. The delight of victory would usually paper over the cracks, but I was sensitive to any kind of divisions, and I resolved to address the causes.

The division may have been reflected most vividly in what had become an uncomfortable relationship between Tony Diprose, the most prominent English player and captain of the team, and me, the coach from South Africa. I regarded 'Dippie' as a talented player with the clear potential to establish himself in the England team, and I desperately wanted to develop the kind of trusting, open and honest rapport with him that I had always felt should exist between every coach and captain.

Tony is a strong man, in body and mind, and it was at my insistence that he had retained the captaincy at the start of the season. I wanted to see him, and help him, develop both as a player and a captain. My primary aim in coming to Saracens had never been to carve out personal glory for myself, but to help build a structure which would propel the other players, like Tony, Richard Hill and others, to the highest levels of the game.

And yet I repeatedly received the impression Tony did not want my advice, and there were occasions when it seemed he was reluctant to accept any of my suggestions simply because they were *my* suggestions. I started to sense his resentment, and our relationship suffered as a result.

The tension came to a head when, after one game, Tony Diprose was asked live on television for his opinion of me as a person. He replied: 'He loses his head like the rest of us, but he has some good qualities.'

I was flabbergasted by a remark which I heard when I was watching a repeat of the match the following day. It seemed so unnecessary and, after a while, I called Tony in and told him his comments suggested he had no respect for me. We spoke frankly, and I tried again to convince him how much I wanted him to succeed. I said it was my dream to see him lift two trophies at the end of the season. He listened, but I never gained the impression of actually getting through to him. There remained a distance and a coolness which I found frustrating.

Not long afterwards, during training, we started a drill where groups of players would pass the ball under challenge from other players holding tackle shields. The aim was to develop an ability to hold the ball under challenge, and the penalty was that each group would have to start all over again each time they dropped the ball. The exercise could be exhausting.

When Tony Diprose's team dropped the ball once, and again, I could see him becoming irritated. The next time, it happened to be me who knocked the ball down with the shield, and I could see Tony was furious.

'You're going to get it,' he told me, with fire in his eyes. I didn't stand back from the impending confrontation because, for some time, I had wanted to see 'Dippie' angry, I wanted to see him stand up for himself and show some fire in his belly.

On the next run, he charged directly at me with his elbow high, passing over the top of the shield and striking me square on the lip. I dropped the tackle shield to the ground and threw two punches. Tony was startled, but he collected the ball and continued the drill. The players were briefly stopped in their tracks. Their coach and their captain at each other's throats on the training field: it did not augur well.

Such emotional flare-ups are relatively common on the practice field in rugby, and it remains a contact sport, but it had been unusual for me to get involved and I soon regretted my actions. Taking the initiative, I walked over and apologised to 'Dippie' for what had happened. We shook hands on the incident, uneasily and uncomfortably.

In his role as judge of the disciplinary committee, Tony Copsey bought us both a rattle which we were instructed to tape to our water bottles during the following week, in his words 'just to remind us not to throw our toys', and his humour diluted some of the tension, but I could not forget what had happened. On the one hand, I blamed myself for losing control, on the other, I felt Tony had deserved what he got, but I was frustrated.

I wanted us to be successful, I wanted us to become a family, I wanted 'Dippie' and me to trust each other, I wanted to help him become a regular international, I wanted to take the club to the next level of performance and it seemed as if the entire process was being held back by what amounted to a relationship issue. The process should have been much easier, so much less complicated. I felt as if I could glimpse an ideal environment where we would realise our potential, but we seemed unable to get there.

The fact that the coach and captain could not work effectively together was an issue which would need to be resolved but, at an advanced stage of the season, I decided it would be more sensible to manage the situation as well as I could for the time being.

And the storm did pass, as it always does. The team continued to perform well on the field, and as matches were played, any sign of conflict was completely submerged by the routine. There were cups and leagues to be won, so we started to pull together.

It had become clear the success of our entire season would hinge on two hugely significant fixtures to be played in the space of just four days: we would play away to title rivals Newcastle in the league on the Wednesday evening and then travel to play Northampton away in the semi-final of the Tetleys Cup on the Saturday afternoon.

Two victories would keep us on course for a remarkable double; two losses would leave us staring at an empty trophy cabinet. As a club, we took a conscious decision not to complain about the congestion, but to regard the obstacle as a challenge. We planned meticulously, treating the two games as a kind of mini-tour. The chips were thudding down.

Once again, the players responded to the occasion and we deserved to defeat Newcastle on the Wednesday, but Rob Andrew's team were driven by the same pioneer spirit. The top of the league was also uncharted territory for them and, as time ebbed away, Pat Lam, the hugely effective Western Samoan who would soon be named Player of the Year, was able to create a match-winning try for the home side. There had been only five minutes to play, and we ultimately lost the match by a couple of points.

Disappointed by defeat, our primary challenge was now to lift the side again for the semi-final at Northampton 72 hours later, and I was delighted by the players' positive and professional response.

Experienced players took time to support and encourage the younger guys, and we developed a shared resolve that Northampton must reap the backlash of our defeat at Newcastle. We arrived at Franklin Gardens to find no fewer than 3,000 Saracens 'fezzed' fans had travelled from north London to support us. This may have been a tiny group in comparison with travelling support for English soccer clubs, but it represented a huge leap forward for a club which had recently drawn far fewer spectators at home.

The players were clearly lifted and we let nobody down. A powerful forward display laid the platform and, once Matthew Singer had arrived as a substitute and scored two tries (he would become known around the club as Supersub), the match was over as a contest. We won by 20 points and duly secured our place in the showpiece event of the English rugby season. Faced by the prospect of seeing our season evaporate, the team had absorbed the pressure and produced a top-class performance. We were developing the hallmarks of a winning combination.

Newcastle, meanwhile, continued to lead the League by a narrow margin and, whatever we tried, we seemed unable to close the gap. Michael Lynagh kicked yet another late drop goal to secure victory over our title rivals before a rollicking Saracens crowd of more than 20,000 at Vicarage Road – once again, the genius Wallaby had risen to the big occasion, and produced the world-class kick when it mattered – but I sensed we were always chasing the league, ever hoping Newcastle would slip up and allow us to snatch the title from their grasp.

Both sides still had to play Gloucester away, a tough challenge in frequently wet and muddy conditions: we performed poorly and lost, while Newcastle squeezed out a win when the home fly-half, Mark Mapletoft, missed what would have been the winning drop goal by inches.

By such margins titles were won and lost and, approaching the last round of league matches, we still trailed Newcastle by a single point. Even if we defeated Northampton away from home, we would only claim the league title if Rob Andrew's determined side lost to Harlequins. There was hope, but I recognized Newcastle were holding all the trumps.

Those matches would be played in the week following the traditional climax of the English club season, the Tetley's Cup Final, a London derby between Saracens and Wasps before a happy, colourful crowd of 65,000 on a warm, sunny early summer's day at Twickenham.

Currie Cup Finals in South Africa had always seemed to be relatively brutal occasions where the winner takes all, but it seemed to me as if English people tended to adopt more of a 'let's enjoy the day' approach to a final. The match became an occasion. As we advanced through our preparations, rugby's showpiece event began to feel more and more like one of the FA Cup Finals that I had watched on television so often in my youth: a thrill for the players and a great day out for the supporters.

My first priority was to be fit enough to play in the final, to recover from a hamstring strained during the home match against Newcastle. As ever, Ron Holder sprung to my assistance, guiding me through intensive treatment during the week I spent in South Africa for Kitch Christie's funeral, and it was with relief that I was declared fit three days before the final.

Kitch, my coach and mentor, had died a fortnight before and I urgently wanted to win the trophy for him. As we planned our training strategy and developed our game plan, he was never far from my mind. What would he have done in this situation? How would he have reacted to that?

When the players were kitted with special suits to be worn on the big day, I imagined Kitch laughing at us, saying we were getting all dressed up and we had won nothing yet. 'You'll look like monkeys if you lose,' he would have teased, ever with a broad grin on his face. But the suits, complete with flowers in buttonholes, made the guys feel special, and we looked fantastic as we arrived at the stadium. While the Wasps guys wore their normal club attire, people told me we appeared up for the day.

'You look great!' These were the opening words of my team talk as I tried to reflect where we had come from during the season, from the start of the new facility at Bramley road, through the great results and the narrow defeats. I wanted the guys to appreciate we had played through a fantastic season and that this final represented the reward they deserved. I said we had earned this moment, and we should enjoy it to the full.

Then I showed a video montage of the season, set to music from the film *Les Visiteurs*. I had been introduced to the song by Etienne de Villiers during one Sunday lunch at his house, and he had volunteered to edit the images and words together as a kind of motivational item. We had used the same strategy before the second Test against the All Blacks in 1994, and I knew the players would be lifted. Etienne and his team at Disney produced something outstanding in every respect.

Players sat wide-eyed, almost entranced by the music and the images invading their senses. This was to be our day. I watched Kieran Bracken and Paddy Johns, and saw the hunger in their faces. For so long a bridesmaid club on the periphery of the major occasions, this was the day when Saracens would walk tall at Twickenham.

As the team bus approached the stadium, I gazed out at the hordes of Sarries supporters on the pavements and spilling out of the pubs, virtually all of them wearing the team jersey or the distinctive red fez on their heads. This was their reward as well, this was their end-of-season party.

Nigel Wray was so excited by the throng and occasion he

decided to watch the Final, not from the calm comfort of the Royal Box where the club chairman was generally expected, but from the open stands, sitting with his family amid the bustling red-and-black sea of smiling, cheering Saracens supporters. He had always spoken of encouraging a family atmosphere at the club, and this was precisely the way he wanted to enjoy the day. More than anyone else in the ground, he deserved to enjoy the day.

Our core strategy to defeat Wasps was to restrict their skilful backline by imposing pressure on their fly-half, Alex King. The first time he touched the ball, we caught him late but did not concede a penalty. Three minutes later, I caught him again, accidentally opening up a cut above his lip.

We had kept the game tight in the opening stages, but then exploded into action after ten minutes when Phillippe Sella broke through three tackles and, under challenge, flipped over to score an opening try. Five minutes later, Gavin Johnson scored our second from a rehearsed backline move which we had bungled on numerous occasions during the season, but which we happily executed to perfection on the big occasion. It was our day.

We won 48–18, claiming the club's first major prize in 127 years. It was reward for an outstanding team performance and, amid the unbridled celebrations of our fans, Tony Diprose did raise the trophy, just as I had envisaged he would throughout the season. I had insisted that he lead the team, and I felt vindicated in my decision.

I heard the match had been broadcast live in South Africa, attracting a much larger rugby audience to SABC Topsport's Mabaleng show than tuned in to watch a live Super-12 match at Newlands being shown at the same time on another channel. I was pleased to think the watching millions could not but have been impressed by our performance, exposing a common South African consensus that English club rugby was somehow inferior.

History records the game as the penultimate competitive

match in the careers of two modern rugby legends: Phillippe Sella and Michael Lynagh. The entire club had been determined to send both players into retirement on the highest possible high and this was duly achieved. I count myself highly privileged to have played in the same team as them.

Michael Lynagh is first and foremost a thoroughly decent person who, even after he retired, would regularly contact me with congratulations or consolations. Living near to each other in Hampstead, we have remained in close contact, becoming friends far beyond the game.

He had, of course, left a deep impression on the game of rugby union. A wonderfully talented fly-half with terrific hands, he had perhaps the most impressive big match temperament I have ever known. If I was ever awarded the penalty kick to save my life, there is no doubt in my mind that I would throw the ball to the record-breaking Wallaby.

Phillippe Sella had been the idol of French rugby for many years, but he became a hero to me during the 1997/98 season. He had torn a groin muscle early in the campaign, and worked hard to recover as quickly as possible. The club rules stipulated he would have to prove his fitness in a 2nd XV match and, at that moment, it didn't matter that he held the world record for the most Test appearances at 111, a mark that is unlikely ever to be beaten. The centre accepted the fact without complaint.

Named in a team of unknown youngsters to play the Bath second side, he remained unmoved when it was announced the Recreation Ground in Bath was in poor condition and the fixture would be moved to a virtual paddock outside the town where the grass had not been cut for weeks.

Under such conditions, anyone might have expected *le grand Sella* to go quietly through the motions. I had travelled with the team and stood on the touchline as he hurled himself into the contest, giving his all and making as many big hits as if he were playing a Test at the Parc des Princes, always encouraging and goading the youngsters around him. That wet day in a field outside Bath, I recognized greatness in the man.

Michael and Phillippe would play their final match in our last league game, away to Northampton on the Tuesday after the final, and I could sense they were both feeling not only emotional at leaving the game which had been such a huge part of their lives, but also nervous. They wanted to go out at the top, with a victory; and the rest of the team formed a guard of honour as the two men ran onto the field for the last time.

Once again the players rose to the occasion, overwhelming the home side with a performance of accuracy and energy, although it was not enough to deny Newcastle the league title. They comfortably defeated Harlequins the following night, leaving us in second place by a single point.

Various functions followed, a black tie banquet to celebrate victory in the Tetley's Cup Final and a lunch to bid farewell to Lynagh and Sella, and the Saracens season duly ended in high spirits. I knew how close we had come to winning the double, and I was frustrated to have missed out so narrowly on such an honour in my first full season, but I was satisfied with the progress of the side. The following season, we would have to be stronger.

Through the year, I had repeatedly told the players that success for the club would result in recognition for them at international level, and I was genuinely delighted when no fewer than five of our players – George Chuter, Danny Grewcock, Steve Ravenscroft, Tony Diprose and Richard Hill – were named in the England squad to tour Australia. If Kieran Bracken had been fit, our contingent would have risen to six. In my mind, this represented an important measure of the club's progress.

Nerine and I took advantage of the break between seasons to spend a few weeks in South Africa, where I was surprised and encouraged by the tide of public support which still surrounded me. People would approach me in the street and ask when I was coming home or when would I play for South Africa again, and I would be encouraged by the enduring warmth of strangers.

I would have liked to have retained such an amicable relationship with the officials of South African rugby but this seemed impossible within the context of my deteriorated standing with Louis Luyt, and the stark, inevitable reality was that both the Transvaal and Springbok squads had since moved on ... with new players and without me.

The past was the past. I could accept that. Every sportsman must accept that. But there were a number of incidents which cast an unnecessary shadow over my ongoing relations with South African rugby. In 1997, I had asked SARFU if I could buy some tickets for two of the three Test matches between the Springboks and the Lions because Nerine and I were hosting Nigel Wray and his family on their first visit to South Africa. Rian Oberholzer, the CEO, responded by informing me no tickets were available. I was amazed and hurt, and it was left to Louis Luyt junior and Brian van Zyl, CEO of the Natal Rugby Union, to assist me.

So I sat in the stand before the Newlands Test against the Lions and watched as Mluleki George, SARFU vice-president, took part in a ceremony on the field to hand back the Webb Ellis trophy to the International Rugby Board. Much had happened since we won the World Cup two years before, but the thought did strike me that I would have dearly liked to have asked to play some role in the proceedings.

I had also wanted to retain warm relations with the Springbok team, coached first by Carel du Plessis in 1997 and subsequently by Nick Mallett. I sent faxes wishing them well before Tests, but these never elicited a reply, and my general sense of unease with the Springboks was compounded by two unfortunate misunderstandings with the squad during their tours to Britain, both at the end of 1997 and 1998.

When the Boks arrived In 1997, I had suggested in a newspaper article that a possible problem for South Africa could be an over-reliance on Gary Teichmann's leadership in an otherwise inexperienced squad, and I contrasted this situation with the All Blacks where Sean Fitzpatrick had the benefit of being surrounded by many experienced players who were leaders in their own right.

Nick Mallett responded by calling a press conference where he said how disappointed he was that I had seen fit to criticize his squad. The truth was that I had not criticized anyone, and I would never do so. That was my firm policy. I had been on the receiving end of such criticism, I had been the captain of a Springbok team under fire and I understood the feeling. I wanted to contact Mallett to reiterate this fact, but was unsuccessful.

The following year, I was contracted to work as part of the ITV rugby presentation team and this meant being at Murrayfield to watch a World Cup qualifying match between Scotland and Spain, a match being broadcast by ITV on the day South Africa played Wales at Wembley. I would obviously have wanted to watch the Springboks, but had no option, and this resulted in more negative press coverage at home – 'Pienaar boycotts Boks'. Again, if I had been paranoid, I would have sensed a vendetta.

Then, before the Test against England, Gary Teichmann was asked by a Sky Sports presenter for his reaction to my prediction that the Springboks would lose. He seemed shocked, but not as shocked as I was when I heard about the incident because I had never made any such prediction. Sky Sports duly apologized for the error and I spent most of Sunday on the telephone to Gary and Nick Mallett trying to clarify the situation; they assured me they understood but, again, I sensed the damage had been done.

At some stage in the seasons ahead, I am certain I will be able to make some sort of contribution to South African rugby. The Springbok team will always mean a tremendous amount to me. The officials know they can call on me at any time to assist in any way. Yes, the past is the past, but the past can sometimes help to enlighten the future.

For now, my challenge remains at Saracens and it was clear our first task in preparation for the 1998/99 season would be to find replacements for Michael Lynagh and Phillippe Sella, a mighty challenge.

In searching for a world-class fly-half, we investigated Neil Jenkins, of Wales, Thomas Castagnede of France, Henry Honiball of South Africa, and Diego Dominguez of Italy but opted to secure Alain Penaud, a brilliant footballer from the French club Brive, who had played for France in my first series as Springbok captain. Hugely gifted, imaginative and entertaining, Alain seemed to suit our attacking style of play and, we hoped, would prove a big success in English rugby. Arriving with EC workers' rights, moreover, he would not count as one of the two 'foreign' players allowed to represent a club on the field at any one time.

Our quest for a centre took us past John Leslie, the New Zealander on his way to represent Scotland, to Jeremy Thomson, the Springbok centre who had played alongside me at Transvaal. Quick and incisive in attack and solid in defence, he also benefited from carrying a British passport.

We were obliged to make a third major signing when Mark Evans, now working as director of rugby, and Nigel Wray combined to sign the Wallaby utility forward Troy Coker to fill the gap depressingly created by the sudden departure of Ben Sturnham to Bath.

The loss of Sturnham, a young player in whom we had invested great effort to the point where he made his Test debut for England, appeared to be symptomatic of a complacency which had crept in to the club. I had suggested months before that Ben should be signed on a new contract, but negotiations had stalled and he proved easy pickings for Bath.

I must also shoulder my share of the responsibility. When we should have been assessing our squad, we simply concluded the previous season had been successful and retained everyone on our books. This was lazy and unprofessional, and we would pay the penalty later in the year.

Any professional sporting squad is like a rose bush. If it is to bloom year after year, it requires prudent pruning by a skilled hand. With the benefit of hindsight, as coach, I lacked the willingness to make the tough decisions and let players go. Once again, I was trying to keep everyone happy, and this was not conducive to creating a lean and hungry squad.

A pre-season tour was arranged to Biarritz, where the guys enjoyed playing touch rugby on the beach in warm weather, and the week appeared to be successful in establishing morale and spirit. We overwhelmed Llanelli and Pontypridd in pre-season friendlies, playing great rugby, and were widely tipped as the hot favourites to win the league.

Alain Penaud became a swift sensation, winning the man of the match award regularly as we overwhelmed our opposition with a fast brand of aggressive rugby which created situations where our forwards would run at the opposition's backs, and our backs would run at their pack. Decisive home victories over Northampton and Leicester appeared to confirm our status as the dominant club in the country, the team to beat.

We felt confident, and prepared to face a Harlequins side which had lost each of their first five matches. Zinzan Brooke's team clicked into top gear on the day, scoring 25 points in the space of 20 minutes. The match was lost 41–28 and, strangely, our season started to fall apart.

Our defensive pattern was failing because Alain Penaud preferred a rush defence when others wanted to maintain the 'one and a half' drift defence that we already had in place. The lack of co-ordination left gaps in our midfield and we were conceding soft tries.

The issue came to a head one morning on the training field. Again pre-occupied with trying to keep everyone happy, I suggested that, whatever we do, the crucial factor in any defence is that everyone does the same thing. I added that if Alain feels more comfortable rushing forward, I said, we should all rush forward. A general discussion followed, but I sensed some general misgivings about my approach to the problem.

In my mind, I was trying to accommodate Alain who had

just arrived from France but some of the players interpreted my approach as a sign of weakness because I was prepared to change the team strategy to suit an individual player. They wanted me to be more decisive, to say this is how we will play and there will be no more debate. Whether I was right or wrong, the team started to become insecure around such issues.

We proceeded to suffer two crushing defeats, the first against Wasps, 31–17 at Vicarage Road when both our defensive and kicking pattern virtually disintegrated, and then away to Newcastle by the humiliating margin of 43–13. Our team spirit had seriously fractured and I won't easily forget the sight of our utterly resolved hooker, George Chuter, sitting in the changing room with tears in his eyes. A crisis was developing at the club.

At five o'clock each Monday afternoon, I had a standing appointment with Nigel Wray to discuss the latest developments at the club and I became determined to resolve the problems and bring him the good news which the sheer size and nature of his investment deserved.

I wondered what was going wrong, and recalled once reading that the first place to look for a problem is within the management. The old principle that a fish rots from the head often holds true, and I realized that I had taken my eye off the ball during the latter part of 1998 by devoting too much time to discussions with the club owners over the future of the game.

While I was contemplating new league formats and preparing a full presentation to the owners, I was taking the structures and personnel at the club for granted. Minor problems went unresolved and swiftly became major problems. Whatever happened, I was confident we could be successful.

Just as easily as we had won in September, we started to lose as the winter closed in. Playing away at Gloucester, where no team in which I have been involved has ever won, we trailed

24–0 at half-time, staged a second half recovery but still lost the match 28–27. I was furious.

Ironically, despite the fact that we had performed so far below our potential, the nature of the season was such that we remained firmly in touch with the leaders. No club had taken the competition by the scruff of the neck and, into the new year, we were still in contention. So we worked harder and tightened our defensive strategy, and a second win away to Bath seemed to have resurrected our campaign from the ashes of December.

It proved a false dawn as the team plummeted to a new low, losing to London Scottish, a team we had led by 50 points at half-time at the start of the season. Once again, the wheels seemed to be falling off. Kieran Bracken, our England scrum-half, was concussed and, amazingly, Alain Penaud left the field injured for the fourth time in five games.

Something had to be done. Before the season, both Nigel Wray and Mark Evans had suggested that I should captain the side on the field to keep continuity between training and matches, but I had resisted their proposals because I wanted Tony Diprose to develop as a captain. I still believed we could work effectively together to the benefit of the team.

However, the defeat against London Scottish had created a situation where we needed to change something to inspire the spirits and reset the engines for the remainder of the season, so I reached a decision to take over the captaincy from Tony Diprose.

The move was intended purely to streamline the channels of communication within the club and, to his credit, Tony accepted the decision. I told him he should concentrate on getting his own game back to where it should be and regaining his place in the England side, and he seemed willing to give me his unequivocal support.

We began to perform more consistently but Leicester had started to take control of the league and we looked towards a successful defence of the Tetley's Cup to salvage our season. That avenue ended with defeat on a wet and windy afternoon at

Newcastle, when the former All Black winger Va'aiga Tuigamala bullocked his way through our defence to score two tries.

Our only remaining goal was to finish among the top six in the league, and thereby guarantee the enormous financial rewards of securing a place in the 1999/2000 season's European Cup. This seemed a formality in March, but further defeats against Wasps, Harlequins and Leicester appeared to put even this modest ambition in real jeopardy. Yes, we were missing as many as eight first choice players, but this was hardly an excuse. With more than one million pounds of European Cup income hanging on the results of our last five matches, our performances became nervous and fraught.

The away fixture against London Irish was always going to be decisive and we managed to eke out a win against a competitive side. Two wins from our remaining three matches would then be sufficient to secure a place in the top six. To my intense relief, we defeated Gloucester at Vicarage Road and, without playing well, won 25–18 at Richmond 12 May to confirm our place in the top six. We had flirted with catastrophe.

It had been, beyond any question, the most disappointing season of my career. My own form had been affected by a series of injuries ranging from a cartilage problem at the start of the season to a strained calf muscle that ruled me out of the closing matches, and I had become consumed by our poor form, worrying about rugby 24 hours a day and, I regret, becoming an occasionally grumpy father and husband as a result.

The realization did, however, start to dawn that difficult decisions needed to be made to reverse the club's apparent decline. Some players needed to be released and the coaching structure needed to be changed. These were not easy decisions; these were not easy times.

When the club owners agreed to implement a £1.8 million salary cap on the total salary bills of each club, I recognized we would have to cut the players' salaries by around 15%. This was not an easy process, but we were less hard hit than other clubs by a general trend in which the market value of England players, for example, seemed to drop from around £90,000 per year to something like £75,000 per year.

Our challenge, of course, is to learn lessons from the disappointing season and to make informed decisions and signings for the next campaign. Despite our mediocre performance on the field, our core support remains loyal and enthusiastic and, I am certain, the future is bright.

Indeed, perhaps the only positive aspect of 1998/99 was that we could have performed so indifferently and yet remained in contention near the top of the league for so long. If we do hit a sustained run of form, or rather when we hit a sustained run of form, we will be hard to catch.

My own commitment to Nigel Wray and Saracens remains as strong as the day I first walked into the owner's office and shook him by the hand. I want the club to grow, I want the club to win the league and I want the club to be successful on the European stage. I must believe great days lie ahead for the fans in the fezzes, and I am determined to play my part in full.

# CHAPTER TWELVE

# *Blueprint for the Future*

*You will have wonderful surges forward. Then there must be a time for consolidating before the next forward surge. Accept this as part of the process and never become downhearted*
Eileen Cuddy

It might be difficult for the current masters of the rugby world to accept, but there is no doubt in my mind that power is shifting to the north. The timescale of this shift is hard to predict but the greatest potential for the game's growth as a commercial product lies almost exclusively in Europe.

The southern hemisphere's big three, South Africa, New Zealand and Australia, have reigned during the 1990s largely because they adopted professional values and disciplines at a time when France and the home unions seemed more concerned with preferential parking passes and faceless committees. At times, the contest did resemble men against boys.

Each of the northern countries have suffered 50-point defeats against the Springboks, All Blacks and Wallabies, and the scars have taken time to heal, but I suspect the future will belong to those countries with the capacity to take the game forward to another level, to grow most quickly.

In South Africa, for example, the white community has long dedicated itself to rugby union, producing powerful national and provincial teams year in and year out. They will surely continue to do so, but the challenge facing South African rugby is to expand beyond its traditional boundaries. The plain demographics of the country do not bode well. I am no prophet of doom, but the problems are clear.

The government seems to be losing patience with a sport

which does not reflect the entire population and, should this continue to be the case, the pressure for the introduction of racial quotas at senior level will continue to grow inexorably. It is my conviction that quotas can play a constructive role in junior rugby but that the central, fundamental excellence of the game relies on pure merit selection at the highest levels.

Yet it is not enough for South African rugby simply to oppose quotas and grimly defend its position. It is required for South African rugby to adopt a visionary five-year blueprint for the development of the game and to embrace the government as a partner in this process.

New Zealanders face a similar dilemma insofar as rugby could hardly be more popular in these islands than it is now, and the simple limits of size and population suggest further growth will be hard. The All Blacks will still compete as a magnificently physical and powerful team, and the marketing of the team around the world has been exemplary. Sales of the famous black jersey under the slogan 'All jerseys keep you warm but only one makes you shiver' are even soaring in America.

Rugby union in Australia faces no such problems. There is plenty of scope for growth because it remains relatively small alongside the status of rival brands of football. Indeed, generations of Wallabies have complained about the lack of support their code has received in relation to rugby league or Australian rules, let alone the global brand of soccer. The 1991 World Cup seemed to offer a platform for growth, but opportunities were missed in what remains a ferociously competitive sporting environment.

If rugby union was the only form of football played in Australia, there is no doubt the Wallabies would be the dominant side in the world, such is their incredible depth of talent and facilities, but the reality is substantially different. Rugby union will continue to fight for its space in a crowded market place and, again, the potential for growth seems limited.

I believe the situation is dramatically different in the northern hemisphere where, to date, the game has been marketed with indifference and played in the coldest, wettest months of the year. I do not wish to demean the virtues of the amateur era, but rugby was primarily viewed as a sport for a clubbish elite, cherished and guarded by the few.

Money was almost universally regarded as an evil to the extent that no effort was made to increase revenue, no incentive was offered to the players to improve their performance and the largely poor condition of club grounds was viewed as being part and parcel of the game's charm. The character of rugby during the amateur era could be likened to a world-class athlete who refuses to join formal competition because he considers it vulgar. A hearty contest, a beer in the bar, friends for life: this was enough.

The potential for growth must be enormous now that the game has decided to engage the real world, to strive for excellence and actively to sell itself in the mass, affluent markets of Europe.

If the code gets its act together, I strongly believe rugby union can be the boom sport in Europe as the new millennium dawns. The variety, the pure physical confrontation, the power, the speed, the tactics, the courage and the movement: all combine to offer an incomparable, gladiatorial spectacle – and the northern hemisphere offers the perfect enviroment for growth.

If rugby gets its act together...

The essence of this challenge is to regard the game less as a social pastime for the few and more as a product that needs to be run in such a way that increasing numbers of people want to buy the product. The jolly, old game needs to be transformed into a slick, attractive, cool brand.

As Peter Deakin, the marketing director at Saracens, amply proved in 1997 and 1998, crowd figures can be dramatically increased by innovative and attractive initiatives among untapped markets. So, with no shortage of bold, bright minds in Europe, where are the obstacles?

Anyone who has followed rugby in the northern hemisphere during the past three years will not need to be told that the game has become regularly bogged down by dispute after dispute. The arrival of professionalism in one fell swoop, rather than as part of a carefully planned evolution, propelled the sport into a tailspin of administrative egos and red tape.

In my view, the game has been held back by administrators clinging to the rowing boats of amateurism and refusing to leap aboard the speedboats of professionalism, often for nothing more than old time's sake. If it was good enough in their day … it is almost certainly not good enough now.

The sport must move forward, away from the days when good old boys ran the committees, to a professional structure where corporate CEOs run the business and report each month to an elected Board. In this sense, rugby has an opportunity to jump directly from 1950 to the year 2000.

I believe the power brokers – the unions and the club owners – should seriously consider implementation of a new structure for the game.

The basic proposition is to adopt a global rugby season, in line with the southern hemisphere, which starts in January and ends in November. An opportunity exists to align the calendar in such a way that the basic causes of conflict within the game are simply removed, but there must be a shared will to wipe the slate clean, think afresh and for the resolve to be bold.

January and half of February would be a designated preseason, with the Six Nations championship, scheduled to be played over five successive weekends starting in the third week of February. It would be important for the Six Nations coaches to gather their squads together fully three weeks before the first match to build morale and further improve the quality.

While the Six Nations unfolds on one level, the 16 top club teams in England would compete in a League Eliminator series, being divided into two eight-team pools to play each other once on a bonus point system. Those clubs who finished higher in the previous season would have the advantage of playing four matches at home, while those who finished in the lower half would be drawn to play three matches at home.

The top four clubs in each completed pool would then move forward to make up an eight-team Division One, while the bottom four clubs in each pool would contest a Division Two competition. Division One would offer what the spectators and the television networks desperately want: big matches with big crowds every week in a strength versus strength situation. Division Two would benefit from the same intense competition.

It is not, of course, ideal that clubs should address this crucial phase of the season without their international players, and it would be preferable for the Six Nations championship to launch the season and then be directly followed by a conventional league, but there are commercial deals in place which make such a structure impossible in the short term. The price of swift progress and change must be compromise, nothing less.

Both Divisions would be run on a home and away, round robin basis, and would be scheduled for completion in the third week of August. The only break would be during June when four weekends would be set aside for tours either to the northern hemisphere or the southern hemisphere. This window would ensure compliance with all the IRB's obligations.

The Tetley's Cup would move through its preliminary rounds during the season, but would approach its closing stages after the league has been won and would be arranged for the last 16, quarter-finals, semi-finals and final to be played on successive weekends. This would ensure continuity and a much higher level of public awareness for the competition.

The final event of the year would be a World Club Championship, starting in mid-October and featuring the top four English clubs, the winners of the English Division Two, two Currie Cup finalists from South Africa, the NPC winner and runner-up from New Zealand, one team from Australia, five teams from France, one Italian club, two Welsh clubs, one Scottish club and one Irish club. These 20 teams would split into five pools and compete in the same format as the fully-fledged 1999 Rugby World Cup with the final due to be played in the last week of November.

There would be no Springbok, Wallaby or All Black tours to Europe at the end of the year because these are generally resented by tired southern hemisphere players at the end of their season (just as exhausted Northern hemisphere players resent their tours south in June), and would be better arranged during June, when players from both countries are fresh and in form. Under this proposal, December would be a month of rest for all rugby players.

Crucially, this revamped season presents opportunities for the sport to increase its television revenue because it offers compact competitions with their own time and space, in contrast to the current muddle.

Furthermore, the sport could escape the worst ravages of winter when conditions dull the skills and demean the game. In essence, the sport would be swapping jolly July for dismal December, not a bad deal.

Another element in the blueprint was a firm commitment to improve the quality and consistency of referees at the highest level. It was proposed that an international panel be assembled and nurtured where the referees would be constantly evaluated, rigorously trained and co-ordinated and, above all, paid according to the highest professional standards.

Etienne de Villiers introduced to me as the son of Kitch Christie's great friend Marquard de Villiers, had become president of Walt Disney's international television division, and I was extremely grateful when he assisted me in calculating the income and costs of such a season. We worked tirelessly on the model, tweaking and refining it until, together, we presented the complete proposal to the club owners at a meeting during October 1998. The instant response was overwhelmingly positive. I was hugely encouraged. But nothing has transpired since.

Some owners expressed concern that the sport attracts support from the A/B income bracket and too many of these people would be on holiday when the league reaches its conclusion in August. I would not know if this would necessarily be true, and nobody will ever know until they try.

Another point raised was whether clubs would be able to live with the uncertainty of the League Eliminator series at the start of the season. Some owners stated they would have far too much to lose if they failed to qualify for Division One. They would prefer to be cautious, but there is no format in the sporting world that guarantees prosperity for a club that does not perform on the field. That's life. The new structure does involve risk, but it offers rewards for success rather than subsidies for mere existence.

Implementation is, however, unlikely until club owners take note of the broader interests of the sport rather than the narrow needs of their own club. Vision and compromise are qualities that have not exactly flowed through the corridors of rugby union power in recent times, but they must flow soon. The solution is not to mimic English soccer, but to develop our own answers.

The sport can contemplate a dynamic future in the northern hemisphere, but the introduction of a new structure is imperative. Enough time has been wasted. Rugby union is staring opportunity in the face.

Let's seize that opportunity now.

# *Epilogue*

Dear Jean and Stephane,

By the time you read this, hopefully, your dad will still have a couple of decent knees. Guys, I want to tell you about rugby.

Most people are under the impression that the game of Rugby Union started when an English schoolboy named William Webb Ellis famously picked up a soccer ball at Rugby School and ran.

In fact, the sport was founded soon after the first Olympic Games were staged in ancient Greece. It happened that the world's finest athletes were sitting together once all the medals had been won, wondering what they were going to do for the next four years until the next Olympic Games would be held.

An administrator named Aristotle Rugbypopulos stepped forward and proposed the development of a new game which would embrace all athletes from every Olympic code, ensuring nobody would be left on the side. Fat or thin, young or old, slow or fast – this was a game which everyone could play.

Magically inspired, he set about his task.

Looking at the weightlifters and shot putters, he declared they would be called 'props'. The rangy, agile high jumpers were told to be second row forwards, and the slow sprinters were instructed to be the loose forwards. To the archer he said: 'You're the fly-half'.

The chariot riders would be the centres, and the fastest sprinters were obviously asked to be the wings. The egg-catcher was dispatched to full-back, and he sought out the two cockiest wrestlers and named them scrumhalf and hooker.

For many years, this game was played without a ball – or so it seemed! – and the players were content to knock the living daylights out of each other. The game was refereed by retired administrators who could rarely make a decision. And yet, even after the most brutal match, the players would gather around the fire, laugh and drink together, developing a special spirit within the game. The sport took them around the world, enhanced their lives.

As the years passed, they began to attract crowds, and epic matches were played between teams of the northern hemisphere and teams from the southern hemisphere. The game grew, and grew, and knew no bounds, becoming the finest sport of all.

Guys, rugby has given me many wonderful experiences. It has given me many friends. It has enabled me to tour the world and see many beautiful places. I have played rugby for nothing, and I have played rugby for a great deal of money.

For me, the university of life has been the university of rugby, and it has taught me many valuable lessons because the values so inherent within the game apply equally to every walk of life. Rugby has shown me that you only take out of any situation whatever you have put in. Take my word for it. That's the fact.

Above all rugby has taught me the value of three qualities in a man: the first is respect, for his teammates and for the game because no individual can ever be bigger than the game; the second is pride, pride to wear the jersey of your country; and the third is humility, to realise that some people will like you and everything you do but others will not like you no matter what you do.

As you grow up, guys, I'll never be far away but maybe these words of Rudyard Kipling will help you as they have helped me, because rugby may be a team game but every team is made up of individuals. In the final analysis, my sons, the game is about you.

*When you get what you want in this struggle for self,*
*And the world makes you king for a day,*
*Then go to your mirror and look at yourself,*
*And see what the man has to say.*
*For it isn't your father, your mother, or wife,*
*Whose judgement of you – you must pass,*
*The fellow whose verdict counts most in your life,*
*Is the guys staring back in the glass.*
*He is the man you must please – never mind all the rest,*
*For he's with you clear up to the end.*
*And you have passed your most difficult and dangerous test,*
*When the man in the glass is your friend.*
*You can be like another and chisel a plum,*
*And think you're a wonderful guy,*
*But the man in the glass says you're only a bum,*
*If you can't look him straight in the eye.*
*You can fool the whole world, down the pathway of years,*
*And get pats on the back as you pass,*
*But your final reward will be heartaches and tears,*
*If you've cheated the man in the glass.*

Love,
Dad

# Career Highlights

Born 2 January 1967, eldest of four boys
Married 20 January 1996, to Nerine Winter

Country Districts, Nuffield Week cricket, 1984
South Eastern Transvaal, Craven Week rugby, 1985
RAU, National club champions, 1990

**Transvaal**
100 caps (87 as captain)
First match: vs Northern Free State, Ellis Park, 1989
Last match: vs Natal, Ellis Park, Currie Cup final, 1996

*Major finals:*
1991  Currie Cup, vs Northern Transvaal: Lost 15–27
1992  Currie Cup, vs Natal: Lost 13–14
1993  Currie Cup, vs Natal: Won 21–15
1993  Super-10, vs Auckland: Won 20–17
1994  Currie Cup, vs Free State: Won 56–33
1996  Currie Cup, vs Natal: Lost 15–33

**South Africa**
29 Tests, all as captain (5 tries): Won 19, Drew 2, Lost 8
584th Springbok

26 June 1993 Durban, vs France: Drew 20–20
3 July 1993 Johannesburg, vs France: Lost 17–18
31 July 1993 Sydney, vs Australia: Won 19–12
14 August 1993 Brisbane, vs Australia: Lost 20–28
21 August 1993 Sydney, vs Australia: Lost 12–19

6 November 1993 Buenos Aires, vs Argentina: Won 29–26
13 November 1993 Buenos Aires, vs Argentina: Won 52–23
4 June 1994 Pretoria, vs England: Lost 15–32
11 June 1994 Cape Town, vs England: Won 27–9
23 July 1994 Wellington, vs New Zealand: Lost 9–13
6 August 1994 Auckland, vs New Zealand: Drew 18–18
8 October 1994 Port Elizabeth, vs Argentina: Won 42–22
15 October 1994 Johannesburg, vs Argentina: Won 46–26
19 November 1994 Edinburgh, vs Scotland: Won 34–10
26 November 1994 Cardiff, vs Wales: Won 20–12
13 April 1995 Johannesburg, vs Western Samoa: Won 60–8
25 May 1995 Cape Town, vs Australia: Won 27–18
3 June 1995 Port Elizabeth, vs Canada: Won 20–0
10 June 1995 Johannesburg, vs W Samoa: Won 42–14
17 June 1995 Durban, vs France: Won 19–15
24 June 1995 Johannesburg, vs New Zealand: Won 15–12
2 September 1995 Johannesburg, vs Wales: Won 40–11
12 November 1995 Rome, vs Italy: Won 40–21
18 November 1995 London, vs England: Won 24–14
2 July 1996 Pretoria, vs Fiji: Won 43–18
13 July 1996 Sydney, vs Australia: Lost 16–21
20 July 1996 Christchurch, vs New Zealand: Lost 11–15
3 August 1996 Bloemfontein, vs Australia: Won 25–19
10 August 1996 Cape Town, vs New Zealand: Lost 18–29

**Saracens**
*Major finals:*
1998 Tetley's Cup, vs Wasps: Won 48–18

# *Index*